THE NEW RIDER'S
HORSE
ENCYCLOPEDIA

ELWYN HARTLEY EDWARDS

THE NEW RIDER'S
HORSE
ENCYCLOPEDIA

ELWYN HARTLEY EDWARDS

First published in Great Britain in 2003 with

Publisher: Sean Moore

Produced by
studio **cactus** ltd

13 SOUTHGATE STREET WINCHESTER HAMPSHIRE SO23 9DZ
TEL 01962 878600 FAX 01962 850209 ISDN 01962 859277
E-MAIL MAIL@STUDIOCACTUS.CO.UK WEBSITE WWW.STUDIOCACTUS.CO.UK

Design Team
Senior Designer: Sharon Cluett
Designers: Claire Moore, Sharon Rudd,
Dawn Terrey, Laura Watson

Editorial Team
Managing Editor: Mic Cady
Editors: Sue Gordon, Kate Hayward,
Elizabeth Mallard-Shaw,
Laura Seber, Aaron Brown

Art Director
Amanda Lunn

Editorial Director
Damien Moore

Photography
Peter Cross, Bob Langrish

Picture Research
Jo Walton

First American Edition 2003

2 4 6 8 10 9 7 5 3 1

Published in the United States by
Hydra Publishing, 50 Mallard Rise,
Irvington, New York 10533

Printed in Great Britain by
Butler & Tanner Ltd., Frome and London.
Colour reproduction by Radstock Reproduction Ltd.

Contents

Author's Introduction

The riders of Vienna's world-famous Spanish Riding School, who uphold a 400-year-old tradition of classical riding in its purest form, display their artistry in the baroque splendor of the Winter Riding Hall at the Hofburg Palace. The Lipizzaner stallions, with their eerily still riders, enter the hall under the light of glittering chandeliers. The white horses wear black bridles adorned with gold fittings and carry the traditional white buckskin saddles, the *selle royale* of classical equitation. Riders are quietly resplendent in tail-coats, buckskin breeches, high black boots, and bicorne hats, which are raised in the traditional salute to the portrait of the School's founder, Charles VI.

The program: the flowing School *Quadrille*, the electrifying leaps above the ground, and the graceful *Pas de Deux*, performed to the music of Bizet, Chopin, Mozart, and Strauss, all are a tribute to "the most noble partner of man." Although the setting and performance are magnificent, at their core is a simplicity that transcends the splendor. Each rider carries a long birch switch, such as might be cut from a hedgerow. He does so as a symbol of humility before the creature that has supported all man's endeavors through his history.

In India, at the Hindu festival of Dassehra, the horse is honored as the supreme weapon of war and companion of man. He is garlanded with saffron-colored flowers, his feet are washed with coconut water, and the colored tilak is applied to his forehead.

In this book the history of the horse is traced from his beginnings as the small, multi-toed, browsing animal of 60 million years ago to the competition horse of today. In between, we examine the evolution of the modern breeds and the methods of management relevant to the 21st century. Unusually, we also include a series of ten riding lessons which, as much as anything, is the manifestation of our partnership with the horse.

It is all offered in the spirit of humility—the greatest attribute of the true horseman.

The Honored Horse
Throughout India, at the festival of Dassehra, the horse is recognized and honored. He is extravagantly caparisoned and is the center of religious rituals, his feet being washed with coconut water.

INTRODUCTION

Today's Horse
These young Lusitano horses are descendents of creatures that lived on Earth perhaps 60 million years ago.

In the Beginning

Less than 200 years ago—the "blink of an eye" in terms of the evolution of life on Earth—a book was published that was to open a whole new dimension to the human concept of life. Indeed, the book, *On the Origin of Species by Means of Natural Selection*, has had an influence on the way we view and understand the living world that cannot be underestimated.

The book was written by the British naturalist Charles Darwin (1809–82) and published in 1859. Darwin, and Alfred Russel Wallace, worked independently on the theory that all living creatures evolved over millions of years by a process of what Darwin called "Natural Selection," by which is meant not so much "the survival of the fittest" but the development and change of an individual species over succeeding generations.

Before Darwin published his book, many people believed that life was unchanging: horses and humans had been created as such, as related in the beautiful story that is the Bible's Book of Genesis, "the beginning." From the information contained in rock formations and then from the more recent fossil formations (beginning about 600 million years ago), a pretty authoritative history of the Earth can be obtained.

It is largely as a result of work by American scientists that we can trace the development of the horse from the Eocene period (although the species has its origins long before that) up to the time of its domestication at the end of the Neolithic period, 5,000 or 6,000 years ago. Indeed, research is ongoing, and significant advances have been made by the Smithsonian Institute, for example, to present an enlargement of the fundamental understanding put forward here in simplistic form. There will never be a definitive explanation of the evolution of the horse. At best, our knowledge is extended by intelligent conjecture and meticulous scientific study.

The Dawn Horse

A nearly complete skeleton of the early horse was discovered in Wyoming in 1867 and was catalogued as *Hyracotherium* (the hyrax being a rabbit-like mammal), the name given to an incomplete skull found a few years earlier in Kent, England. The American scientists, more romantically, called their discovery *Eohippus*, the Dawn Horse.

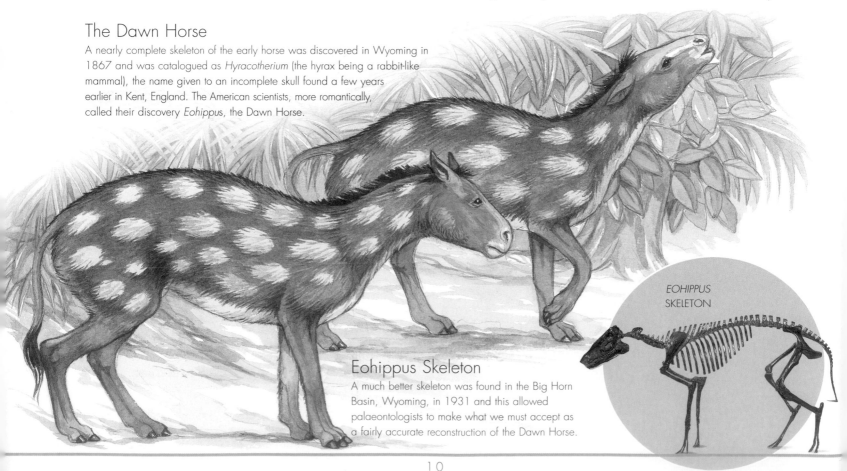

Eohippus Skeleton

A much better skeleton was found in the Big Horn Basin, Wyoming, in 1931 and this allowed palaeontologists to make what we must accept as a fairly accurate reconstruction of the Dawn Horse.

EOHIPPUS SKELETON

Eohippus

The "Dawn Horse," *Eohippus*, was a somewhat round-backed animal with four toes on the front feet and three on the back. The base of the foot was a pad like that of a dog or tapir—a distant relation of the horse. It survives in the modern horse as the "ergot" (*see* p.96).

The creature weighed about 12lb (5.4kg) and stood about 14in (36cm) at the shoulder—no bigger, in fact, than a middle-sized dog. The formation of the feet enabled *Eohippus* to move on wet, soft ground, like that found in jungle. It is suggested that the coat was in texture like that of a deer, a characteristic retained by the Tarpan millions of years later (*see* p.159). Probably in the interests of concealment, it was blotched, spotted or even striped.

The eyes were in the middle of the head, for the jungle animal had no use for the lateral vision developed much later by its scrubland- and plains-dwelling descendants. The short-crowned teeth were quite unlike those of the modern horse but well suited to a diet of soft leaves growing on low shrubs. They were not suitable for grazing—but then there was no grass!

However, there was a wide variation in size, probably from 10in (25cm) at the shoulder to 20in (50cm), which implies that the largest animal was eight times heavier than the smallest one. There may have been bigger specimens in Europe, which was then as one with the American continent. The Eurasian versions, spreading eastward and westward from the cradle of the New World by way of land bridges, became extinct some 40 million years ago, and the progression toward *Equus caballus*, the modern horse, lay almost entirely on the American continent. Even there, no ordered development occurred and very few of the numerous strains would lead to the ultimate emergence of a single-hoofed animal.

Mesohippus and Miohippus

In the Oligocene period, 40 million years ago, *Eohippus* was succeeded by *Mesohippus* and *Miohippus*. The two may possibly have overlapped.

They had a more advanced dentition than *Eohippus*, with premolars, or incisor teeth, which could be used in a powerful chopping action to consume a greater variety of leafy foliage. In addition, both now had three toes on each foot, the central one of which was the most prominent. The leg was longer, and the rounded back less noticeable. The height had increased

Merychippus

At 36in (90cm) at the shoulder, *Merychippus* was no bigger than today's Shetland pony. It was, nonetheless, a recognizable horse in its structural shape.

MERYCHIPPUS SKELETON

to 18in (46cm) and the skull was becoming larger, with the eyes set increasingly towards the side of the head.

Environmental Change

The change in physical detail points to an altering environment in which jungle was being replaced by scrub areas that supported bush and shrubs. The loss of the fourth toe suggests changes in the ground condition. Although still wet, it was firmer underfoot.

Longer legs imply greater speed, to suit a more open country, while the changes in the skull allowed for the increase in lateral vision. In fact, the defense system was adapting to the new factors involved. Up to this point defense had depended on concealment; now the emphasis was moving towards a system reliant upon detection and flight. In consequence the blotched coat pattern may have begun to fade.

Merychippus

By the beginning of the Miocene period, about 25–20 million years ago, *Eohippus* and his early relations had disappeared from Eurasia, giving way to browsing animals that had come from the American continent.

Meanwhile, the next major advance towards *Equus* was being made in the Old World with the appearance of *Merychippus*.

Towards *Equus*

The Miocene period, and *Merychippus*, marked a watershed in the development of the horse. Gradually, in the way of evolution, significant changes were taking place in the environment, compelling the animals dependent on it to adapt. The jungle and forest that had supported browsing, multi-toed animals was giving way to plains or steppelands, mostly treeless and covered with a low growth of wiry grass.

Savannah Horse

To survive, *Merychippus* developed longer legs, with leg ligaments, to give an action nearer to that of a modern horse. At 36in (90cm), it was a larger animal than its predecessors. Increasingly the weight was carried on the center toe, although the outside toes, now less pronounced, remained. The neck became longer—so that the animal could graze—and, when raised, it gave greatly improved vision, a feature much assisted by the altered shape of the skull and the positioning of the eyes on the side of the head.

In order to eat the hard savannah grasses, major changes developed in the teeth and jaw. The teeth became stronger and higher-crowned, and were covered in protective enamel. They had a heavy filling of "cement," necessary to prevent wear caused by the grinding action of the molars.

Defense Mechanism

The defense mechanism was now to all intents in place, with the animal equipped to detect predators and to run away from them at speed.

At the same time these early horses were developing the heightened senses that are still characteristic of today's naturally highly strung animal.

Multi-toed animals in less advanced stages of development would have survived in Asia and Europe certainly up to the end of the Miocene period and possibly for much longer. One of them was the huge *Megahippus*, many times the size of the modern horse, which may have survived in both continents during the Miocene period.

Pliohippus

The final prototype for *Equus* arrived in the mid-Pleistocene period, about six million years ago. This was *Pliohippus*, the first single-hoofed "horse" with fully developed leg ligaments. It stood about 48in (1.2m) high or, in our terms, 12.2hh.

Pliohippus was the source of the other branch of the equine family, the zebras, asses, and hemionids or "half-asses" (*see* pp.118–19)—and, very importantly, it was the forerunner of the "true" horse, named *Equus caballus*, which developed five million years later, during the second half of the Ice Age.

Equus Caballus

Equus caballus spread to Asia, South America, Europe, and then to Africa, over the still existing land bridges, up to approximately 9000BC. Then the last land bridge, across the Bering Strait, disappeared with the receding ice packs, and the American continent was isolated.

Pliohippus

This was, it is believed, the lead-in to *Equus caballus* and the first single-hoofed "horse."

PLIOHIPPUS SKELETON

not return to America until the species was re-introduced into Mexico by the Spanish conquistadore Hernando Cortes (1485–1547) in the early 16th century. Cortes embarked on his conquest with a complement of 800 soldiers and 16 horses.

The Modern Horse

It is thought that at the end of the Ice Age four distinct but related forms of Equus remained, distributed as follows: horses inhabited Europe and Western Asia; asses and zebras survived in the north and south of Africa, respectively; and the onager (wild ass) thrived in the Middle East. Modern horses are now generally considered to have originated in three "primitive" types of horse that developed subsequently. Only one of these, the Asiatic Wild Horse (p.158) survives. The Tarpan (p.159) and the Forest Horse (see Poitevin, p.143) are extinct in their original form.

In very simple terms, today's heavy horses can be related to the Forest Horse, with some outcrossing to the Asiatic Wild Horse. The modern light horses (riding/driving types) are seen to have originated in the Tarpan and Asiatic Wild Horse and their crosses.

"Primitive" Horses
The Asiatic Wild Horse of Mongolia is the only surviving foundation horse. It is also known as Przewalski's Horse, after the explorer Nicolai Przewalski, who discoverd a wild herd in the Gobi Desert in 1870.

About 1,000 years later, as the result of some as yet unexplained natural disaster, the horse became extinct in North America, along with many other creatures, including the sloths and mastadons. *Equus caballus* did

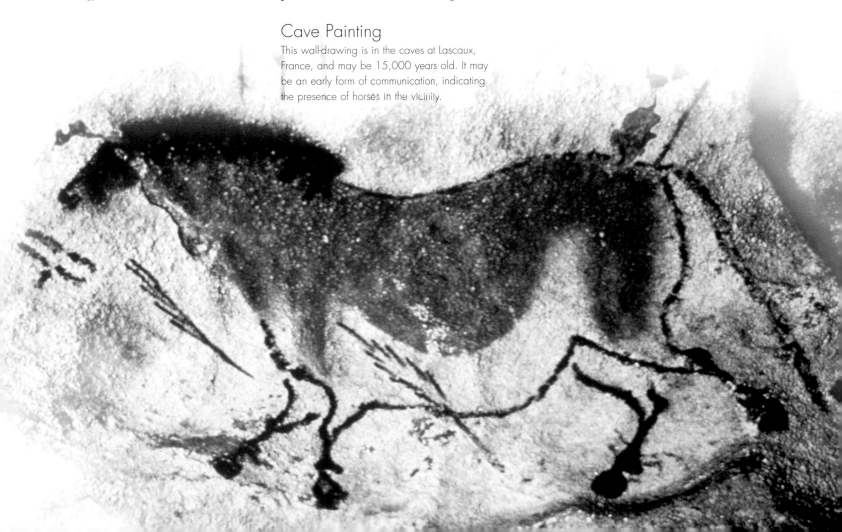

Cave Painting
This wall-drawing is in the caves at Lascaux, France, and may be 15,000 years old. It may be an early form of communication, indicating the presence of horses in the vicinity.

Legend and Literature

No subject, except love, has amassed so vast a fund of legend and literature as the horse.

Horses in Ancient Mythology

In the mythology and legend of the Eastern religions, for instance, horses draw chariots through the sky and partner the gods in magical feats, while for over 2,000 years horses were a central element in the civilization of Ancient Greece.

Horses—always white ones—were sacrificed to the Greek god Poseidon, who as well as being god of the sea was creator of horses. Helios, god of the sun, used winged horses to pull his chariot of gold, but it is Poseidon who was said to have created the great winged horse, Pegasus. Another story claims this fabulous horse sprang from the blood of Medusa when the demigod Perseus cut off her head.

Pegasus flew to Mount Olympus, the home of the gods, and was housed in the stables of Zeus, for whom he carried thunderbolts, the guided missiles of the day. Pegasus also visited Athena, the goddess of wisdom, at Mount Helicon, where affection was lavished upon him.

Once, when he was thirsty, Pegasus stamped the ground and immediately water gushed out for him to drink. The spring was called Hippocrene, the "fountain of inspiration," and anyone drinking from it was inspired to create poetry.

Only one human rode Pegasus—the young hero Bellerophon. King Iobates of Lycia set him three tasks, including a battle with the Chimera, a fearsome monster with the head of a lion, the body of a goat, and the tail of a snake. His reward was the hand of the King's daughter and half the kingdom.

Tiring of killing monsters, the young hero rode Pegasus to Olympus, and that was his undoing. To punish such temerity, Zeus caused a hornet to

Pegasus
Perseus, mounted on the winged Pegasus, carries aloft the severed head of Medusa. Pegasus had been created from Medusa's blood.

Timeless Tale

Black Beauty is one of the world's best-loved stories. Here, the actress Judi Bowker appears in a popular 1970's television series based on the novel.

sting Pegasus, who kicked out and threw Bellerophon back to Earth.

Pegasus returned to Mount Helicon, to live happily ever after with the nine Muses, the goddesses of all the arts and sciences.

Black Bess

Dick Turpin's ride on Black Bess from London to York, a journey of 190 miles (300km) in a single night, is a classic tale and a masterpiece of equestrian literature.

W. Harrison Ainsworth described the ride in his novel *Rockwood*, published in 1834. The story is so good that most people believe it is true. It isn't, of course, but there was a real Dick Turpin, born in Essex, England, in 1705, who did perform some astonishing equestrian feats in his time. Turpin, a horse thief and a highwayman, was hanged at York, England, on April 10, 1739, for the murder of an Epping innkeeper.

Black Beauty

One of the most successful horse books ever written anywhere in the world is *Black Beauty*, by Anna Sewell. First published in Britain in 1877, it is still in print today and has sold millions of copies. This life story of a carriage horse, told from the horse's point of view, was Anna's protest against the ill-treatment of horses in the mid-Victorian era.

The Maltese Cat

The master storyteller, Rudyard Kipling, wrote the wonderful story *The Maltese Cat* in 1895. A wise little, flea-bitten grey pony brought to India from Malta, where he was found pulling a vegetable cart, the pony was the architect of the Skidars' epic victory over the Archangels in the Upper India Free-for-All Polo cup. He was "desperately quick on his feet" and " ... as everybody knew, Past Pluperfect Prestissimo Player of the Game." The story has been described as "the finest description of a game in the English language."

National Velvet

Enid Bagnold wrote *National Velvet* in 1935, and since then millions of children have thrilled to the story of 14-year-old Velvet Brown, who won a horse called The Piebald in a raffle—he was so called because he was black and white. After the usual ups and downs, Velvet contrived to ride the horse in the world's most famous steeplechase, the Grand National—and won! She fell off exhausted after the race and she was disqualified for being a girl, but she was first past the post. The film of the book was made in 1944.

Don Quixote and Rosinante

The Spanish writer Miguel de Cervantes (1547–1616) gave us the immortal story of the often ludicrous and deluded Don Quixote, his squire Sancho Panza, and Rosinante, his broken-down horse.

In *The Adventures of Don Quixote of La Mancha*, which was first printed in 1605, the "sad and foolish knight" journeys in search of daring deeds and damsels in distress. His misadventures include a famous battle with windmills (which he mistook for giants), in which, as usual, the Don came off the worst.

Poor Rosinante, all skin and bone, is hardly the noble charger of chivalry, but he was that and much more to Don Quixote, who spent four days of deliberation before giving him the name Rosinante (from *rosin*, a common drudge horse, and *ante*, before). "He had only been a rosin ... before his present condition and now he was before all the rosins in the world."

Don Quixote

Many stage and film versions of *Don Quixote* have appeared over the years. The novel was originally devised as a parody of the chivalry romances that were fashionable in Spain at the time.

Horse Behavior

Behavioral patterns, apart from those implanted by domestication, are always instinctive in the horse, never rational. For the most part, their roots are in the defense mechanism formed millions of years ago, when the horse herds were preyed upon by carnivorous predators, but they persist even in the domestic state.

The horse is a herbivore and, although it is very big and powerful, it is not an aggressive animal—unlike the dog, for example, who is a descendant of the savage wolf packs that hunted for their food.

Like many other herbivorous animals, the horse's defense lies in an inbuilt early-warning system that enables it to detect danger—real or imagined—and a physique that allows for swift and immediate flight.

As a result, a set of finely tuned, heightened senses developed, far exceeding our own. The horse's hearing, for instance, is acute. The ears, controlled by 13 pairs of muscles, are incredibly mobile

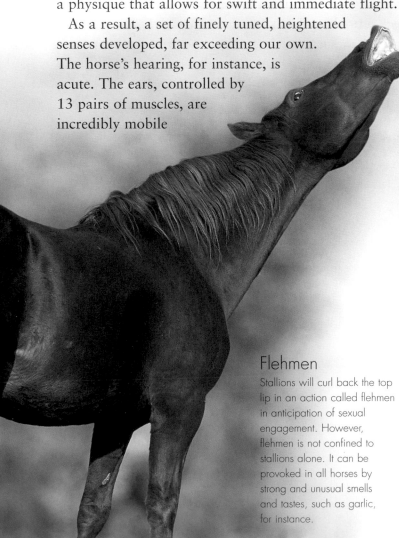

Flehmen
Stallions will curl back the top lip in an action called flehmen in anticipation of sexual engagement. However, flehmen is not confined to stallions alone. It can be provoked in all horses by strong and unusual smells and tastes, such as garlic, for instance.

and can be rotated at will through almost 360 degrees. Because of the position of the eyes, the horse has virtually all-round vision, even when grazing.

The horse is also possessed of an exceptionally keen sense of smell. It is a part of the defense system, but its greater role is in the social make-up of the herd, including mating.

The Herd Instinct
Fundamental to the horse is the herd instinct—the need to belong to a group of its own kind. The gravitational pull of the herd may be subdued in part in the domestic state by training but it is never eliminated entirely, and the successful trainer will recognize that inescapable fact.

A herd is made up of groups, often led by an older mare. Members of a group are identified by a corporate odor. Foals, of course, instinctively recognize the smell of their dam. Horses, like other animals, produce and receive pheromones, smell messages, made by the skin glands. Smell is an important part of sexual behavior. A mare gives out pheromones when she is in oestrus, ready to mate with the stallion, and reinforces them with physical messages indicating her willingness to accept the stallion. Conversely, she communicates just as clearly if she is not ready by squealing, kicking, making threatening faces and biting.

Vocal Communication
Horses do communicate vocally with each other, but only in a limited way. Mares whicker softly to their foals, and many horses make the same sound in anticipation of feeding time. The whinny may be given in excitement or when the horse is separated from companions. Snorting occurs if danger is sensed, or if something of special interest is encountered. Squeals

for hearing, but they tell us, and other horses, a lot about their owner's state of mind. Pricked forward, they indicate strong interest in an object to the front. They go back when the horse is attracted by something behind. Laid back, they indicate temper, displeasure and aggression. When the ears are lowered and allowed to become limp, the horse is relaxed or dozing. Ears twitching back and forth when the horse is ridden tell us that he is paying attention to the rider—a comforting thought.

Stamping, shaking the head, and/or swishing the tail are signs of irritation. In relaxation, the head hangs down, the lower lip may hang, a hind foot is rested, and the eyes are partly closed. Tension is made equally evident in the posture.

Mutual Grooming

The sense of touch is important to social relationships. Horses indulge in mutual grooming, nibbling each other behind the withers, in the same way that a mare nuzzles her foal. It is a way of creating a friendly relationship.

and grunts are signs of aggression or excitement. Horses will also respond to the human voice, which is, after all, one of the natural "aids" (see pp.168–69). Used intelligently, the voice is a valuable tool. It can be used to calm and reassure, to encourage, reward and, on occasions, to reprimand. Of course, it is the tone that is all important; the words matter not at all.

Body Language

Body language in horses is, indeed, a pretty sophisticated means of communication. The ears are

Bucking and Rearing

Horses may rear when startled, excited, or in play. The buck is a bit different. It is the final defense, to be used when a predator lands on the horse's back. There are no predators left for domestic horses, but the buck remains as an expression of resentment. Or it may be just a bit of fun between friends.

Pecking Order

Horses quickly establish a pecking order, the more dominant asserting their authority and their place in the group. Just like humans, some are nice, easy-going characters while others are bad-tempered and difficult.

Domestication

The dog was the first animal to be domesticated (in about 12000BC), but another 6,000 years was to elapse before men of the late Neolithic period were in a position to benefit from domestic horse herds. In the intervening years many other animals, from sheep and cattle to poultry, had been drawn into the domestic fold, including the ill-tempered onager and, more significantly, the reindeer.

Man has had a relationship with horses as a source of food for many thousands of years. The huge depositories of bones at Solutré and Lascaux in France make this very clear. The cave-drawings in France, Spain and elsewhere, which may be as much as 15,000 years old, might be taken as evidence of man herding horses rather than hunting for food, but in the conditions existing then, and taking the terrain into account, it would have been impractical and without advantage to herd and control such big, unpredictable animals.

Horses were first tamed, the evidence suggests, by the nomadic steppe people of Eurasia, notably those Aryan tribes who moved round the steppes of the Caspian and Black seas. These people were used to herding animals, even if that meant little more than following wild flocks of sheep or goats or herds of reindeer.

Reindeer Herding

Of those animals reindeer would have best suited the tribal lifestyle. They do not wander, nor do they need to be moved to new pasture. Instead, as migratory animals, they follow purposefully the growth of "reindeer moss," which is their staple food.

There are other good reasons for supposing the reindeer to have been the lead-in to the domestic horse. Notably, the reindeer lived in the areas subsequently frequented by nomadic horse-peoples, that is from the Great Wall of China to Outer Mongolia. Only later did the reindeer shift further north towards the Arctic. Reindeer herders in these steppelands had worked the herds for probably 2,000 years and were entirely familiar with them.

Herding horses has advantages over the reindeer culture, and when horses became more numerous in the steppe areas it would have been sensible to make the change from one to the other. Horses do not follow the migratory cycle and could be driven to chosen locations. Moreover, they could find and dig for food in the snow better than the reindeer.

The "saddlery" of the reindeer people had its origin in the time before horse domestication and is hardly different today. Furthermore, it varies little from that used in the early horse cultures.

Reindeer

A reindeer, or, as they are known in North America, caribou, pulls a sleigh in Finnish Lapland. We know that reindeer were certainly pulling sledges in northern Europe in 5000BC and may also have been ridden and more or less selectively bred.

Travois

The *travois* originated in Eurasia and reappears as part of the equipment of the Native American much later. A platform strung between two poles could carry baggage, teepees, and people.

Horse Herders

The Kabardin people of the northern Caucasus pasture their horses on the high ground in summer, bringing them to the foothills in the winter.

The Pazyryk Tombs

Another connection between horses and reindeer is to be found in the remarkable artifacts of the Pazyryk Tombs. In 1929, Dr. S. I. Rudenko excavated a group of deep-frozen tombs in the Altai Mountains of eastern Siberia in what was to be one of the most significant archaeological discoveries of the 20th century.

The tombs belonged to a Scythian tribe, the most notable of the horse-peoples. They revealed, in remarkable detail, a history of horse husbandry going back to about 3000BC. An important chieftain, a Scythian "rancher," was buried here with all his possessions: his steppe-wagon, food, weapons, and utensils as well as his horses. Everything was preserved in the ice exactly as on the day of interment. Notably, some of the horses wore face-masks that transformed the heads into those of reindeer, including the antlers. Clearly there was a strong connection. Were the masks

a recognition of an earlier culture when the Scythian horsemen were tenders of reindeer? It is certainly not impossible.

Herd Management

The composition of early domestic herds would have excluded stallions because of their disruptive potential. A common breeding practice was to tie out in-season mares who would attract wild stallions to mate with them. The young males provided meat, mares were milked, and hair and hides were used for making clothes and shelters. The dung provided fuel for fires—there was no wastage. Old people, the baggage and the tents (*yurts*) could be moved on a horse-drawn sled, the prototype *travois* of the Native American, who just could be a descendant of the Scythian nomads.

Horse-riding, we must presume, started by chance. A boy, perhaps tending the herd, jumped on the back of an old mare and discovered the advantage given to a mounted man. Riders could more easily hold and direct the herd, in the fashion of the Western cowboy, than could men following on foot.

Fairly soon, one imagines, riding became a part of the nomadic life, and along with the ability to move possessions by means of a horse-drawn *travois*, increased the tribe's mobility a thousand-fold, giving a new perspective to their lives.

From these beginnings in the Central Asian steppes, the domestic horse spread outwards, east, west, and south, to cover the known world of the day.

Horses in History

Every age has men who stand head and shoulders above their fellows, controlling and influencing the course of world events. Of course, the ages have their quota of famous horses, too.

In general, famed horses belong to famed soldiers, men like Wellington, with his horse Copenhagen, and Napoleon with Marengo, but a few make their name far from the battlefield, like Tschiffely's Mancha and Gato whose story is told here.

First of the horse heroes has to be the black horse, Bucephalus, the mount of Alexander the Great (356–323BC). His name means "ox-head" and refers to the broad forehead and concave profile of the Thessalonian breed. Alexander acquired the horse at the age of 12 when his father King Philip had

bought him for the equivalent of $10,000. The horse when brought out, could not be mounted. The young prince saw that the horse was afraid of its own shadow and those of the men seeking to restrain him. Alexander turned the horse to face the sun and calmly mounted him. Thereafter, Bucephalus would permit no one but Alexander to sit on his saddle. The grooms had to exercise him bareback.

After conquering the Persian Empire, Alexander turned his attention to the conquest of India, defeating the Indian King Porus at the Hydaspes River (*Jhelum*) in

327BC. At the end of the battle Bucephalus, now aged 30, died of his wounds. He was buried with full honors, and a city, Bucephalia, was founded on the site. Alexander died three years later at the age of 32.

Chetak

In Rajasthan and throughout India the name Chetak is revered, but outside the sub-continent few know of the gallant Marwari horse (*see* p.129) who was the mount of Maharana Pratap of Mewar.

At the battle of Haldi Ghati in 1576 Mewar, riding Chetak, confronted in single combat the commander of Akbar's armies, Raja Man Singh, mounted in the *howdah* of his war elephant. They attacked with a stupendous leap which allowed Mewar to use

Alexander the Great
Detail showing Alexander the Great from an ancient Roman mosaic of the Battle of Issus, 334BC. Alexander rode his horse Bucephalus in all the campaigns against the powerful Persian Empire ruled by Darius, finally crushing the Persian armies at Arbela in 331BC.

Marengo

Napoleon on his favorite horse, the grey Arab Marengo, at the St. Bernard Pass, painted by Jacques-Louis David in 1800. The horse was named after the site of one of Napoleon's greatest victories, which opened up the whole of northern Italy to him.

his lance; the thrust was parried, but Chetak continued to leap at the elephant, drumming his forefeet on its head. In the heat of the fight Chetak's hind fetlock was slashed off at the joint, probably by a stroke from the heavy sword held in the elephant's trunk.

Forced to flee, Chetak galloped away on three legs, escaping his pursuers by a last, mighty leap over the gorge at Haldi Ghati, where the great-hearted horse died with his head in his master's arms.

Chetak is commemorated at Haldi Ghati with a memorial platform, the Chetak Chabutra, and today there is a Chetak Horse Society.

Comanche

Less illustrious but no less famous was the dun-colored Comanche, the hero of the US 7th Cavalry and for 15 years its "second commanding officer."

The horse got his name when he was wounded by a Comanche arrow in his first action against the Indian tribes. Comanche had stumbled momentarily when he was hit but continued to the end of the engagement. Owned by Captain Myles Keogh, he was wounded three times in the course of many engagements over a period of eight years up to June 25, 1876, the date of General Custer's ill-judged Last Stand at the battle of Little Big Horn. After the battle, Comanche, the sole survivor, was found covered in blood and badly wounded.

With great difficulty the cavalry got him by steamer and wagon to Fort Lincoln where he was nursed back to health.

Comanche stayed in retirement with the 7th Cavalry as an honored veteran, having the run of the lines, dying in 1891 at the age of 29.

Mancha and Gato

Very little can approach the epic ride from Buenos Aires to Washington DC, a distance of 10,000 miles (16,090km), made by the Swiss traveller and writer, Aime Felix Tschiffely (1895–1954). His

companions were two tough Criollos (*see* p.138), Mancha and Gato. Mancha was a pinto, while Gato was of the famed *grulla* or *gateado* (cat-colored) color, a coffee or mouse-dun shade. When Tschiffely left Buenos Aires on April 23, 1925 Mancha was 16 and Gato 15. Their journey took two-and-a-half years over some of the most dangerous country in the world.

The horses retired to a South American *estancia* where Gato lived to be 36 and Mancha died at the grand old age of 40.

Age of the Chariots

In rough, mountainous country the only practical option for fighting troops was ridden horses. But in the flat, open country of Syria, Egypt, and Iraq, the wheeled vehicle was more effective. The horses may have been too small to ride, in some instances, but a pair or, better still, four horses harnessed to a light chariot could carry a three-man crew easily and at great speed.

Before 3000BC horse-riding nomads were moving out of their steppelands in a continuing war of expansion against the settled communities beyond their borders. By that time Kassites and Elamites, nomads from northern Iraq, had conquered northwest Persia, while the Hittites, a highly successful horse-people, had penetrated into Asia Minor and were occupying what is now Turkey. But in the rich, flat valley lands of the Middle East, along the Tigris and Euphrates rivers, warfare was to be governed by the chariot, a weapon of war more suited to the terrain.

The spoked wheel was in use in Mesopotamia by 2500BC, and by 2000BC Aryan chariot forces had over-run Persia and India, the Celts were pressing through Europe, and the Hyksos, another nomadic people, had occupied Upper Egypt. It was the Hyksos who introduced this new concept of warfare into Egypt, along with the wheel and, of course, the chariot.

The Hittites

Nonetheless, it was the Hittites who were to be the greatest exponents of chariot warfare and the most formidable of Egypt's enemies. They had extended their empire into northern Syria and had taken Babylon by 1595BC, all the time being in a state of war with Egypt. The final battle was at Kadesh in Syria in 1286BC, when they defeated King Rameses I in the greatest chariot confrontation of the ancient world, the equivalent of

Temple of Amon

This Egyptian relief from the Temple of Amon shows the bitting arrangement necessary to control spirited horses and gives a good indication of the horses employed.

the tank battles of World War II and over much the same ground. The Hittite army was composed of 17,000 foot soldiers, while the number of chariots, at 3,500, exceeded the number of tanks engaged here in World War II.

The Hittite chariot, the light tank of the time, was drawn by four horses that were small by our standards. Two were harnessed to a central pole and two were hitched to the outside of them with an outrigger. Over the level ground they could be driven at a considerable speed—almost as fast over short distances as the World War II tanks some 3,000 years later.

The Hittite chariot was the first to employ the three-man crew: driver, shield-bearer and either an archer or javelin thrower. The Hittites put great emphasis on horse-management, designed to increase the fitness of their chariot horses. Indeed, it was they who produced the world's first horse-training manual. It was written by Kikkuli the Mittanian in about 1360BC and, in a surprisingly modern way, gave detailed instructions on the regular feeding of grain, lucerne and chaffed straw. Moreover, feeding was carefully related to systematic exercise. Chariots and harness, also, were carefully maintained, and the skilful management of the well-drilled chariot formations in battle was an example followed by all the subsequent chariot-driving people.

Chariot Harness

The control of a fit, four-horse team, even though made up of relatively small horses, was a matter of vital importance. Jointed bits, acting across the lower jaw, were in use from early times. At first, they were made from hardwood and then from bone and horn, but by 1200–1300BC metal bits were in general use. As bigger, stronger horses became available, a variety of

Hunting Chariot
In this illustration, depicted on a casket found in the tomb of Tutankhamun, the detail of the royal hunting chariot and the superbly accoutred horse in all its finery is shown very clearly.

tight nosebands and martingales were used to support the bit, which could be made more severe by serrated mouthpieces or the addition of "hedgehog" spikes.

Chariot harness was adapted from the yoke that had been used with oxen for centuries. Because of the horse's different shape, it had first to be bowed and made lighter, then fitted with pads lying over the withers so that it could be fastened to the central pole. It was kept in place by a girth and a strap fastening round the neck, so that the horse was actually pulling the load from that part of the anatomy. The addition of a martingale from the neckstrap to the girth corrected the worst effects of the yoke harness, but was not an ideal solution. Nonetheless, the chariots were light, and the addition of an outrigger on each side of the pole pair increased the pulling power.

All the chariot people—Hittites, Babylonians, Assyrians and Egyptians—followed this practice, and so in later years did the Romans with their *quadriga*. The Hittite Empire was no longer of any consequence by 1190BC, but the use of the chariot as an integral part of warfare was to persist for centuries to come.

Greek Pottery
This piece of pottery, though immensely stylized, is interesting for its depiction of the four-wheeled vehicle drawn by two horses employed in funerary and other processions.

Nomadic Horsemen

The nomadic horsemen of the steppes began their incursions into the territories of their more settled neighbors over 3,000 years before the Great Wall of China was even contemplated. Quite simply, that remarkable structure was created to keep out the Asiatic Huns, and this is a measure of the effect these restless nomads had upon the world's developing civilizations.

Foremost of the early nomadic horse-people were the Scythians, a generic term applied to loosely related races of southern Russia, who were, without doubt, the archetypal horse-people of the world (*see* pp.18–19). They reached Egypt in 611BC and then spread outwards on to the Hungarian Plains and the Carpathians.

It is to the Scythians that we owe the convention of Western male clothing and the beginning of a saddle, too. Their clothes were entirely suitable for "a people born on horseback."

The Scythians

The Scythian saddle was far in advance of the cloths used by the civilized Greeks and Romans. It was made of felt and leather and comprised two oblong pads, or cushions, stuffed with deer hair. The pads were joined by a connecting strip of felt or leather laid from end to end, or they were joined by wooden arches at front and rear. Thus the rider's weight was carried on either side of the spine, just as we recommend today. The saddle, worn over a felt numnah, was kept in place by a girth and breast-band, with or without a breeching fitted round the quarters. The saddle of the Argentine gaucho is not much different in its essentials, stirrup apart, and when the gaucho needs a vantage point he stands on his saddle, a foot on each pad. So did the Scythian and his successors, the Huns and Mongols.

The Scythians used both sword and dagger but the principal weapon of these supreme light horsemen was the short bow. Moving swiftly, they avoided closing

Did you know?

The Mongol Empire lasted from 1206 to 1405 and at its peak was the greatest land empire in the world, stretching from China to the Arctic Circle. It was created by an illiterate nomad of the Gobi Desert, Genghis Khan.

Scythian Tapestry
The Scythians wore woollen trousers, leather boots, and warm, hooded tunics, while Greeks and Romans wore robes of fine cloth—elegant, but hardly suitable for riding.

Steppe Horsemen

Throughout the Eurasian steppelands there are horsemen like this one, descended from the old nomadic tribes and carrying on the traditions of their horsemanship.

with the enemy, firing hails of arrows out of the range of javelin throwers or swordsmen—and they never, ever charged in line abreast!

It was a martial society of merciless warriors. They scalped (like the Native American of a later century) or beheaded the fallen, hanging the scalps from the saddle bow and bridle. They made the skulls into highly decorative drinking cups, lined with gold. They were hunters, horse-breeders, and dealers, and they gelded the male horses they did not wish to retain as stallions.

The Parthians

The Parthians, deriving from the Scythians, had made a kingdom in Iran during the third century BC and they terrorized their neighbors and the Roman Empire for centuries after. Indeed, they defeated the much-vaunted legions at Carrhea in 50BC. They, too, were horse-archers, using a short, double-curved horn bow and employing the same hit-and-run tactic as the Scythians. They gave us the term "the Parthian shot": feigning flight, they turned in the saddle and fired arrows over the horse's tail when their pursuers came within range.

Yeh-lu T'su T'su, a Chinese general of the period, said of them: "On horses they go to war, to banquets, to public and private tasks and on them they travel, stay still, do business and chat." Like the Scythians, they would mount a horse to go 100 yards rather than walk.

Genghis Khan

The Scythians, Parthians, Huns and Mongols were in their time the apocalyptic horsemen of the world, and none more so than the Mongols of Genghis Khan. Theirs was the final and most terrible assault by nomadic barbarians on the civilized world, and they were almost totally destructive.

Their empire was built, maintained and administered from the backs of horses. Genghis Khan was an inspired leader and a cavalry commander of absolute genius. Mongol armies were wholly mounted. Each man had five horses, changing to another as necessary and covering over 80 miles (124km) a day. The "hordes," under strict discipline, lived off the land.

They were masters of the *tulughama*, the swift, encircling movement that took the enemy in the rear.

Although, in nomad fashion, the Mongols took what they could use and destroyed all else, including great cities and whole populations, they created a system of communication, the *yam* (a network of defended routes) that reached to every part of the vast empire and was unsurpassed for two centuries.

But in the end the Mongol contribution to the world was minimal, just a sort of earthquake, violent and destructive, in the ongoing affairs of mankind.

As Yeh-lu T'su T'su said, "The Empire was won on horseback, but you cannot govern on horseback."

THE WORKING HORSE

The Royal Force
Canada's Royal Mounted Police is the most famous of all mounted police forces and still maintains a ceremonial unit.

Horses at War

The English poet Rudyard Kipling (1865–1936) put the horse firmly and finally into the context of world history when he wrote: "Four things greater than all things are—Women and Horses and Power and War." All have been with the human race from the beginning, before ever those horse-people broke out of the Eurasian steppes (*see* p.18) and all, unconsciously, changed the course of world events forever.

In the history of the world there has never been a time without conflict of some sort in one or other of the five continents. Just as certainly, no major war, and few of the lesser ones, has been conducted without the employment of horses, often in overwhelming numbers.

World War I

By the 19th century the armies of Europe were employing cavalry on a huge scale, and in World War I (1914–18) millions were used, a very large percentage of them dying from exposure in the morass of the Western Front. Many horses were employed in cavalry units, but far more of them dragged guns and ammunition through axle-deep mud, while others brought up baggage wagons, pack loads, field kitchens and ambulances. Some motor vehicles were used, but horses were more effective, and the war depended to a very large degree on their exertions.

Into Battle
Unionist cavalry played a hugely significant role in the Civil War (1861–65). This evocative picture is by the artist of the West, Frederic Remington (1861–1909).

Ready for Anything
This German trooper of World War II and his horses are equipped to meet the emergency of a gas attack. Germany employed upwards of 80,000 horses at the outbreak of war, many of which were used to transport heavy artillery, while the Russians had over a million.

In Palestine, General Allenby's victorious campaign against the Turks is now regarded as the classic cavalry campaign. It ended in October 1918, when the 20,000-strong Desert Mounted Corps, comprising Australian, New Zealand, Indian and British regiments, occupied Aleppo, the city that had been founded by one of the earliest horse-people, the Hittites. Lloyd George, the British Prime Minister, paid fulsome tribute to both horses and men. However, he then allowed 20,000 of the horses to be sold into Egypt to suffer brutal neglect and callous cruelty, being worked to death in the streets of Cairo. The betrayal led to the foundation of the Brooke Hospital for Animals in Cairo, which opens its doors to all sick animals. It was the brainchild of Dorothy Brooke, the wife of Sir Geoffrey Brooke, who commanded the Cavalry Brigade in Egypt in 1930, and it still functions today (*see* pp.34–35).

World War II
When World War II broke out in 1939, horse-power was still a factor in the armies of Europe. The Poles went to war with a complement of 86,000 horses. In 1939 they lost 2,000 of the Pomeranian Cavalry Brigade in half an hour, when they were attacked by German dive-bombers. The German Wehrmacht employed almost as many horses, while the Russian Army could field 30 cavalry divisions, supported by horse artillery and 800,000 draft horses—making a total of 1.2 million war horses. In November 1941, the 44th Mongolian Division, in the face of the German advance to Moscow, charged entrenched infantry with sabres drawn. Within minutes, 2,000 horses and men lay dead and dying. As Maréchel Bosquet remarked of another cavalry disaster, the "Charge of the Light Brigade" at Balaclava in 1854: "*C'est magnifique, mais ce n'est pas la guerre*" (It is magnificent, but it is not war).

Modern Warfare
Transport mules were used extensively in other theaters of war, particularly in Italy and Burma. In the early 21st century, both India and China patrol their long frontiers with mounted forces, and there are horse units in Kashmir, Afghanistan and Bosnia, working in country inaccessible to motor vehicles.

Indeed, even in the later hostilities in Afghanistan both sides relied heavily on horses in the notoriously difficult terrain. At one point even American special troops were moving up to Kabul in a loose mounted formation.

Mounted Snipers
Two Afghan snipers maintain mobility on a single horse near Herat, Afghanistan during the Soviet invasion of 1980. Crack shots, Afghan snipers were very effective in harassing Soviet troops with continual small-arms fire during lightning raids on Russian positions. Their Kabuli horses are sure-footed and very tough.

Horses in Agriculture

It was not until the 8th century AD that horses began to be used in agriculture in Europe and then only on a small scale. Before that, horseshoes and harness had not been developed sufficiently to allow for heavy tractive work, and, secondly, the horses were neither big enough nor sufficiently strong, nor was agriculture advanced enough to make use of them.

By the 11th century the demand for a more substantial warhorse led to the development of the modern heavy-draft breeds we know today, and by then there had been significant improvements in draft harness, largely due to the inventive Chinese.

Sophisticated, wheeled vehicles were in use in China as early as 1300BC. It was the Chinese who invented the single-horse vehicles drawn by lateral shafts. They were also the first people to drive horses in tandem, one harnessed behind the other. A breast harness, like the ones in use today, was used in China by 250BC, and after that came the indispensable breeching strap, allowing the horse to brake the vehicle. Finally there was the invention that changed the face of the civilized world, the horse collar, acclaimed as one of the world's greatest inventions because, quite simply, it allows the most efficient tractive force to be exerted with the minimum of effort.

Developments in Europe

It took time for these momentous improvements to reach Europe and even then, it was not until the 18th century that the horse finally took the place of oxen for cultivation of the land. Oxen, indeed, continued to be used in Europe until after World War I. In the Middle East and Asia the horse was far too valuable a

As Big as They Come

This set of disc-harrows is an impressive example of the advances that were continuing in the manufacture of farming equipment during the 19th century. It is heavy enough to require a team of four horses to draw it.

Unusual Combination

A farmer is aided by a horse to plough a field near Mouta, Jordan. Horses are not generally used for cultivation in the Middle East, but this horse appears to be doing the job. The harness is rudimentary and is similar to that used on oxen. It employs neither a breast harness nor a collar.

commodity for menial tasks, and frequently it was not best-suited to the work conditions. The mule and donkey carried out the work satisfactorily enough—as, indeed, they often do today.

The turning point came with the introduction in the 18th century of improved methods of cultivation, in particular the three-crop rotational system (cereals, roots, then a return to grass) and the development of machinery to meet the demands of more intensive farming methods. Integral to the new systems, of course, and to a degree influenced by them, was the breeding of a powerful agricultural horse capable of heavy draft. The horse was better suited than slow-moving oxen to the new equipment. Moreover oxen, because they are slow, need pasture close to their work and, very importantly, as ruminants they must be given time to chew the cud.

The Industrial Revolution

In Britain, the Industrial Revolution of the 18th and early 19th century—and it was a revolution—led to a rapid rise in population. People moved in droves from the then impoverished countryside to the industrial centers. There was also a corresponding increase in demand for food. More grasses and clovers were therefore needed to feed the horses that were integral to both industry and agriculture, as well, of course, as the beef cattle and sheep raised for human consumption.

Advances had already been made in the manufacture of agricultural implements. The Rotherham plough was made in Britain in 1730, an improvement on the existing Dutch design and a forerunner of the Arbuthnot swing plough, which turned the spit (the slice of soil turned by the furrow) better than anything else of its time. Jethro Tull's horse-drawn seed drill was made in 1731 and was followed by a horse-hoe.

By the 19th century, the agricultural machinery industry in Britain was in full swing, producing machines that stood the test of time and could be improved upon only in detail. Threshers, corn grinders, elevators, multi-furrow ploughs, sub-soil ploughs, reapers, cutters, and binders were all made available. In the USA giant combine harvesters worked by 40-horse teams were used.

Only the heaviest and strongest animals were a match for what was often brutally hard work (*see* box, below).

American Multi-horsed Implements

A horse-drawn combine harvester and thresher cuts wheat in a field near Moro, Oregon c. 1880. America rapidly acquired unrivalled expertise in the operation of the multi-horsed implements, which were necessary to cope with the huge wheat acreage there—half as large again as the entire cultivated area of Britain. As a result, the US horse population had risen from 7 million in 1860 to 25 million by 1914. By 1890 the western prairie lands were being harvested by combines 40ft (12m) wide and weighing 13.5 tons (13.7 tonnes). These were drawn by as many as 42 horses, controlled by six men. However, with special harnessing, one man could drive a 36-horse team pulling a set of drills or harrows. The massive ploughs that cut into the virgin prairie land were especially hard for horses; drawn by a team of eight they earned the name of "horse-killers."

The Heavy Horse

Heavy breeds, already existing in France, the Low Countries, Germany, and Scandinavia, were further improved to produce, for example, the heavyweight Brabant or Belgian Heavy Draft and the French Percheron (*see* pp.140–41). Both these breeds were exported in large numbers to the USA and Canada in the 19th century.

The British breeds, too, were especially notable: the massive Shires, the Clydesdales, and the clean-legged Suffolk (*see* pp.140–43). It was these tremendously powerful breeds that underpinned the advances in agricultural practice in Western Europe and elsewhere up to the 20th century.

The Percheron was perhaps the most in demand, and between 1880 and 1920 was exported heavily to the USA, Australia, South Africa and South America. In fact, to meet the demand and to replace the enormous loss of horses in World War I—more than half-a-million in total—Britain imported Percherons and part-bred Percherons from both the USA and Canada. Thousands were to go to France in 1915, destined to form a large percentage of the horse casualties.

In the last years of the 19th century, the going rate for a Percheron in the USA was $5,000. Between 1900 and 1910 there were 31,900 registered Percherons, and the price for a top horse was around $40,000.

Percheron Pair

A pair of French Percheron draw the plough. The Percheron (*see* p.141) remains one of the most popular of the heavy breeds and is certainly the most versatile. In its time it has served as a coach horse, farm horse, and gun horse. It has even been ridden under saddle.

Eastern Europe

In Eastern Europe, where farming was, and to an extent is still, less advanced and the acreages are smaller, a much lighter, all-round farm horse was favored over the big, heavy horse that was expensive to keep and hardly necessary on the mostly light soils.

While the horse remains a part of the Eastern European agricultural economy, the tractor has now replaced the heavy horse teams elsewhere. Tractors do the work more quickly than horses, and the land used for growing horse-feed is released for other purposes.

Carting Hay

Above, a group of Russian farm hands transport hay in a horse-drawn cart. In Eastern Europe generally, a much lighter horse is used for all-round farm work in an agricultural economy that is less developed than elsewhere in Europe and where, for the most part, the soils are light and not suitable for intensive cultivation.

However, tractors cause atmospheric pollution and, unlike horses, do not reproduce themselves. Nor do they create a waste product that will enrich the land without the need for artificial fertilizers.

Horses are frequently used in commercial forestry for clearing and hauling (*see* below).

Logging

Horses are less intrusive and damaging of the environment than tractors, more efficient and more economical. The increased use of horses in forestry plantations, where the inclines are steep and the ground soft, is now becoming noticeable and the practice attracts much favorable media coverage. In Britain, the horses employed are usually Shires or Shire crosses (*see* p.142); In America, other breeds, such as the Percheron or even the Belgian (*see* pp.140–41), might be considered for this specialized work. To handle a horse effectively in a forest environment calls for very considerable skills. It goes without saying that the horse needs to be calm and steady as well as sure-footed in what are often extremely difficult conditions.

The Brooke Hospital

One of the greatest victories of World War I (1914–18) was that of General Allenby's Desert Mounted Corps, which in the world's last classic cavalry campaign defeated the Turks in Palestine in 1918. The politicians were fulsome in their praise, and the British Prime Minister, David Lloyd George, spoke of the "conspicuous example of the services which cavalry can render in war," saying the horses were "as unbeatable as the riders."

However, in a shameful act of betrayal, the British government then abandoned these "unbeatable" cavalry horses. And it was because of this that the Brooke Hospital for Animals in Cairo came into being.

After the war, over 20,000 horses of the Desert Mounted Corps were sold to peasants for a pittance or were left to fend for themselves, in both cases being condemned to lives of brutal neglect and callous cruelty.

The local people were poor and depended on a single animal to scratch a pitiful living for their families. There was no room for compassion, and as long as a horse, a mule or a donkey could move, whatever the pain or effort, it had to work, usually being given only bare scraps of food to eat.

In the city lame, emaciated and exhausted horses, cruelly abused and often savagely beaten, were used to draw the carriages, called *caleches*, that carried tourists.

To the Rescue

It was left to a dedicated lady to save what she could of the old cavalry horses and to campaign for all the other neglected horses, mules and donkeys. She was Dorothy Brooke, wife of Major-General Sir Geoffrey Brooke, who commanded the Cavalry Brigade in Egypt in 1930 and was one of Britain's greatest horsemen.

Dorothy Brooke raised money, by organizing appeals and dipping deep into her own resources, to buy the crippled horses for sums that would go a long way to help the owners buy a healthy replacement.

Five thousand animals were bought. They were then made comfortable, and most were put down humanely.

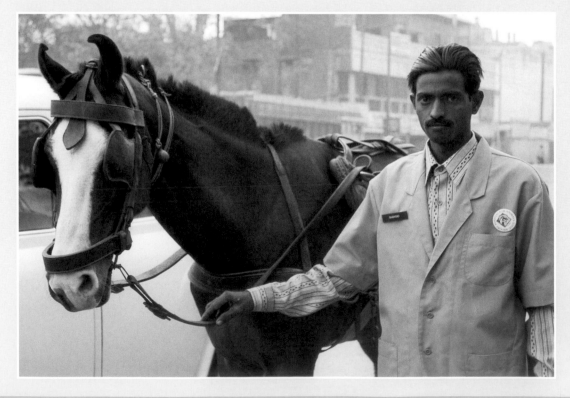

Veterinary Workers
Mohammed Shamsed is the equivalent of the medical community nurse, providing a follow-up service and after-care for animals that have received treatment.

Mobile Unit
Mobile units are able to visit animals in need of attention and treatment, and provide a very valuable service for those most in need.

Prevention
On the principle that prevention is better than cure, the Brooke Hospital provides the vital worming treatments necessary for the animals' health.

Education
Education is the key to better management and, consequently, better health in the animals. The hospital conducts regular public instruction with the aid of visual material, such as this puppet show.

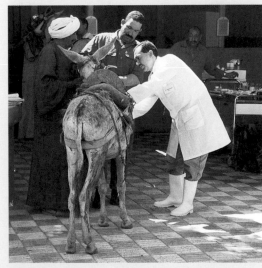

Veterinary Clinic
Veterinary workers in the Luxor out-clinic. Luxor is one of six out-clinics set up by the Brooke Hospital as an extension of the work done at the principal Cairo Hospital.

The Hospital Opens
By 1934 Dorothy Brooke had bought premises and opened the doors to all sick animals, who were to be treated without charge. She continued her work until she died in Cairo in 1955. By then the hospital was soundly organized and its services much expanded. Today it employs a veterinary staff, and the original building has been extended to include an operating theater, dispensary, farrier's shop, stable blocks and offices. It maintains its own ambulance. Clinics, run on the same lines, have been set up in Luxor and Alexandria, and it is the Brooke Hospital that is responsible for the provision of water troughs in Cairo and Luxor and near the Pyramids at Mena and Sakkara.

It is still necessary to put horses down, but many more are nursed back to health. Each year thousands are treated for every sort of ailment.

The Hospital's Role Today
The problem for all forms of animal welfare in the Middle East is a combination of *poverty*, *attitude* and *ignorance*. The hospital, apart from providing the means, through sound, healthy work animals, can do no more to alleviate the first but, inevitably, *attitude* and *ignorance* have given rise to a strong educational element in the hospital's work: education by example, if you like, along with a little persuasion.

Today the hospital is one of the most famous and respected animal charities in the world. It remains as a working, ongoing, memorial to its dedicated founder and, perhaps, a reminder to us all of man's inhumanity to the animals that serve him so well.

Horses in Industry

The period between 1700 and 1850 goes down in history as the Industrial Revolution. Spearheaded by the British, brimming with confidence in the growth and wealth of their expanding empire, the Industrial Revolution marked a fundamental change in the societies of the Western world that had repercussions in almost every other country.

The Industrial Revolution was about coal and steam, iron and steel, and machinery that took over work once accomplished laboriously by hand. But just like the business of war, industry was dependent on horse-power. Horses then were crucial to the moving of raw materials and finished goods between cities, towns and railheads.

In Britain, in 1769, James Watt perfected his steam engine, the power of which, with perhaps unconscious irony, was measured in units of "horse-power"—the power required to raise 550lb (250kg) one foot in one second (equivalent to 745.7 watts) being one horse-power. (Until well after World War II the power of motor-car engines was also expressed in terms of

horse-power rather than cubic capacity: a 1600cc car, for instance, was known as a 16hp model.)

Although machines would, in the end, make horse-power redundant in industry they did, just as certainly, encourage and promote specialist breeding of horses—particularly the heavy breeds and the vanner (a light draft horse)—and did so right up to the 20th century.

Pit Ponies

Coal was the great source of power and in the concentrations of pits in Britain alone, thousands of horses and ponies were employed. In Scotland, Shetland ponies were used, their small stature—enabling them to work in the low-roofed drifts—being quite disproportionate to their remarkable strength.

In Wales, it was the Welsh ponies and the smaller cobs, known as "pitters," that were in demand and were frequently bred for the purpose.

Ponies continued to be used in British mines up to 1972, when the five ponies working the Wheldale Colliery, Castleford, were retired.

Horse Mills

Farm machinery—including grist mills, root choppers and the like—was naturally horse-powered, but there were also many hundreds of horse mills, worked often by blind or lame horses, in conditions where wind- and watermills were impractical. Horse mills were usually round structures—often attached to barns—inside which the horse walked round and round attached to a system of cogs and gears so as to provide motive power.

Canal Horses

In Britain, a network of canals was established in the 18th century. Canals also existed in mainland Europe, but nowhere, within so small a compass, was the system so comprehensive as in Britain. The barges carried both freight and passengers and were hauled principally by horses, but mules might be used occasionally, and even donkeys. There was no particular breed or type of barge horse; the "boaters," as they were known, were usually strong vanner sorts or smaller part-breds of Shire type. Because of the height of the bridges over the towpaths, horses could not be over 15.2–15.3hh., but they had to be very strong, as well as intelligent and versatile.

The boater hauled a load of 50–60 tons (50.5–60.5 tonnes) at a speed of about 2mph (3.2km/h), but when relays of trotting horses were used in short stages, the barges could cover over 50 miles (80km) a day.

In 1810 it was estimated that one horse and three men could move as much by barge as 60 horses and ten men could pull in a wagon. Fifty years earlier, barges with a 200-ton (202-tonne) load were hauled up the River Thames by teams of 14 horses. Before then, they were dragged slowly and painfully by 80 or more men.

Down the Mines

In the mining industry, horses worked at pit heads turning the windlass of the hoist, and hauling the heavy coal wagons, while the small but sturdy ponies (see inset) worked underground drawing the coal tubs, and were stabled there during their working life.

Boat Horses and Railway Horses

The pride of the canals was the high-speed passenger and light-freight fly-boat. It made its debut at the end of the 18th century and ceased to operate just after World War I. The fly-boat was a light, shallow craft drawn by pairs of horses hitched fore and aft. One horse was ridden by a postillion, and the pace was a steady canter that produced an average speed of 10–12mph (16–19km/h) The horses were used in relays over stages of 3–5 miles (5–8km) and teams could be changed in under a minute by the expert horsemen employed for the purpose. Fly-boats had priority over all other traffic, and to reinforce their standing were often fitted at the bow with sharp scythe blades with which they could cut the tow rope of barges slow to give way to them.

The boater learned to cope with bridges and tunnels and also with the gates and stiles on the towpath that marked boundary fences. These obstacles, often as much as 3ft (90cm) high, would be jumped by a good boater—a not inconsiderable feat for a horse in harness.

Pack Horses

Another early transport network was that provided by the pack-horse routes. Pack trains were in use in many parts of the world where there was a minimal road system and mountainous terrain.

Dales and Fell ponies (*see* pp.152–53), as well as Britain's premier carriage horse, the Cleveland Bay (*see* p.106), were all used in pack, while in the 17th century the Pack Horse Service between Bampton, Devon and London employed a good, all-round trotting horse, the Devonshire Pack Horse, a bigger version (about 15hh.) of the Exmoor and Dartmoor pony (*see* pp.146–47). The breed, or more correctly, the type, has long gone, but it gave good service in its day.

The Railways

The early railways consisted of horse-drawn freight and passenger coaches travelling on a track (known as tram- or dramways) over short and medium distances. The first-recorded British line on which the carriages

Boat Horses

Boaters, as the canal horses were called, are still to be seen on the waterways drawing holiday barges, or narrow boats, but the work is far easier than it used to be and they are not expected to jump turnstiles! This horse is being driven but boaters usually work untended.

Street Car

This early American street car or tram ran on a track (tramway) and was one of the fleet operated by the Minneapolis Street Railway. Unusually, it is drawn by a pair of mules rather than the vanner type horses typically favored in Europe. Dirt on the rails made the trams particularly heavy to pull into motion.

were drawn by horses was the Surrey Iron Railway, opened in 1803, and running between Wandsworth and Croydon.

A similar branch line in Northern Ireland, terminating at Fintona Station, survived up to 1957, while a number of horse lines were operating in mainland Europe far into the 19th century.

The grandest horse railway of them all was Austria's long-distance Linz–Budweis Line. It carried salt to Bohemia and was also much used by passengers. In its heyday it carried on its 124 miles (200km) of track 100,000 tons (101,600 tonnes) of freight and 150,000 passengers a year. It was opened in July 1832 by the Emperor Franz I, who with the Empress made the trip between Urfahr and St. Magdalena in a splendidly upholstered state landau fitted with flanged iron wheels for the occasion and driven by a uniformed coachman. Alas, this Ruritanian enterprise closed in 1872.

George Stephenson opened the first steam-powered railway in 1825, making a 20-mile (33km) journey covering Stockton and Darlington, UK. By 1845 the railways were well on the way to bringing the road-coach era to an end and were beginning to emerge as the greatest employers and owners of horses in Europe.

Most of the railway horses were used in cartage and delivery. Shire teams were needed for heavy industrial goods, vanners for light goods deliveries and cobs for express parcel delivery. Horses also shunted rolling stock. The last one in Britain—at Newmarket—did not retire until 1967, a year before the last steam train was withdrawn from the railway system. His job was to move horse boxes round the sidings.

Wagon Train

It was wagons like these, drawn by teams of as many as six horses, that carried settlers into the American West in the 18th and 19th centuries. They were the main means of long-distance transportation for both people and goods before the advent of the railways.

City Horses

Buses and Trams

The omnibus started up briefly in Paris as early as 1662, but the first regular service, also operating in Paris, was started by Stanislaus Baudry in 1828. The idea was copied by George Shillibeer, who was running a London service in the following year. For a time, the vehicles were called "Shillibeers," the name gradually being replaced by "omnibus" or simply "bus."

By 1890 London had 2,210 buses, worked by 11,000 men and twice that number of horses. Many of the bus horses were Clydesdale (*see* p.141) and a percentage were the strong Irish Draft, the basis for the celebrated Irish Hunter.

The tram, running on rails, followed the bus, but it was much harder on the horses, and tram horses were soon worn out. After that came electric trams, trolleybuses and finally the petrol- and diesel-driven vehicles of today. By the twilight of the tram, horse-drawn public transport had lasted for just 70 years.

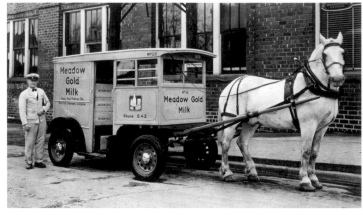

Milk Float

Until well after World War II, many cities had their milk delivered by a smart horse-drawn milk float. The one illustrated here was in use in 1945 at Bloomington, Illinois, and was drawn by a strong type of vanner. In London, the milk rounds were serviced almost entirely by Welsh cobs, renowned for their stamina and for being easy to manage.

Growing Cities

In the 1890s and 1900s, cities such as London, Paris, Berlin and New York teemed with horses used for all sorts of purposes. There were cab horses (London had 11,300 cabs and twice that number of horses to keep them in service), funeral horses, carriage horses, and horses for the coal carts and for all sorts of general deliveries. And then there were the horses employed to bring in enormous supplies of fodder and those needed to remove the subsequent waste product, which in some cities posed a serious health hazard. New York City had a horse population of 150,000–175,000 in 1880, while small-town Milwaukee, in Wisconsin, with a population of 350,000, had 12,500 horses, producing, it is reported, 131 tons (133 tonnes) of manure every day.

The life of a city horse was hard, although, in fairness, the railway companies were exemplary owners and kept their horses to a high standard. But many horses, the cast-offs in every category, were worked to death, cruelly mistreated by small traders and the like.

London Omnibus

Horse-drawn London buses, originally called "Shillibeers" after George Shillibeer, were a popular form of transport right up to the end of the 19th century and contributed in no small way to the traffic jams which were a less than attractive feature of the city. To move a fully loaded bus was hard work for a two-horse team, and the working life of the horses was short in consequence, even though they were usually well looked after.

Fire Engine

Then, as now, the Fire Service was operated by an elite body of dedicated men. The fire engines were drawn by teams of well-conditioned horses that galloped to the scene of the fire to the accompaniment of the vehicle's loudly-ringing warning bell.

The unhappy truth is that, on the whole, men exploited the horse as much in times of peace as they did in times of war.

The End of the Line

Most horses ended up in what was commonly known as the "knacker's yard"—a slaughterhouse dealing exclusively with the disposal of horses. In these highly organized abbatoirs, numerous by-products were made: bones were ground for fertilizer, grease was extracted for candle-making, manes and tails went to upholstery and the making of violin bows. The hides were used to manufacture leather goods, while hoofs and skin were made into glue. It was a thriving industry in which little or nothing went to waste.

Did you know?

The working life of a bus horse was reckoned at around four years, while that of a tram horse was usually three years. The horses used to draw buses and trams were always mares.

Lines of Communication

Across the world, in every nation, until the arrival of motorized vehicles, it was the horse that provided the essential lines of communication. Horses were the means by which the early civilizations were administered. They carried supplies and goods of all kinds and in later years they were integral to organized postal services as well as providing transport for the individual.

By the end of the 2nd century BC the Persians had established a mighty empire and, with it, the means of communication that was necessary to administer it. They built roads with posting stations one day's ride apart. In this way, the royal messengers could cover 1,500 miles (2,415km) in 7 to 14 days—although the stirrup had not yet been invented! Presumably either Persian horsemen rode pacing horses, whose lateral gait provides a virtually level platform for a rider, or they avoided the uncomfortable trot by walking, cantering or galloping.

A millennium or so later, early in the 13th century, Genghis Khan (*see* p.25) installed a similar system in his own vast Mongolian empire—but his couriers had the advantage of the stirrup.

Inauguration of the Penny Post
Britain's Penny Postage system, a descendant of Palmer's earlier mail deliveries, began with the delivery at Waterloo, London, in 1840. In that year alone, it dealt with 169 million letters.

Delivering the Mail

What was probably the most significant advance in communication was made in Britain in 1784, when John Palmer, the Postmaster General, initiated a regular mail service that was superior to anything in Europe or, indeed, in the world at that time.

Before that date, mail packages had been carried by postboys on horseback. The boys were given the worst horses, common-bred and rough-actioned. To ease their discomfort, they introduced the practice that we know as rising or "posting" to the trot—when the rider lifts his seat off the saddle at alternate strides. Later, there were mail carts, which were more reliable than postboys but very slow.

Did you know?

The post-chaise was a small but luxurious horse-drawn carriage that could be used by passengers as well as mail. It was fast, but also very expensive.

John Palmer's first mail coach ran from Bristol via Bath on the night of August 2, 1784, arriving at the General Post Office, London, at 8am the next morning, after completing the journey in 15 hours— exactly on time. This could only be achieved with the meticulous organization of the staging halts at chosen inns, or "hostelries," where teams of ostlers (working in the manner of today's racing car pit-stop) changed a team in under 60 seconds.

Improving Roads

Organization and management played a large part in the success of the mail coaches, but it would have been to no avail had there not been state-of-the-art vehicles, with harness to match, and a network of surfaced roads.

In Britain, the roads were largely the work of Thomas Telford, bridge- and road-builder extraordinary, and John McAdam, whose contribution was the macadam or tarmacadam surface. There were 20,000 miles (32,000km) of good roadways in 1830 and a supply of suitable horses to draw the coaches over them. There was, by then, a surplus of English Thoroughbred horses, as well as stallions that could be crossed with Cleveland Bays, for example, to produce the lighter, faster Yorkshire Coach Horse.

Early Passenger Services

Encouraged by the success of the mail coaches, private operators began to put on passenger coaches, maintaining the same high standards as the mail.

In Britain, around the start of the coaching era, records show that in 1825 the passenger coaches were travelling at 10mph (16km/h), while the Royal Mail averaged 12mph (19km/h).

The American coaching era began at about the same time and was dominated by the Concord coaches. As befitted the rough roads, these were very tough vehicles. Drawn by six-horse teams, the Concords could travel at 15mph (24km/h).

The Pony Express

It was America that gave the world the most romantic venture of them all, the legendary Pony Express. Epitomizing the "frontier spirit," it took its place at the very heart of America. The Pony Express was the brainchild of William H. Russell, acclaimed "the Napoleon of the Plains." He inaugurated his service in 1860.

The route, through six states, was between St. Joseph, Missouri, and Sacramento, California, a distance of 1,966 miles (3,164km). A series of riders, "young, skinny, wiry fellows," each armed with a Bible, a pair of revolvers and a rifle, took the mail in relays through often hostile Indian territory. Each man rode 60 miles (96km); 400 ponies—Mustangs and Morgans—were used between 190 relay stations located every 5–20 miles (8–32km). These were manned by 400 staff. The journey was made in ten days.

The Pony Express lasted less than two years, but even that was long enough for it to become an essential part of the American legend.

Pony Express Rider

An artist's impression of a Pony Express rider carrying the mails leaving St. Joseph, Missouri, where the service first began in 1860. It took ten days to reach Sacramento, California.

Pomp and Pageantry

Horses have become the natural accompaniment to ceremonial state occasions, adding immensely to their color and endowing them, like nothing else, with a suitably heroic image. While few countries today maintain a cavalry force of any appreciable size, many retain ceremonial mounted troops, and most have a force of mounted police, who are indispensable to any great occasion.

Perhaps no other country in the world has a calendar of spectacular events to match that of Great Britain—from the daily Changing of the Guard at Buckingham Palace to annual military shows.

A Royal Birthday Parade

In London, one of the most colorful ceremonial occasions is the Trooping the Color. This is an annual ceremony that is carried out on the sovereign's official birthday by troops from the Household Division in the presence of the sovereign and royal dukes at Horse Guards Parade. One of the five regiments of the Foot Guards "troops" its "color": the color (or flag) that originally formed a rallying point in battle is

marched through the ranks of the regiment (the object, in days past, being to familiarize the soldiers with their flag).

Also taking part in the Trooping the Color are the mounted troops of the Household Cavalry. This includes squadrons of the Blues and Royals, who are distinguished by their blue tunics and red-plumed helmets, and the Life Guards, who wear scarlet tunics and white plumes. The squadrons are mounted on black chargers, while the trumpeters ride grays, and the horses ridden by the drummers are traditionally skew- or piebald.

The King's Troop, Royal Horse Artillery, with its guns and limbers drawn by six horses, parades past

The King's Troop

The King's Troop, Royal Horse Artillery, perform their breathtaking ride at full gallop at agricultural shows all over Britain during the summer.

the sovereign, too. It is responsible for firing the royal salute. The King's Troop is engaged in ceremonial duties and displays all year round, and at royal and state funerals, the coffin is, by tradition, carried on one of its gun limbers drawn by its horses.

The Household Cavalry squadrons provide escorts for visiting heads of state and carry out the daily Guard Mounting at the Palace of Westminster, in the heart of London.

Mounted Troops Across the World

The equivalent of the British Household Cavalry on the other side of the world is India's President's Bodyguard, raised at Benares in 1773. Magnificently turbaned and uniformed, the men carry lances and ride Indian-bred bay horses with no white markings. Like Britain's Household Cavalry, the President's Bodyguard takes part in all state occasions and, similarly, its personnel are trained fighting soldiers. In the case of the President's Bodyguard each trooper is also a paratrooper and able to man armored cars.

In Europe, France maintains its legendary Garde Republicaine, the only surviving cavalry regiment in the French army. It contributes brilliantly to the pageantry of the state occasion, but also has serious policing duties and, with other units, has a responsibility to maintain law and order. Its dress uniform is that of 1873: crested, plumed helmets, blue tunics with scarlet facings and blue breeches. White breeches are worn only in the presence of the President of the Republic.

Canada's Royal Canadian Mounted Police, the Mounties, were formed specifically to police the huge tracts of country that make up the Northwest Territories. Between the two world wars the force still used horses on general duties, but today the mounted section is kept up solely for ceremonial and display purposes. The Mounties ride black horses, of good hunter type, bred specifically at Fort Worth. Their world-famous Musical Ride is performed wearing the distinctive uniform of a red tunic, a very smart version of the bush hat, gold-striped blue breeches and, unusually, brown boots.

Canadian Mounties

The red-coated Mounties and their purpose-bred black horses perform their fast-moving Musical Ride at venues throughout the world, and they are always a popular attraction. The constables all carry lances.

Circuses and Tricks

Horses have been circus stars ever since Roman times and one famous act, "Roman riding," in which the artist gallops two horses round the ring with one foot on the back of each, has been performed all over the world for over 2,000 years.

The creator of the modern circus (the word comes from the Latin meaning "ring"), was an Englishman, Philip Astley (1742–1814). He opened his first circus near Waterloo in London in 1769 and it was Astley who was responsible for the size of the standard circus ring. His riding circle was 42ft (13m) in diameter and that has been the size ever since.

By experiment, Astley, who was a skilled horseman, found that by galloping round a ring of that size it was much easier to keep one's balance when standing on the horse's back, because the angle at which the horse inclined to the center remained the same throughout.

Astley's Circus

Astley was a real showman and soon added to his horse acts, clowns, jugglers, tightrope acrobats, and dogs. He himself had a horse called Billy, which

Palomino

This striking and talented Palomino is presented in an act on the long lines and executes movements worthy of the most advanced dressage horse. The color is a very popular one among circus folk.

was advertised as "The Little Learned Military Horse" (Astley had served in both the British army and the forces of the King of Prussia). Billy could unsaddle himself, wash his feet in a bucket, perform some mental tricks, counting and the like, and also wait at the dinner table.

Philip Astley's other horse was the white Gibralter, given to him when he left the British forces, and in the early days Astley earned his living giving demonstrations of acrobatics and trick riding with Gibralter, who became very much a star in his own right.

Circus Horses

Circus horses belong to one of three main groups. There are the highly schooled Haute Ecole (High School) horses (*see* p.64), which are capable of performing the classical movements under their spectacularly costumed riders, as well as one or two circus additions. Usually, the High School horse is an elegant Thoroughbred (*see* p.104).

The Liberty horses, working in groups, on the other hand, are generally Arabs (*see* pp.102–103). They are extremely beautiful and not so long in the body as the Thoroughbred who takes up more ring space as a result. The third group are the vaulting horses, sometimes called rosin-backs. These are broad-backed, heavily built horses. They are very steady and reliable and work at a smooth, rhythmical canter. Circuses have always favored spotted horses for these acts, like the old Knabstrup breed (*see* p.121), but the showy, coal-black Friesians (*see* p.109) are also popular.

Trick Horses

The "trick" horse certainly appeared as a circus act but more often gave individual demonstrations. One of the first was the celebrated Morocco, who in the 1590s toured Europe with his master, a Scotsman called Banks. Morocco could count the numbers on thrown dice, tell you the value of coins accurately and identify in the audience owners of property brought up to the stage.

He was famous enough for Shakespeare to mention him in *Love's Labour's Lost*, but, alas, he and his master may have come to a tragic end. It is said that both were burned at the stake as witches.

Princess Trixie

Four hundred years later W. Harrison Barnes' part-bred Arab mare Princess Trixie performed at the Palace Theatre, London, in a "run" that lasted two years.

Trixie could spell, do arithmetic, and pick out colors. Asked, on one occasion, to spell football, she picked out the correct sounding letters: FUTBAL. Barnes claimed she had the mental ability of a child of six and scientific tests could find no evidence of trickery.

Karl Krall

The act of the German trainer Karl Krall employed two Arab stallions, Muhammed and Zarif, and a Shetland pony called Hanschen. They learned to solve mathematical problems, including fractions, square and cube roots; they could recognize pictures and also identify colors and scents. Krall claimed he used the same methods as those employed when teaching children.

Liberty Horses

This beautiful team of Liberty horses are all pure-bred Arabs. They work through their act at Billy Smart's Circus in complete unison, obeying the whip gestures and quiet words of their trainer.

The Roman Ride

This classic equestrian circus act has been performed all over the world since Roman times. It is executed here, at Austin's Circus, with absolute confidence, the artist dressed in colorful Cossack costume.

Pony Club

Here is the Pony Club version of the Roman Ride. In its way, it is just as difficult to perform, even with the help of the riders on the ponies—and it is certainly just as much appreciated.

THE SPORTING HORSE

Racing in the Snow
Equestrian sports feature strongly at the winter resort of St. Moritz in Switzerland, where both flat- and harness-racing fixtures are held.

Racing on the Flat

The sport of racing is founded on the business of gambling, the incentive that led the sporting English gentlemen of the 17th and 18th centuries to develop the English Thoroughbred racehorse (*see* p.104).

Today racing is an enormous, multinational industry, with a turnover of billions in all sorts of currencies. It employs thousands in stud farms, racing stables, race tracks and ancillary industries, including feedstuffs, saddlery, veterinary medicines and so on, as well as in gambling. Towns such as Newmarket, Suffolk, in the UK, and Lexington, Kentucky, in the US, revolve around the horse.

Organized racing on the flat, under the patronage of the English Kings, James I (1603–25), Charles I (1625–49), and Charles II (1660–85), has its roots in Newmarket, the acknowledged headquarters of British racing and the home of the sport's governing body, the Jockey Club. The Jockey Club, which owns the training grounds of Newmarket Heath and the site of the two racecourses, was founded in about 1752 by a group of wealthy landowners. All racing countries have similar organizations.

The UK has more racecourses and stages more races than any other country, but that includes National Hunt courses and races (*see* pp.52–53).

English Classics

Modern races are much shorter than those that were run in the 18th century, when the emphasis was on distance races up to 4 miles (6.4km). The longest of the English Classic races for three-year-olds is the St. Leger over 1¾ miles (2.8km). There are five Classic races,

Epsom Derby

Probably the most famous race in the world, the English Derby at Epsom was first run in 1780 and has since been held annually on the first Wednesday in June.

American Racing

Racing is carried on at centers throughout America. Unlike in the UK, the practice in America is to stable and train horses on the track and race on specially prepared "dirt" surfaces.

America, centering its industry in the bluegrass state of Kentucky, is probably the strongest force in modern Thoroughbred racing and has its own Classic races, running the famous Kentucky Derby (on the usual American "dirt" track) at Churchill Downs, Louisville.

In Europe, the most prominent racing countries are the UK, France, the Republic of Ireland and Italy, all making unique contributions to the sport.

The Maktoum Family

At the end of the 20th century a new dimension was added to flat racing by the Maktoum family, the rulers of Dubai, in the United Arab Emirates, with their very successful Godolphin enterprise based in the UK in Newmarket as well as in Dubai.

The Maktoums have become patrons of the sport in the manner of the early aristocrats who laid the foundations 300 years ago on Newmarket Heath—and are worthy successors.

Their breeding program, along with such astute purchases as Daylami, Kayf Tara, the phenomenal Dubai Millennium and the Derby winner Lammtara, who was sold to Japan for $30 million, has produced some remarkable horses. These and the establishment of their state-of-the-art racing complex at Dubai have placed the Maktoums in the forefront of modern racing.

three of them comprising the Triple Crown, racing's greatest accolade. They are the 2000 Guineas, the St. Leger and the world-famous Derby, replicated in the Classic races of all racing countries. The Derby might have gone into history as the Bunbury, for the name was settled on the toss of a coin between the 12th Earl of Derby and Sir Charles Bunbury before it was first run at Epsom in 1780.

English colonists took their love of racing to the New World, and it was Richard Nicolls, New York's first governor, who laid out the first American track in 1664.

St. Moritz

Racing at the popular winter resort of St. Moritz in Switzerland is held on snow tracks with the horses being specially shod for the purpose. Attendances are large and gambling is as popular as it is elsewhere.

Weighed Out and In

Before each race every jockey must be weighed *out* with his equipment by the Clerk of the Scales to ensure that his horse carries the stipulated weight. As a further precaution, it is obligatory for all jockeys to be weighed *in* immediately after the race finishes.

Steeplechasing

Steeplechasing belongs firmly to the UK and Ireland, to the inclement weather and soft going that marks the hurly-burly of racing over fences. It suits the robust Thoroughbred (*see* p.104) that can still be found in considerable numbers in both countries. Steeplechasing is the winter sport and is a world away from the Royal Enclosure at Ascot, in the UK, with the women in their summer hats and finery.

America has its Maryland Hunt Cup, run over post-and-rail fences—obstacles that demand a special technique—but the American sport cannot approach the UK/Ireland equivalent in terms of courses, races and popularity.

In Europe, France stages jumping races at Auteuil and, particularly, at Pau, at the foot of the Pyrenees, where horses race over the famous banks. The most spectacular of the European races is the Czech Republic's Gran Pardubice, a very formidable race over natural obstacles—but the average Pardubice entry would be outclassed in races such as the UK's Grand National or the Cheltenham Gold Cup.

In the UK, the sport is governed by the National Hunt Committee, which was appointed in 1863. A century before that the first "match' took place in Ireland, when Messrs O'Callaghan and Blake raced their horses over the 4½ miles (7.25km) between the steeples of Buttevant and St. Leger churches—hence the name steeplechasing. As early as 1811, four fences were built on the Bedford, UK, flat-race course for races restricted to hunters.

Maryland Hunt Cup

America's Maryland Hunt Cup is the most prestigious of the American "chasing" events. Run through natural country over timber fences up to 5ft 6in (1.6m) in height, only amateurs are eligible to race. There is no organized betting, no admission charge, and no grandstand. Jay Trump won the race in 1963 and 1964 before going on to win the UK's Grand National in 1965.

Point to Point

In both the UK and Ireland, there is the thriving amateur sport of point-to-point racing, open to both men and women. Every recognized hunt puts on its point-to-point (a major source of income) at some date between February and early May. Horses must have been "fairly hunted" with a recognized pack of hounds. The course was once over natural country, but today's point-to-points are run on oval courses over built-up fences, no fewer than 18 of them. The minimum distance is 3 miles (4.8km). During the season, more than a dozen point-to-points are held each weekend, and they attract huge crowds determined to have a good day out—and a picnic to match!

The Grand National

The Grand National has its own unique aura and is enormously popular throughout Britain, perhaps because the result, after 4 miles 856 yds (7.22km) and 30 awesome fences, can never be predictable.

Six horses have won the race twice, but the greatest performer, who made Aintree his own, was Red Rum (*see* p.62), who won the Grand National in 1973, 1974 and 1977.

While the Grand National has a unique reputation and its own peculiar romance, the most prestigious of the UK chases is run at Britain's biggest jumping meeting, the Cheltenham National Hunt Festival. Here the big race is the Cheltenham Gold Cup, followed very closely by the Champion Hurdle,

Cheltenham

The racecourse at Cheltenham in the UK is famous for its testing, uphill finish and, of course, the prestigious Gold Cup. The Gold Cup was won by the Duchess of Westminster's legendary Arkle in 1964, 1965 and 1966. In 1983 the great trainer Michael Dickinson made racing history when he saddled the first five horses to pass the post.

another of the special events of the racing year. Hurdle races are shorter (the Champion Hurdle is over 2 miles—3.2km) and the flights of hurdles are lower and give way if hit hard.

Only the legendary Golden Miller won both the Gold Cup and the Grand National. He came first in the Gold Cup five years running, between 1932 and 1936, and he won the National in 1934.

There are 25 National Hunt courses in the UK, and a further 18 courses stage both flat and jumping meetings.

Did you know?

The St. Albans Steeplechase was the first regular event to be held in Great Britain. First run in 1830, it was superseded nine years later by the world's greatest steeplechase, the Grand National, which is held at Aintree, Liverpool.

The Grand National

The UK's Grand National is one of the world's greatest and most challenging races. In 1929, no fewer than 66 horses lined up for the start, the largest entry ever. They had to start in two rows

The Horse in Art

Horses were a feature of prehistoric art and remarkable depictions appear in the caves of Lascaux (*see* p.13), Pech-Merle, Santander, and other sites in Europe. Whatever their significance, religious or otherwise, they are works of art in their own right.

Power and Glory

At every stage in our human progress art, in every medium, has reflected social history and provided inspiration, culminating, perhaps, in the glorious affirmations of faith represented by the great cathedrals of Europe, their spires and towers reaching up to the Heaven that was the dearest, heartfelt desire of medieval and Renaissance man.

On a much lower, mortal plane, kings and great men sought immortality in the paintings and sculptures created by the most gifted artists of the day, and almost every one magnified his heroic image by being portrayed on the back of a nobly proportioned horse.

However, there were many, many painters and sculptors drawn to the horse by the challenge of expressing its vitality and beauty of form on canvas or in bronze.

Sporting Scenes

Other artists were absorbed in portraying the sporting horse and around them there grew up in Britain a unique school of sporting art, unrivalled in its variety and output. It may not always have been great art, certainly not on the level of Velasquez (1599–1660), Rubens (1577–1640), Goya (1746–1828), or Rembrandt (1606–69), for example, but it was good art, faithfully reflecting the Englishman's joy in field sports. In George Stubbs (1724–1806) it produced a master of horse portraiture of world standing.

19th-century France

Of the 19th-century French school, Delacroix (1798–1863) was perhaps the greatest exponent. Wild-eyed Arab stallions appear again and again in his work. Among the Neo-classicists, David (1748–1825) was unrivalled in his day. His *Bonaparte Crossing the Saint-Bernard* (*see* p.21) shows the Emperor Napoleon mounted on his favorite horse, the grey Arab Marengo.

Europe produced notable animal sculptors, such as Herbert Haseltine (1877–1962), who was responsible for the statue of *Man o' War* in the Kentucky Horse Park, and in the continent today there are sculptors of rare quality.

American Art

America, which was denied the tradition and inspiration of the Renaissance artists, nonetheless produced its own recognizable, home-spun art, which at its best is memorable indeed.

Outstanding among the American artists was Frederic Remington (1861–1909). He understood the West and loved it with a passion that shines through his work (*see* p.28). One of his greatest painting is *Dash for the Timber*, which was first exhibited at the National Academy of Design in 1889, while his magnificent bronze *The Mountain Man* ranks with some of the best of all time.

"Free Spirits At Noisy Water"

This monumental sculpture comprising eight horses on a man-made mountain is by the American sculptor Dave McGary (b.1958) and is to be seen at the Hubbard Museum at Ruidosa Downs, New Mexico. It depicts seven American breeds, plus a Paint foal. As an engineering achievement—the horses weigh up to 5,000 lb (2,275 kg) and are supported on only nine feet—it is no less than remarkable. Whether or not it is great art is, perhaps, debatable.

Equestrian Monument

The statue of Bartolomeo Colleoni, radiating power, dominates the centre of Venice, Italy. It is the work of the Renaissance genius Andrea del Verrochio (c.1435–88).

Impressionist School

Edgar Degas (1834–1917) had the ability to impart to both ballet dancing and racing scenes an incredible sense of movement. This scene at Longchamps typifies his extraordinary work.

The Horse Artist

No one portrayed the horse with such anatomical accuracy as George Stubbs. This picture of the Duke of Dorset with his favorite hunter exemplifies his genius.

Hunting

Hunting, either on foot or on horseback, was one of the earliest of human pursuits. Despite the controversial nature of the subject in the politically correct 21st century, hunting with hounds (never called dogs), as it developed from the 17th century onwards, has been a major factor (along with the practices of war) in establishing modern horse sports.

Hunting is the best of training grounds for cross-country riding and provides the criteria and encouragement for the breeding of cross-country horses. Furthermore, the sport has been a powerful influence on conservation and rural life.

Galway Blazers
A stylish young "thruster" on a grand pony tackles the stone-wall country of Ireland's famous Galway Blazers.

Hunting is generally regarded as the pursuit of the fox, the predominant quarry in the UK and the Irish Republic, where hunting is an important part of the equestrian industry. It is also increasingly popular in America, Canada and Australasia, where the gray fox, in the absence of the red fox, and the coyote are more likely to be the quarry. In fact, hunting in America, strictly on the British pattern, began with the early colonists in Virginia, Maryland and Pennsylvania. By 1747, Thomas, Lord Fairfax, owner of an enormous tract of land in Virginia, was hunting the first American pack. George Washington was also an enthusiastic foxhunter and, despite his high office, still found time to be a Master of Foxhounds.

Hunting in France
France has the oldest tradition of organized hunting, and much of the language of the chase is based on

French Hunt
Unlike the English hunting field, where jumping is an important element in the day, "leaving the ground" is not involved in French hunting. Nonetheless, days are long and stamina is at a premium for horse and rider.

French words and terms. Today, the French tradition continues with some 75 packs hunting stag, *equipage*, and wild boar, *vautrait*.

French hounds have great "nose" (scenting ability) and are bred for the quality of their "tongue" (voice).

Members of the Hunt

The area over which a pack hunts is called the hunt "country," while the hunt is under the jurisdiction of a Master or Joint Master, one of whom, the Field Master, will be in control of the field, that is, the mounted followers. The Masters appoint the hunt staff, including the Huntsman and his assistants, the Whippers-In. Only the Huntsman carries a horn, which he uses in specific calls to communicate with his hounds, his Whippers-In, and the field.

Alternative Hunts

In areas where foxhunting is impractical, the sport of drag-hunting provides an exciting substitute. Here hounds—a pack of five "couple" (ten hounds) is sufficient—hunt a "drag," a strong-smelling lure laid over a predetermined line that usually involves plenty of jumping.

Another form of hunting uses bloodhounds, whose quarry is the "clean boot"—the scent left by a man, and an athletic one, too. It is slower, but there is the bonus of hearing the persistent bloodhounds' wonderfully resonant tongue while watching them puzzle out the line.

Did you know?

The famous hunting cry of "Tally-ho!", which is given when the fox is seen to be running, is a corruption of the French *Ty a haillaut*, or *Il est hault* ("He's off!").

The Meet

English hunting has its own long tradition but is less formal than its French counterpart. Only the huntsman carries and blows on the hunting horn.

Showjumping

A French cavalry manual of 1788 included recommendations for jumping training, acknowledging that, in a countryside increasingly affected by enclosures (hedges and fences), the jumping of obstacles would be a necessary accomplishment for mounted troops. But the first-recorded jumping competitions were the "leaping" classes held by the Royal Dublin Society in 1864, in the Republic of Ireland.

The leaping classes held by the Royal Dublin Society included a High Jump, a competition that was retained until the 1950s, and a Wide Leap. Both were devised as a test for hunters and to encourage the Irish horse-breeding industry.

Captain Caprilli

Nevertheless, the most significant factor in the development of showjumping and, indeed, of equestrian theory and practice generally, was the Italian Cavalry School at Pinerolo and the teaching of its chief instructor, Captain Federico Caprilli. Unfortunately for the world, Caprilli died in 1907, at the age of 39, when he fell from his horse apparently after fainting. In his short life, however, he had changed the concept of outdoor riding forever.

Largely because of the Italian revolution in equestrian thinking and the example set by the Italian riders, the sport of showjumping was included in the 1900 Paris Olympics. Two years later, at the first Turin *Concorso Ippico Internazionale*, the Italians demonstrated the superiority of the Caprilli forward system decisively in competition with cavalry officers from Germany, Switzerland and elsewhere.

Did you know?

The German horse Meteor, ridden by Fritz Thiedemann, is the only showjumper to have won medals at three consecutive Olympic games, in 1952, 1956, and 1960.

The Forward Seat

Caprilli's *sistema*, often called "the forward seat," was not aimed specifically towards the fledgling sport of showjumping. Its purpose was to get cavalry across country swiftly, efficiently and with minimal strain on the horses. Coincidentally, it encouraged a new sport that quickly became widespread throughout the world.

Caprilli trained his riders over the sort of country in which they might be called upon to operate.

Instead of the dominated collection of the military schools, where horses were ridden in a shortened outline imposed by the double bridle at one end and strongly engaged hind legs at the other, Caprilli's horses were ridden in natural extension and in snaffle bridles. The riders conformed to the outline and balance of the horse by riding with shortened stirrups, with an advancing hand, and with the weight perched over the horse's moving center of balance, where it would be the least possible encumbrance to the movement. Whatever the obstacle, the seat remained the same, and the performance was improved immeasurably as a

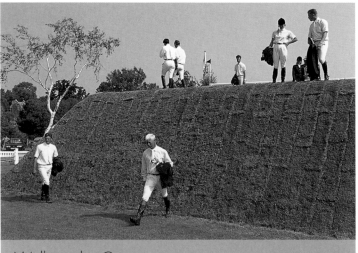

Walking the Course
Competitors examine the notorious Derby Bank at the Hickstead All-England Jumping Arena, which is a popular feature of the British Derby Meeting. The first Derby course, incorporating cross-country type obstacles, such as banks, ditches, water, and so on, was staged at Hamburg in 1920. The British Jumping Derby was introduced to Hickstead by its owner, Douglas Bunn, in 1961.

consequence. Before Caprilli, horsemen in Europe—but not in Asia—had sat back and hung on with raised hands. The system may have been adapted to meet new circumstances but, essentially, over fences and other jumps, we continue to sit forward in the Caprilli manner.

Showjumping Competition

International competitions multiplied between the two World Wars, although largely dominated by the military, but it was not until after World War II that competition rules were standardized by the FEI, the international federation founded in 1921. However, despite the introduction of these regulations, the British and Americans continued to use outdated national rules that excluded timing and retained the ridiculous slats laid on the fence (marks being deducted for their displacement). Largely as a result, the sport declined in both the UK and the USA and did not revive until the introduction of better course-building and, importantly, easy-to-follow rules that enhanced the sport's spectator appeal.

Modern Events

Today, everyone understands four faults for a knockdown; three and six for the first and second

Royal Dublin

The Dublin Arena in Ireland is one of the most famous in Europe and, indeed, the world. The international Dublin Show is held here every August. The ring still includes the testing bank obstacle, which is a natural feature of many Irish hunting countries (the area covered by a hunt).

refusal respectively, elimination for the third; a fall incurs eight faults, and in timed jump-offs or competitions faults are expressed in seconds. Nowadays, showjumping once again attracts big audiences to what, to all intents, is a show-business sport offering big rewards to the top riders. The sport also offers the best of TV viewing and big events get good coverage.

Sydney 2000

An American competitor, Laura Kraut, jumping at the 2000 Sydney Olympics, Australia. Her style, so typical of the American riders, would be difficult to fault, as would that of the bold horse.

Horse Trials

The French call the sport *concours complet*, which is an appropriate title for the ultimate test of the all-round horse and rider. Indeed, it was the French who devised the *Championnat du Cheval d'Armes*, a comprehensive military exercise comprising four phases: a "dressage" test; a steeplechase; a 30-mile (50km) ride over roads and tracks; and then a jumping competition.

That was in 1902, and the *Championnat* served as the basis for the three-day event (another title) for military riders that was held as part of the 1912 Olympics. In fact, the event was known as the "Military" for some time and was confined to service riders.

Open Competition

Civilians first competed in horse trials after World War II. Surprisingly, in what had been an entirely male-dominated sport, the majority of competitors were female and, not surprisingly, British, for it was in the UK that the sport first became established in its modern form. Standards of performance and the design of cross-country courses, which are largely interdependent, increased dramatically, but without losing sight of the objectives of the military event. These were defined as being a means of testing the horse's endurance, speed, stamina and obedience under pressure, while testing the rider's judgement and ability at the same time.

The Winner

Pippa Funnel, one of the foremost British riders, rode Supreme Rock to win the 2002 Badminton Horse Trials, defeating the international entry with a brilliant "clear" across country.

High-risk Sport

The sport falls firmly into the high-risk category and great emphasis is, therefore, placed on safety and on the building of "horse-friendly" courses. Horses are graded according to performance records, and there is a careful progression from one-day, pre-novice events to full-blown three-day championships. Nonetheless, every competition will have its quota of falls, many, like the one shown here, caused by horses tipping up when landing in water. A fall can result in the elimination of both the horse and the rider.

with a ride over the roads and tracks leading to the steeplechase course, followed by another section of roads and tracks. After a compulsory break of ten minutes, competitors set off on the cross-country course. After the veterinary inspection on the final day, the arena jumping phase concludes the event. The course set is not a difficult one, but it fulfils the object of confirming that the horse remains "fit for further service" after the exertions of the cross-country phase.

At Badminton the endurance phase takes 1½ hours to complete and is 16 miles (25km) long. The first section of the roads and tracks is 3 miles (5km) and the second is 6 miles (9km); in between is the 2-mile (3km) steeplechase. The cross-country has 32 fences, a number of which are combination fences, and is 4½ miles (7km) long. Time limits are applied to all sections of the endurance phase and, of course, to the arena jumping.

American Competitor

Australian, New Zealand, and American riders are regular supporters of the British events. Here, an American competitor, Wash Bishop, brings his horse down the imposing steps at the Gatcombe Trials in Gloucestershire.

The growth of the sport owes much to the now-famous Badminton Horse Trials, first held on the Duke of Beaufort's Badminton Estate, Gloucestershire, UK, in 1949 with the active involvement of the duke himself. It remains a focal point for the world's event riders and is the country's premier three-day horse trials.

Event Classification

The dressage test in one- and two-day events is the first phase, followed by arena jumping, and then the cross-country course, which is at the heart of every event, whatever its classification.

Similarly, the three-day event opens with the dressage test, but then the formula changes. The second day is devoted to the speed and endurance phase. It begins

Roads and Tracks

The roads and tracks section provides a warm-up for horse and rider before the steeplechase section. It also, of course, allows the team a well-earned 'breather' before the frequently gruelling cross-country phase of the competition.

Sporting Greats

Arguably the greatest of the greats was the racehorse Eclipse, so named because he was born on April 1, 1764, the year of the great eclipse. He goes down in history as the founder of the most influential Thoroughbred blood-line—his descendants have dominated the English Derby since its inception in 1780. He is immortalized in the words of his owner, Dennis O'Kelly, "Eclipse first, and the rest nowhere."

In two years, 1769 and 1770, Eclipse won all his 18 races, pulverizing his contemporaries. He went to stud in 1771 only because no opponents could be found for him. Eclipse ran in four-mile (6.5km) races, often run in heats during the same afternoon, and he carried 168lbs (76.5kg).

Not a prepossessing horse, he was thick-winded and roared like a bull in his gallop. Moreover, his temper was such that at first he was almost impossible to train. Nonetheless, his conformation—he was higher at the croup than the wither—accounted for the huge length and speed of his stride, while his above-average heart weight of 14lb (6.5kg) was in part responsible for his extreme stamina.

Big Red

Without doubt America's "mostest horse," and best loved, was Man o' War or Big Red, whose statue by Herbert Haseltine dominates the Kentucky Horse Park, outside Lexington, Massachusetts. In his racing career Big Red was beaten only once (as a two-year-old) in 21 races, and he was often mobbed by his fans. Born in 1917, he died in 1947. At stud at Faraway Farm, he was visited by his thousands of admirers. His birthday was celebrated each year, they made him an honorary citizen of Lexington and he was the honorary Colonel of the US First Cavalry. When he died, over 10,000 people attended the wake and the funeral.

Red Rum

Steeplechasing seems to have attracted even more national heroes. Red Rum, the three-time winner of the Grand National (*see* pp.52–53), had a fan club rivalling that of a pop star. In retirement he appeared as a celebrity at charity events all over the country. Trained by "Ginger" McCain in a small yard in the seaside town of Southport, Lancashire, in the UK, he was bought for 6,000 guineas (a guinea, a predecimal unit of currency, was the equivalent of £1.05) by the redoubtable Noel le Mare when the latter was 84!

Arkle

Red Rum was the Aintree favorite but it was Arkle who was king at Cheltenham, the course he made his own and where he won the Gold

Eclipse

This is the painting of Eclipse by George Stubbs (1724–1806), one of the world's greatest horse painters. The skeleton of this remarkable horse is preseved at London's Royal Veterinary College.

Man o' War

America's "mostest horse," Big Red attracted as much publicity in his time as a modern day pop star. He died in 1947 at the age of 30 and is buried in the Kentucky Horse Park, Lexington.

Red Rum

Red Rum wins his third Grand National in 1977. When he died at the age of 30, Red Rum was buried beside the finishing post at Aintree and is commemorated by a statue on the course complex.

Shergar

Shergar was one of a select group to win both the Irish Derby at the Curragh and the English Derby, a feat accomplished in 1981. Retired to stud in Ireland, Shergar disappeared—and the mystery has never been solved.

Desert Orchid

The brilliant gray was the hero of the 'chasing crowds. He won the King George VI at Kempton, in the UK, in breathtaking style in 1986, 1988, and 1989, the same year that he triumphed in the UK's Cheltenham Gold Cup.

Cup in 1964, 1965, and 1966. He won 24 other races, all in his own fluent flashing style, and his prize money totalled £75,206 ($115,000), a huge sum in those days.

Anne, Duchess of Westminster, bought him as a three-year-old at Dublin in 1960. Of Arkle, she would say: "I will never let my Arkle run in the Grand National, because I adore him, because he is one of the family, and because he is too precious to me."

In December 1966, in the King George VI Chase at Kempton Park—

the race he had won so majestically in the previous year—Arkle broke the pedal bone in his off foreleg, but still galloped on to finish only a length behind the winner, Dormant. He stayed at Kempton for six weeks with his leg in a plaster cast and was treated as a VIP, with press releases on his progress being issued for the benefit of his admirers. Perhaps he could have raced again, but the Duchess would not let her "pet" take the risk, and he retired from the racing game to a life of ease in his native Ireland.

Dubai Millennium

Dubai Millennium, winner of the English Derby 1994 with the irrepressible Frankie Dettori in the saddle, was a product of the Maktoum's Godolphin empire and was claimed by many to be the ultimate Thoroughbred.

Dressage

The Renaissance was the period roughly between the 15th and 16th centuries that saw a huge resurgence in learning and the appreciation of the arts in Europe, including a renewed interest in the art of riding.

The Byzantines of the eastern part of the Roman Empire were skilled horsemen who founded centers of riding in Naples in the 12th century. It was there that the world's first great riding school was opened by a Neapolitan nobleman, Federico Grisone, in 1532. It was to be the foundation of what we call "classical riding," which is preserved in the Spanish Riding School at Vienna. It is the classical schools that provide a background for the modern sport of dressage, a word that is derived from the French *dresser*, which means training as applied to the riding and harness horse.

Indeed, the advanced dressage tests include the classical movements of *piaffe* and *passage*, which were practised by Greek and Roman horsemen in the pre-Christian era. Both demand a high state of "collection," i.e., when the horse's body is compressed towards

the center—the base shortened, the croup lowered and the hind legs engaged well beneath the body, while the neck is raised and the head held vertically. *Piaffe* is the high, cadenced trot executed virtually on the spot. In *passage* the horse moves forward majestically in the same lofty action.

Dressage Classes

Dressage at every level is probably the fastest-growing sport of all, with tests ranging from those for Pony Club children all the way up, through a carefully graded progression, to the international competitions and the ultimate Grand Prix test, ridden at the Olympic Games.

Pirouette

The pirouette, either a demi-pirouette or a full turn, is a turn made on the quarters or a half-pass made on a very small half-circle or circle. It is executed in walk or, as in the Grand Prix tests, at canter. It can only be made at trot from *piaffe*. In any event it calls for a very high degree of collection if the sequence and rhythm are to be sustained.

Passage

An Olympic competitor performs the majestic, elevated movement of *passage*, in which the horse advances slowly to his front. In *piaffe*, the movement is executed on the spot.

Lower-grade tests are based on the ability to ride elementary school figures within an arena measuring 130ft x 65ft (40m x 20m) at walk, trot and canter, showing some lengthening and shortening of the stride. More advanced tests from medium level upwards, including the international tests, are ridden in a bigger arena, 196ft x 65ft (60m x 20m). Horses are expected

Passage

An Olympic competitor performs the majestic, elevated movement of *passage*, in which the horse advances slowly to his front. In *piaffe*, the movement is executed on the spot.

to show an increasing state of collection through the test levels, and the figures to be ridden and the variations in gait are far more demanding and complex.

The lower-level tests are judged by a single judge, the more advanced levels by three. Marking is on the scale of 10 excellent, 9 very good, 8 good, 7 fairly good, 6 satisfactory, 5 sufficient, 4 insufficient, 3 fairly bad, 2 bad, 1 very bad, 0 not performed. The total score is usually expressed as a percentage.

The German Influence

The leading dressage nation is Germany, the major force in the sport almost since its inception. Germany not only influences the criteria of judgement but has also had a powerful effect on the type of horse employed and bred. The very strong, athletic German horses with notable elevation in the paces dominate world dressage and so, in general, do German riders, the inheritors of a tradition of indoor, school riding that did not exist in the UK and Republic of Ireland. Nor, of course, was school riding part of the American tradition. However, the USA and the UK are catching up. The Americans, particularly, have some very talented horses and riders.

Novice Dressage

Dressage begins at Pony Club level and is limited to simple movements at walk, trot, and canter, the tests being ridden in the snaffle bridle. Nonetheless, the pony must go forward energetically, and be calm and obedient to the aids and there is certainly no place for anything other than effective riding.

Long-distance Riding

Endurance, or distance, riding is the sporting equivalent of the military rides that were tests of stamina and fitness and, it was intended, an encouragement to good horse management. Like dressage, it is a growing sport and is, indeed, recognized as an International Equestrian Federation (FEI) discipline, with European and World Championships held under the Federation's rules.

In fact, many of the military rides held in Europe were inhumanely severe; but that was not the case in America, where the US cavalry organized endurance tests for Arab and Thoroughbred horses that were models of good horse management.

The Tevis Cup

The rides encouraged the foundation of civilian trail-riding associations, and one of the first major events was the 100-mile (160km) Vermont ride of 1936. Today, there are some 500 distance rides held in the USA each year. The Tevis Cup is the toughest of them all and the one that set the standards of qualification and stringent veterinary supervision for the modern long-distance event.

The Tevis covers over 100 miles (160km) of the steepest and most hazardous country in the world, from Tahoe City, Nevada, to Auburn, California, and the climatic conditions are often extreme. Modern riders cover the distance in 24 hours, but most try to finish in half that time.

Australia's equivalent of the Tevis is the Tom Quilty, run over the same distance and over country just as testing.

100-mile Ride
A competitor, riding an attractive grey Arab, crosses a river on the 100-mile (160km) Exmoor ride, which is held annually in south-west England.

The Arab

Wendell Robie, three times winner of his own Tevis Ride, rode Arab horses (*see* pp.102–103), and it is the Arabian horse that is at the base of endurance riding. Bred to hardship and privation, it is innately tough and enduring and has unrivalled recovery rates in respect of pulse and respiration. No wonder that the Arabian and his close derivatives dominate the sport.

Endurance riding in the UK also evolved around the Arab horse. In the 1920s the British Arab Horse Society organized endurance rides to promote its breed and with a view to using the Arab in the production of cavalry remounts.

The rides they held were over a 300-mile (480km) course and were to be completed in five days. The

Tough Combination
An experienced long-distance partnership keeping up to time with a period of steady cantering. The horse is a pure-bred Arab, the best possible horse to use in this tough and demanding sport.

horses were pure-bred Arabs, standing no more than 15hh., and they were required to carry 182lb (82.5kg).

Endurance Riding Societies

There are now endurance riding societies all over Europe. All belong to the European Long Distance Riding Conference, a body that organizes the competition for the European Trophy.

In general, endurance rides begin with Pleasure Rides, up to 25 miles (40km) with a required speed of 5mph (8km/h), and then go on to Competitive Trail Rides, which are run at much faster speeds over 20–25 miles (32–40km). Finally there are the 100-mile (160km) Endurance Rides proper, which are races and are governed by stringent veterinary checks. In all events, penalties are incurred for respiration, pulse, and recovery rates that fall outside the set limits.

Veterinary Check
The compulsory veterinary checks for respiration, pulse, recovery rates, etc., call for the services of a dedicated back-up team at the halts. The team will also see to it that the horse is made comfortable.

The Maktoum Influence

Just as the Maktoum family of Dubai, in the United Arab Emirates, has become a world influence in Thoroughbred racing and breeding, so it has become a powerful force in endurance riding. Sheikh Mohammed and his family participate in the sport enthusiastically and successfully. An endurance riding center has been constructed between Abu Dhabi and Dubai, and Dubai has staged the World Endurance Championships.

The sport remains essentially amateur, but at the higher levels it is becoming increasingly sophisticated. To compete nowadays demands the support of an expert back-up team.

Desert Ride
These Arab horses are at home in the desert environment of the Dubai Ride 2001. The Maktoum family are keen competitors and supporters of this challenging sport.

Western Sports

The Western seat, the tack, the system of training, and the style of riding are all adaptations of the Spanish horse culture brought to America roughly 500 years ago. It is an essentially practical school that evolved from the herding and management of cattle, and at its highest level is quite the equal of the classical schools of Europe.

For many the appeal of "riding Western" is the relaxed informality, the pleasure of riding a smooth-gaited horse, and, perhaps, the comfortable security of the Western saddle. Nonetheless, the show classes and the Western sports are strictly conventional in many respects. Indeed, they can be more formal and demand a greater attention to detail than the equivalent activities in Europe.

Western Pleasure Class

The best introduction to Western riding sports, or classes, is the Western pleasure class. It is ridden with one hand on a relatively loose rein and calls for the horse to be ridden in both directions at the definitive Western paces of walk, jog, and lope, and then to "back-up" quietly (i.e., rein-back in European terms).

In all three paces the horse holds the head and neck low and extended, while remaining in perfect balance (the opposite, in fact, to the "collection" imposed on the European horse). The lope is a relaxed, loose-rein canter with a speed of 6–8mph (9.5–13km/h). The jog is also ridden on a loose rein at about 5mph (8km/h).

Trail Riding

Trail riding is a popular recreational activity, and trail-riding classes, again ridden with one hand, are a feature of the American horse show—as they are of shows held in Europe by various Western riding associations.

In this highly competitive class, horses have to complete a course of obstacles, three of which are compulsory requirements in the course-plan. The first is a gate, which has to be opened and closed; the

Did you know?

The Spanish recognized two riding styles: *a la brida*, the long-legged seat learned from the Christian Crusaders, and *a la gineta*, the short stirrup adopted by the Saracens.

Western Pleasure Class

The introduction to Western riding sports, although designed for novices, adopts strict judging procedures, which include the performance of the rider and the correct turnout.

Trail Riding

Obstacles in the trail classes are practical tests of the ability of the rider and the training of the horse, which must remain calm throughout. They will require the horse to move sideways and make controlled turns in a confined space.

second is a grid of four logs, which may be set on a straight line or on a curve; the third is an obstacle constructed in one of a number of shapes—L, V, or U-shape, for example, which the horse has to back through or around.

Other obstacles depend on the ingenuity of the course-builder and may include a water hazard, a wooden bridge, a variety of pole arrangements, and so on. They will require the horse to move sideways and make controlled turns in a confined space, as well as "backing-up." They are all intended to test the standard of training and the horse's calm acceptance of the unusual. Very often competitors have to remove and replace a piece of clothing, such as a slicker, and may even have to ground-tie or hobble the horse.

Equitation and Reining

The dressage test of Western riding begins with the equitation classes, in which riders have to perform set movements with absolute precision. The correctness of the rider's seat is assessed by the judges, as well as his or her ability to apply virtually invisible "aids," the signals that in Western terms are called "cues."

The equitation classes can be difficult enough, and the standard at the bigger events is often extremely high, but an even more demanding test is the reining

class, which is quite unmistakably the equivalent of the European dressage classes and is graded in much the same way.

The judging of these classes is strict, and in addition to the demand for high levels of schooling and accurate riding, just as in European dressage, there is the added difficulty of riding the "patterns" at speed and using just one hand on the reins.

Advanced Reining

The advanced reining class includes all the movements of the Western school. The three gaits and the "back-ups" apart, there are spins (the dressage pirouette); changes of the leading leg, including the "flying change" (the change of leg at the lope made "in the air" in a single stride); the roll-back (about-turn on the pivot of a hind leg); fast and slow circles; and the sliding stop, made from the lope with the hind legs locked well under the body and on a loose rein.

Sliding Stop

The approach to a sliding stop is made at an accelerating gallop and the horse may slide up to 30ft (9m) on the locked hind legs, but rein contact remains minimal.

Cutting Horse Competitions

The supreme Western horse is without much doubt the Quarter Horse (*see* pp.130–31), which is used almost exclusively in cutting horse competitions.

On working ranches the most valuable horse in the remuda (the string of horses available to the cowboy) was the cutting horse, whose job it was to "cut" or separate a single animal or a small group from the herd and prevent its returning.

Rules of the Sport
The exciting sport of cutting follows closely the ways of the open range. The difference is that the cutting

Cow Savvy
The cutting horse has what is termed "cow-sense" – it works cattle instinctively, like a sheepdog with sheep. In competition, the rider must not touch the rein or "cue" his horse.

horse is now as valuable as a Thoroughbred racehorse, and prize money, often more than US$2 million, makes cutting the world's richest arena sport.

Once in the arena with the "herd", the rider selects the calf to be cut out and is then not permitted to change to another. The calf will usually attempt to return to its companions and the rider, or rather the horse, must prevent it from doing so. From this point it is the horse that has to control the calf on its own initiative, for the rider

Did you know?

In cutting horse competitions, the horse used is almost always the Quarter Horse. It is far and away the world's most popular breed, with the Quarter Horse register listing millions of horses.

Team Roping

Team roping is a competition for two riders. The "header" ropes the head or horns of the steer while the "heeler" lassos the heels. The two riders then manoeuvre their horses so that they are facing each other, with the steer held immobile on the taut ropes.

must not touch the rein or attempt to direct his mount. The horse, maintaining a head-to-head position with the calf, blocks its every attempt to rejoin the herd, working the animal instinctively, like a sheepdog does. The rider has two-and-a-half minutes to demonstrate the skill and lightning-quick reactions of his horse and has to be a consummate horseman to stay in the saddle as the horse turns and stops and jumps with spine-jarring speed and violence.

Naturally, the cutting horse has to be trained for the work, but he also has to have a highly developed, and possibly inherited, "cow-sense".

Team Penning Competitions

While the spectacle of a single contest between horse and calf is the very peak of Western riding, the team penning competitions, with two or more riders cutting out a group of animals, is just as fast-moving and thrill-packed. It calls for a high level of skill as well as supremely trained horses that are quick, agile, and very intelligent.

Riding the Range

The ideal mount for this Colorado range is the willing, clever, and sure-footed Quarter Horse on which "cowboys" can sit comfortable and secure. The saddle is made for all-day riding, and a thick saddle cloth prevents sores.

The Hollywood Horse

Hollywood is an all-American phenomenon, and in no other country has the movie industry made such extensive use of horses—but then no other country has the story of the Wild West in its history. The Western films were an industry in themselves and used thousands of horses, some of them becoming "stars" as famous as their owners.

An early star of the silent screen was Fritz, the Pinto who shared the billing with the cowboy actor William S. Hart. Hart tried to present the West as it really was (well, nearly) and he and Fritz never used doubles, however dangerous the scene that was to be shot. The pair were masters of the stunt fall at the gallop; they jumped off cliffs; dived into ice-filled rivers, and once jumped through a plate-glass window.

Trigger

Trigger, who partnered Roy Rogers, the "King of the Cowboys," was probably the best known of the equine movie stars, and he had mastered a wide repertoire of 60 tricks over and above the standard Hollywood requirements—lying down, rearing, going lame, etc. Trigger, an exceptionally highly

Roy Rogers and Trigger

Trigger was a highly photogenic and striking Palomino color. The color is popular with the film studios, where an arresting appearance is a real asset. He made 87 films and appeared in 101 television shows. He travelled extensively, always with his own passport and he was at the center of a huge and lucrative fan club.

Tom Mix on Tony

Hollywood stars Tom Mix and Tony the Wonder Horse in their 1923 movie *Soft Boiled*. Like William S. Hart and Fritz, the pair never used doubles, a fact much emphasized by the publicity men.

Stunt Horses

The Western movies created a small industry producing the stunt horses that specialized in spectacular falls at the gallop, usually when engaged in the range wars that were a feature of the Wild West films. Intelligent horses were trained to perform special "tricks."

Sit Down
Trick horses can rear, buck, dance, walk backwards, bow and even sit down to order.

trained horse, was also very intelligent. He enjoyed his work and knew exactly how to behave for the camera—he was, in fact, a natural.

He would yawn, whinny and nuzzle on cue, he had numerous counting routines, performed dance steps, made his celebrated rear a trademark of his performance with Roy Rogers and could walk backwards 150 paces on his hind legs. He revelled in the bustle of the film set and in the publicity that accompanies the show business life.

Trigger died in 1965 at the age of 33, when his name and that of Roy Rogers was forever secure in the annals of the movie business.

Tony

Another of the Hollywood horse greats was Tony, the talented, white-faced sorrel, an eye-catching red roan color (*see* pp.100–101), who was the partner of Tom Mix for 20 years.

Like Trigger, he was unusually intelligent and could perform a wide variety of tricks. He could untie knots to free his master from awkward situations, he could carry messages and gallop for help when Tom was in trouble. He would fight the bad men alongside his master with hoofs and teeth, while Tom knocked out the villains with his fists, for in the Tom Mix-Tony films fists were used more than guns.

Tony starred in his own right in the film *Just Tony*, Tom's tribute to his equine partner. Tom was killed in a car accident in 1940 and Tony died four years later, aged 34.

Equine "Extras"

Many of the horse stars were Saddlebreds (*see* p.133), who appeared, of course, in their natural state, without the show-ring aids. They were considered to have the presence, beauty, intelligence and temperament that are needed for the charismatic horse actor.

But there are also the hundreds of extras of nondescript breeding but of suitably docile temperament. They play the town scenes, tied to the hitching rail of the saloons, they are driven in wagons or make up the sheriff's posse, and without them there would be no stars.

Legs Crossed
"I can't think why humans should want me to stand like this, but it's a job!"

Rodeo

The Rodeo reproduces the old-time skills of the working cowboy within the confines of an arena. It has grown into a show business industry, with great spectator appeal and the prospect of high prize-money for successful competitors.

The six basic rodeo events are saddle-bronc riding, bareback riding, bull riding, steer wrestling, calf roping and team roping. The supporting events, although less dangerous, can be nearly as exciting to watch. Barrel-racing, when riders race singly against the clock around three barrels set on a triangle, is done at breakneck speed. The women are better than the men. The Quarter Horse (*see* pp.130–31) is the best option as a mount because of its electrifying speed and exceptional agility.

Wagons Roll!
The chuck-wagon race has all the spirit of the old West with the wagons being driven at full gallop around the track, encouraged by wild "hollers" from the escorting riders.

The "fun" event of the rodeo, though not without its dangers, is chuck-wagon racing on an oval track, with teams of four horses drawing the somewhat unstable chuck-wagons. A similar event was held in the circuses of Ancient Rome, with teams drawing chariots. It seems to have been even wilder than chuck-wagon racing and was probably more hazardous.

Saddle-bronc Riding
The classic rodeo event is the saddle-bronc riding, for which horses are specially bred. It appears to be a very high-risk contest but, in fact, casualties are rare. The horse is saddled with a tight bucking strap round its loins and wears a headcollar fitted with a thick plaited rope for the rider to grasp. Competitors mount the horse in a closed chute, and when the doors are opened he comes out bucking hard.

The cowboy hopes for a horse that bucks straight and rhythmically, because that is easier to stay with than the wild one who twists. He is marked on style, raking the horse from shoulder to flank with his blunt rowelled spurs in time with the buck. He has to do that for eight seconds, while hanging on with one hand.

Bareback Riding
Bareback riding is the most difficult and dangerous of the bronco events. The rider hangs on for dear life to a hand loop on the surcingle and hopes to stay there for eight seconds as the horse bucks and twists and leaps to remove him.

Barrel-racing

Barrel-racing is a sport where the cow-girls frequently beat the men. Competitors race over the course against the clock and at breakneck speed. To win, or even to compete, at this exciting game you have to be a very good rider on a very good horse.

Bareback Riding

Bareback riding is marked in the same way, but it is more difficult and dangerous, too. The bareback rider relies on a handloop fastened to a surcingle to stay on the horse, for the bareback bronco wears neither bridle nor headcollar.

Bull Riding

The bull riders sit—they hope for eight seconds—on quick-moving Brahma bulls, which have horns and will use them if given a chance. More than any other event, this one has the gladiatorial element of the Roman circus. The event is judged in the same way as the others, but it is necessary to have helpers to keep the enraged bull from attacking the rider when he hits the ground.

Steer Wrestling

Steer wrestling, another elemental contest between man and beast, involves the cowboy leaping on the steer and wrestling it to the ground. The event is judged on time, and usually the steer is down within a mere three or four seconds.

Calf Roping and Team Roping

Calf roping is also a speed event against the clock, the rider roping and hog-tying the calf while the horse, with the rope fastened to the saddle horn, holds it taut. Team roping has two cowboys working in unison to bring the steer down by roping both horn and heels. For both these events the best horse is, once again, the fast, agile and intelligent Quarter Horse.

Calf Roping

Roping a calf was a basic skill for the old-time cowboy and the modern sport is no less skilful and probably considerably faster. The event is against the clock and finishes when the calf is roped and hog-tied.

Harness Racing

Chariot racing was a fiercely contested sport (accidents were frequent and often bloody) in Ancient Greece and Rome long before the acceptance of horse racing. The lightweight, skeletal vehicle developed in the Roman circus was the forerunner of the modern, harness-racing sulky, although the Roman chariots were usually drawn by four-horse teams harnessed abreast.

In fact, harness racing in the USA, Australasia, Scandinavia, mainland Europe, and Russia rivals the popularity of flat racing and offers just as much prize money. In the UK and the Republic of Ireland, the countries that have been the inspiration for so much equestrian initiative, the sport has surprisingly little support from the public.

American Racing

The leading harness-racing nation is the USA, where the sport has an audience of over 30 million people, who can watch and gamble at more than 70 raceways, all of them left-handed, oval in shape, and equipped with all-weather surfaces and flood-lighting for evening racing.

American racing revolves round the world's supreme harness-racing horse, the Standardbred (see p.134), which has influenced the sport worldwide.

Trotters

Most Standardbreds are pacers, moving the legs in lateral pairs, and in America the conventional trotter, which moves the legs in diagonal pairs, is not so popular, although trotters are preferred in Europe, Scandinavia

The Trotter
This harness-racer at the Red Mile Raceway, Lexington, Kentucky, is a conventional trotter, using the diagonal gait. Most American harness-racers go at the preferred lateral pacing gait, whereas conventional trotters are popular in Europe.

Did you know?

The New Zealand Standardbred, Cardigan Bay, one of the world's most famous harness-racers, won 80 races and held two world records. He was the first Standardbred to win US$1m prize money and was commemorated on a postage stamp.

Red Mile

One of America's most famous raceways is the Red Mile at Lexington, Kentucky, which stages the prestigious Futurity, one of the Triple Crown races for trotters. All the American raceways stage evening meetings lit by floodlights, and all offer sophisticated facilities for racegoers, who can watch the "trots" in great comfort.

The Pacer

Below, a pacing Standardbred employs the lateral gate. This horse is fitted with hobbles, which help prevent the horse from breaking into a gallop and being penalized accordingly.

and Russia. Indeed, in France, the strong French Trotter (*see* p.117) is raced under saddle as well as in harness. In no country, however, do pacers race against trotters.

Pacers

The USA, where heavy betting is a feature of the sport, encourages the pacer for the reason that it is less prone to "break" than the trotter. If a horse should break into a gallop, it is obliged immediately to move over to the outside of the field, losing ground as well as any chance of winning the race.

To reduce the possibility of a horse breaking, pacers all wear hobbles, a harness connecting the fore- and hind legs above the knee and hock respectively. Much attention is paid to the meticulous shoeing of the harness horse, to the bitting arrangement (often a very powerful one) and to the provision of protective boots of very sophisticated design. They are necessary, as well as the shoes that encourage an absolutely straight action, to prevent a horse striking into himself. If that were to occur at speeds of up to 40mph (65km/h) the resultant injury would be severe and disastrous. Most horses, incidentally, wear sheepskin nosebands, "shadow rolls," to limit the vision and prevent shying.

The Sulky

The speed of harness racing depends largely upon the design and weight of the bike-wheel racing sulky. The first was invented as long ago as 1892 and immediately

reduced racing times over the mile. In the 1970s, the design was further improved by Joe King, an engineer by profession. He straightened and shortened the shafts and built the sulky from steel instead of wood. As a result, the number of two-minute miles increased from 685 in 1974 to 1,849 in 1976.

Starting Gate

The next vitally important invention related to harness racing was the mobile starting gate, which is basically a pair of retractable wings mounted on a truck. The vehicle is driven in front of the horses up to the start line with the wings extended. Then the wings are closed, and the truck accelerates away from the field to give the horses an absolutely fair start.

Facts and Records

Horse facts are fascinating, and records are always absorbing, even though they are often controversial and provoke pretty fierce competition among devotees of equine statistics.

The longest-living horse that we know about was Old Billy. He was born in Lancashire, UK, in 1760, and worked with the canal barges until 1819. He died on November 27, 1822, aged 62 years. Old Billy seems to have had a Cleveland Bay background.

High and Wide

The official high jump record is held by a 15-year-old ex-racehorse, Huaso, ridden by Captain Alberto Morales. In 1949 at Santiago, Chile, the pair jumped 8ft 1¼in (2.47m). However, greater heights were cleared before official records were kept. The Thoroughbred mare Heatherbloom, for example, with Dick Donnelly in the saddle, jumped 8ft 2in (2.5m) at Richmond, Virginia, in 1902.

The long jump record is held by Something, ridden by Andre Ferreira. In 1975 in Johannesburg, South Africa, he cleared 27ft 6¾in (8.4m).

The record height cleared by a horse ridden side-saddle is claimed by actress and playwright Carolyn Woffard, who jumped the 17.3hh. Polish Warmblood Solidarity (nicknamed "The Giraffe") over a 5ft 7in (1.7m) fence of planks at Birchinlay Manor, Lancashire, UK, in 1996. This is an exceptional feat given that horses ridden side-saddle are not usually expected to clear jumps of more than 3ft 6in (1.07m) or so.

Speed

The world equine speed record was set on February 5, 1945 at Mexico City when the four-year-old racehorse Big Racket was timed at 43.2mph (69.62km/h). R. C. Andrews, studying the Mongolian Kulan (*Equus hemionus hemionus*) in the Gobi Desert between 1922 and 1925, reported that when chased by a car the Kulans set off at speeds of between 35 and 40mph (56–64km/h). One stallion

8ft 1¼in (2.47m)

High Jumper
The high jump was once an organized class in jumping events but is something of a rarity today, although there are still *puissance* classes including a big fence.

27ft 6¾in (8.4m)

Long Jumper
This is the official record but it is likely that it might be equalled, or indeed exceeded, by horses racing at speed over hurdles.

was recorded as averaging 30mph (48km/h) over 16 miles (26km).

Little and Large

The smallest pony is recorded by D. P. Willoughby (*The Empire of Equus*, 1974) as the midget pony mare Sugar Dumpling, who stood 20in (51cm) high at the wither and weighed 30lb (13.6kg). She was bred by Smith McCoy at Roderfield, West Virginia, and died in 1965. Nonetheless, it is claimed that Argentinian Falabellas have measured as small as 14–15in (35.5–38cm).

There have been numerous instances of draught horses standing 7ft (2.13m) at the wither, i.e., 21hh. Dr. Le Gear, a dapple-gray Percheron foaled in 1902, was that height and weighed 2,995lb (1,359kg). Owned by Dr. Le Gear, he died in St. Louis in 1919. Brooklyn Supreme, a Brabant or Belgian Heavy Draught, 1930–1950, foaled in Minneapolis, was 6in (15cm) smaller but at 3,200lb (1,452kg) was probably the world's heaviest horse.

The tallest of all is claimed to be the Shire gelding Sampson (afterwards called Mammoth). He was bred and born in Bedfordshire, UK, in 1946 and as a four-year-old stood 7ft 2in (2.18m), or 21.2hh.

Endurance

In 1935 a group of Akhal-Teke horses made a famous journey from Ashkabad to Moscow, a distance of 2,580 miles (4,128km), 600 miles (960km) of which was over desert. The desert horses covered the route with only a minimal water ration and completed the journey in 84 days.

Tails and Manes

There is an account in the magazine *Nature* of January 1892 of a Percheron with a mane 13ft (4m) long and a tail of 10ft (3m). In 1942 George Zillgitt of Inglewood, California, had a mare, Maud, with a mane that was 18ft (5.5m) long and a tail to match.

Smallest and Tallest
Interestingly, the smallest horse in the world would just about measure up to the knee of the largest and tallest, and no more.

Polo

The game of polo was played in Persia and China as much as 2,500 years ago, by women as well as men. The modern game originates in the Cachar Valley of Manipur, India, where it was played as a national sport on little, agile Manipuri ponies that did not stand much over 12.2hh. (1.27m). The game had come to Manipur from Tibet and was called by the Tibetan word *pulu*.

British administrators in Manipur took up the game, and in 1859 the first European club was formed by Captain Robert Stewart and Lieutenant Joseph Sherer.

From Manipur the game spread all over British India and had made its way to Britain by 1869 when the 10th Hussars, calling it "Hockey on Horseback," played a match at Aldershot. Each side fielded eight players. It soon caught on and was played at Hurlingham, near London, as part of the smart "London season." Subsequently it was the Hurlingham Polo Association that formulated the rules that, with adaptations made in the early years, govern the sport today.

Fast and Furious

Polo, played at the gallop, is the fastest horse game in the world and one of the most physical, with players seeking to deny possession of the ball to their opponents. The strict rules are designed to reduce the risk of injury.

Pony Club Polo

Polo is played enthusiastically and often extremely well by many Pony Club branches, with hard-fought championships being held each year. In this action shot, the ball (which is traditionally made of wood) can just be seen under the small bay on the extreme left as another assault is made on the goal.

Argentine Supremacy

The British established the sport in Argentina in 1877, and in the following year it was being played enthusiastically, and expertly, in America. Since then America and Argentina have been the world's leading polo nations, and Argentinian players and their ponies (see p.156) have been a major influence in the game. From 1886 polo was played by teams of four on a low-boarded ground measuring 300yd × 200yd (273m × 180m).

Rules of the Game

The object is to hit the ball, made originally from willow but now increasingly of plastic, through the opponents' goal with a bamboo mallet. The "ponies" are now bigger, measuring between 15hh. and 15.3hh., but are always called ponies, never horses.

In the team of four, numbers 1 and 2 are the forwards, number 3, who fills the pivotal position, plays the center field, and the back is number 4.

Players are graded according to the handicapping system devised by the Americans from −2 to +10, and there are not many 10-goal players at any one time.

A match lasts a little under an hour and is divided into chukkas of seven-and-a-half minutes.

In high-goal matches, when the aggregate handicap of the teams is 19 and over, five or six chukkas are played, while lower-rated matches are divided into four chukkas. Because of the speed at which the game is played and the exertion involved, ponies are changed after each chukka and no pony plays more than two chukkas in a match. For those reasons players need at least two ponies and in fast, high-goal matches three are certainly needed.

A Complex Sport

Polo is not only fast but also complex, and rules are strictly enforced by the umpire, who will also award penalties for any infringement.

There is no off-side rule as in soccer, but a player must not cross another's right of way. Bumping deliberately, zigzagging to obstruct a player and any misuse of the stick are all penalized. However, it is permissible to hook an opponent's stick and to "ride him off" the ball. Indeed, riding off is an essential skill. This is done by placing the knee in front of the opponent's knee, and then by means of neck rein, weight, and leg, pushing the opponent off the line of the ball (in much the same way as a soccer player barges an opponent to prevent his kicking the ball).

Behind the Scenes

Here, a group of ponies are being exercised by their grooms. Most of them wear Argentinian pattern headcollars and many of the grooms travel with the ponies from Argentina. The grooms are natural horsemen, brought up with ponies and polo, and they are able to school their charges as well as to care for them and keep them at peak fitness through the season. Polo is a hard game and the speed, combined with the frequent stops and turns, puts great strain on the vulnerable legs. Particular attention is given to them and the ponies are always played with carefully fitted boots and/or supporting bandages. Careful bitting is also essential to give maximum control without damaging the mouth.

Asian Games

Games on horseback are traditional in Central Asia, Iran, Afghanistan and in the Uzbek and Tajik lands around the former Soviet border. Some are based, very roughly, on polo, while others are fierce, brutal contests.

Buzkashi is as bloodthirsty as any of them, with 100 riders slashing and fighting for possession of a goat's carcass. More pastoral, in contrast, is *Kyzkuu*, based on the bridal chase of the nomadic horse-peoples and played in a variety of forms throughout Asia. A bunch of men pursue a woman, all intent on claiming at least a kiss from her. However, she is armed with a heavy whip with which she can beat them off on her ride to the finishing post. Or, of course, a favoured suitor might catch her eye with whom she is glad to ride off over the steppe! Wrestling on horseback, called *Oodarysh* or *Sais*, is popular in Kazakhstan and Kirghizia, while some very gymnastic, acrobatic riding is to be seen all over Central Asia.

Pig Sticking

Three thousand years ago men hunted wild boar on horseback, with a spear. British officers and civilians carried on the sport in 19th-century India,

and today the tradition is continued in a smaller way by hard-riding Indian Army officers who organize pig-sticking meets on the Kadir, or riverine jungle country, bordering the Ganges and Jumna rivers at Meerut and Muttra. It would be difficult to imagine a more dangerous sport, or one that called for such courage on the part of man and horse.

Once the pig breaks cover, three or four riders ride flat out in pursuit over rock-hard ground pocked with holes and hazards and intersected with *nullahs* (dried-out streams). They do so virtually blind, for the view is hidden by tall grass and tough bushes of *jhow* (tamarisk). In these conditions the horseman must ride with a loose rein, trusting his horse to keep his feet while he keeps his eye on the boar.

Olga Tartish

Olga Tartish, ostensibly a type of polo, is one of the games played at Kirghiz weddings and involves the possession of a carcass. It is rough, tough, and the rules are not much in evidence!

Polo Pioneers

The people of Manipur, living in the small state between Assam and Burma, introduced the game of polo, in their tongue *Kári-jái-bazee*, to the British in the mid-19th century. It had come to Manipur from Tibet and from Manipur it spread, via British India, throughout the Western world. In Manipur, polo was the national game and even a small village would have its own polo team. The players' polo kit was unorthodox to Western eyes, and they rode with bare feet, although, as the picture illustrates, they wore leg guards and turbans. The ponies were also notable. Nimble, brave, and quite able to carry a grown man, they rarely exceeded 12.2hh. (1.27m). The picture dates from about 1885, a quarter of a century after the formation of the first European polo club in the Cachar Valley.

Kadir Cup

In the days of the British Raj the sport of pig sticking was highly organized around the "tent clubs," so called because members camped out in the jungle. Each club operated within fixed boundaries and was responsible for enforcing the rules. Also, each club employed *shikaries*, gamekeepers, to locate the quarry. The so-called "blue riband of pig sticking" was the contest for the Kadir Cup, which took place near Meerut. It was first held in 1874 and took place annually up to 1939.

Tent Pegging

The related sport of tent pegging is less dangerous and is extremely popular with all mounted military formations, the mounted police and a substantial number of civilians in both India and Pakistan. Indeed, the enthusiastic supporters of tent pegging continually lobby for the sport to be included in the Olympic Games.

Did you know?

The national drink of a large part of Asia is *Kummis*, an alcoholic beverage invented by the Mongols made from fermented mare's milk!

Tent-pegging Rules

The horseman, or a team of four riders, gallops down a prepared track (*pathi*) and the rider has to strike the peg and carry it on the lance for 49ft (15m) to gain maximum points. Marks are also given for style and pace. In the final run the peg may be turned sideways to present a target about 1in (2.5cm) wide. Marwari and Kathiawari horses (*see* p.129) usually make superb tent peggers and feature prominently in the sport.

Like so many of our equestrian sports, tent pegging has military origins. In an attack on an enemy camp, cavalry could gallop through the lines, collapsing the tents by lifting the pegs. The ensuing chaos in the assailed camp can easily be imagined.

Tent Pegging

A rider spears the peg during a game at Windsor in England. The sport of tent pegging has come a long way since its origins as a cavalry war tactic, and enthusiasts continually lobby for its acceptance as an Olympic event.

Gymkhana

The word gymkhana is of Anglo-Indian origin, a combination of *gend-khana* ("ball-house" or "racquet court") and "gymnastics." It came to mean a place for games and athletics, and the traditional Gymkhana Club is still found all over India. Today, however, the Indian clubs are unlikely to stage "mounted games," which is what is now understood by the word "gymkhana."

Mounted games are traditional to Asia, and in India, as indeed elsewhere, games on horseback were seen as useful training for cavalry as well as being an excellent form of recreation.

Throughout Asia, adults take part in mounted games, most of them originating in Mongolia, which has the largest number of horses per person in the world. Associations organize the sport on a considerable scale in Russia and the former Russian republics.

Pony Clubs

In Europe (particularly in Britain), America and Australia, gymkhana games, increasingly termed mounted games, are firmly rooted in the Pony Club, that remarkable international youth movement based on the ideals of good horsemanship and a proper

respect for the welfare of horses and ponies. The Pony Club was founded in England in 1929 and has a membership worldwide that fluctuates around the 100,000 mark. Australia and America have the greatest number of branches (known as clubs in America). They all play gymkhana games.

Mounted Games Championship

In Britain, a Pony Club Mounted Games Championship, held at London's Horse of the Year

Potato Race

To drop a potato accurately into a bucket at full gallop requires suppleness of a high order and a reliable pony, too. This rider is giving a textbook performance, without hanging on to the bridle.

Obstacle Race for Two

Get off, give your pony to your team mate, crawl very quickly over and through an awkward obstacle without knocking it down, get on again, and gallop for the next, when it's your partner's turn while you hold *her* pony.

A Variety of Races

Then there is the stepping-stone race, where riders lead their ponies while running on a line of up-turned pots. There are also sword (wooden) and lance (a light bamboo stick) events, based on the army skill-at-arms competitions, as well as flag races, obstacle races and others devised by the ingenuity of organizers. The list is, indeed, endless.

Of course, a gymkhana is primarily a fun event, however seriously it is prepared for and played. Nevertheless it demands balance, suppleness, agility, riding skills, courage and respect for the pony.

show, is a feature of the Pony Club year and of the show. First instigated by HRH Prince Philip in 1957, it is still called the "Prince Philip Games" in Pony Club circles. To compete, riders must be 15 years or under, and the ponies must not exceed 14.2hh. (1.47m).

The standard of riding and the agility displayed is of a very high order and the performance of the ponies, who know what is required just as well as their riders, is beyond belief. Indeed, a good gymkhana pony, whatever his background—and most have some Welsh antecedents—is a valuable animal.

Principal Games

The number of games that can be played is large. The principal ones are the bending race, an almost universal game, which involves zigzagging at speed through a line of poles; the sack race, in which the rider hops at amazing speed while leading the pony; and every sort of relay race, which often involves the pony carrying two riders who vault on and off with enviable agility. That practice really belongs to the sharpshooter's race, where one rider leaps off the pony to throw a ball at a figure or some similar target.

Stepping-stone Race

You need agility and balance to run quickly along a line of pots, and you have to have a steady, sensible pony to help you. Obviously, these two characters are a good partnership.

Driving

Driving competitions were being held in Europe in the 19th century and were officially recognized as a competitive sport in 1969. The sport has plenty of thrills as competitors cope with the marathon phase, which can also have its share of spills. However, there is an elegance and style about the competition, particularly in the dressage phase.

Driving trials, or competitions, are based on the ridden three-day event, with classes for four-in-hand teams and others for pairs, tandems (one horse harnessed behind the other), and for single horse and pony turnouts.

Dressage Phase

Like the ridden three-day event, the competition opens with the dressage phase, held in an arena 110yds x 44yds (100m x 40m) for the four-in-hands and in a smaller one for the pairs and singles. The movements required are straightforward, but the four-horse team and carriage is about 33ft (10m) in length and so is not

easily maneuvered. The dressage, Competition A, is followed on the next day by Competition B, the marathon phase – the equivalent of the ridden event's speed and endurance. The course is over 15–17 miles (24–27km) and has to be completed in two hours.

Marathon Phase

Section A of the course is a 6¼ mile (10km) route over roads and tracks, driven usually at trot at a speed of 9½ mph (15km/h). Then follows the less arduous Section B, which is also a test of obedience, over ¾ mile (1.2km). It has to be driven in walk at a speed of 4½ mph (7km/h), and is followed by a compulsory halt during which the grooms can check over their teams.

After this, the marathon becomes a serious business as the teams set off on Section C, over a hilly, twisting route that is hard work even for a team of four. No cantering or galloping is allowed, so the pace has to be a good, sharp trot to meet the required speed of 11–12mph (18–19km/h).

It is followed by Section D, another walk stage, and then a veterinary check.

Section E is the main part of the marathon course. It is over 6¼ miles (10km) of varied terrain and includes eight obstacles, which are called "hazards," grouped fairly closely towards the end of the course. It requires great skill to get a four-horse team around the tight turns involved without losing any time, and there is often some "grief" (a horsey word meaning trouble or accident). The speed required for this section is 9½ mph (15km/h).

The Water
Water is bound to be a hazard on the cross-country phase. It requires determination and skill on the part of the driver and a team of bold, ongoing horses that are unlikely to hesitate.

Cone Driving

Competition C is the equivalent of eventing's arena jumping phase, an obstacle course called "cone driving" because it involves getting round up to 20 obstacles created by traffic cones in a very tight time limit.

While Competition A calls for a smart vehicle, the marathon employs a specialist practical turnout—a "battle wagon" in fact, which may, indeed, be fitted with a type of disc brake, like that of a car.

Driving Breeds

The horses are usually Warmbloods, the Dutch Gelderlander, Holsteiners and so on. But Cleveland Bay teams are by no means unknown, as are Welsh Cob and Fell Ponies. The dashing Hungarians, a people with a great driving tradition—they invented the coach, *kocsi*, in the 15th century—use Lipizzaners, bigger and faster than those used at the Spanish School in Vienna, driven Hungarian fashion in breast harness.

Scurry Driving

The groom sits behind the driver. Her job is to lean out, perilously, to one side or the other to preserve the vehicle's stability. Ponies are often of Welsh extraction, but however they are bred they must be fast, agile, and very bold.

Tandem

Driving in tandem is really difficult and if the lead horse were to turn around and lose his nerve all would be lost. It all depends on keeping your leader straight and going forward.

The Scurry

Scurry driving is a hell-for-leather race against the clock in an arena filled, it seems, with obstacles. There are two divisions for pony pairs, one for ponies 12hh. and under and one for those between 12hh. and 14.2hh. They are put to a light, pneumatic-tired, four-wheeled vehicle manned by a driver and groom.

The Horse Show

While the show ring provides a "shop window" for breeders and producers of horses and ponies, it is also a source of enjoyment and purpose for thousands of exhibitors whose concern is far from being commercial. They obtain pleasure from being a part of the show circuit, from the atmosphere and the social contacts made. To those people a rosette is more important than a cash prize.

In Great Britain, classes—for youngstock shown "in-hand," and hunters, hacks, cobs and ponies exhibited under saddle—as well as the harness classes, are judged on the basis of expert opinion and experience.

Classes are judged by one or, at the most, two judges, who receive out-of-pocket expenses and no more. The same system is followed in British Commonwealth countries and in one or two European countries.

In mainland Europe generally, however, the emphasis is on well-organized and stringent performance testing. Where classes more or less follow the British pattern, they are often judged by a panel, each member of which awards marks, which are later averaged, for the principal parts of the conformation, i.e., head and neck, shoulder and forearm, and so on.

In contrast, the American show circuit is nothing short of a major industry on an unbelievably large scale. It is a highly competitive world, and the considerations are unashamedly commercial.

Halter Classes

Thousands of "halter" classes are staged annually ("halter" is used rather than the British term, in-hand), and great attention is paid to detail and to what is, or is not, "correct." There is a huge diversity of classes covering the three riding styles: hunt seat (English), saddle seat, and stock seat. Saddle-seat classes are for the gaited horses – the Saddlebreds, Missouri Foxtrotters, and Tennessee Walkers (*see* pp.133–35), while the stock-seat classes are those ridden in Western style (*see* pp.68–71).

Judging Shows

American judges are paid professionals for whom, in marked contrast to the "amateur" approach of the British rings, the show circuit is very much a business. American judges, unlike their British counterparts, do not touch the exhibits brought before them; and they certainly do not ride them, as British judges do in the ridden classes.

Nonetheless, in its numerous hunter and jumper classes America combines performance with conformational correctness in an extraordinarily effective way, and the classes can be a valuable proving ground for potential showjumpers and eventers.

All American hunters jump in the ring and are schooled to give a polished display. Not unexpectedly, judging in these classes is heavily weighted on the performance element.

Saddlebred
There may be criticism of training methods but there is no doubt that the arresting presence of the Saddlebred and his immaculately groomed rider makes him the star of the show.

"Working-hunter" Classes

The British ring also takes performance into account in its "working-hunter" classes, in which entrants must jump a course of rustic fences—"rustic" as opposed to the brightly coloured fences of the showjumping competitions. A maximum of 60 percent is awarded for jumping and 40 percent for conformation and ride (the horses are still ridden by the judge). However, "show" hunters in the British ring do not jump—a matter that other European horsemen, and Americans, too, find wholly incomprehensible. They are judged on presence (personality), conformation, on the ride they give the judges, and on their good manners (behavior) in the ring. Jumping, it is held, is no more than a natural extension of those criteria.

American Extravaganza

The average American show is big by European standards and the top shows are simply enormous, staging hundreds of classes, many of them wonderfully colorful and very much influenced by a strong sense of theater. It would be difficult, for example, to match the stunning effect of the extravagant parade classes. In fact, for sheer variety and a certain degree of "razzmatazz" the great American horse show is in a class of its own.

Juniors in the Ring
An American show class for children is an attractive sight with youngsters and ponies very formally turned out. Comparisons with English classes are difficult because of the brilliance of the British Riding Pony (see p.157).

Hunter Jumping
Hunters in the American ring always jump, and great emphasis is put on style and performance. The classes are good testing grounds for potential eventers and showjumpers as well as hunters. The style of this combination is perfection.

HORSES OF THE WORLD

Kabardin Herd

The ancient Kabardin breed of the Caucasus is regarded as Asia's best
mountain horse and has an unerring sense of direction.

What is a Breed?

The answer to this question could depend upon which side of the Atlantic it was asked, since breed status in America does not always meet the criteria required in Europe and is frequently claimed for what by European standards are "types." The American color types and crosses such as the Morab are cases in point.

Breeds and the stud books on which they depend are a comparatively recent innovation. Indeed, very few stud books—apart from those of the Thoroughbred and Arab—are more than 100 or so years old.

Before the stud book became a governing factor, a "breed" would have meant groups of animals inhabiting a particular area. Because of the environment and the relationship inevitable between them, they would have shared discernible similarities in terms of height,

Arab Youngstock

Each of these pure-bred Arabians has a pedigree extending over many generations of similarly pure-bred ancestors. Indeed, the principal lines involved can be traced over hundreds of years and, given industry and application, probably much more than that. This is the reason for the unmistakable character of the breed.

conformation, coat color and character. Today, "breed" is the word applied to a group of horses selectively bred over a sufficient period of time to ensure consistency in character, appearance and action.

The Closed Stud Book

Moreover, "breed" horses must be the progeny of parents whose pedigrees (ancestry) are recorded in the stud book of that breed. In turn, their progeny are entitled to be entered in the book. This is the definition of a "closed" stud book—one that is confined to pure-bred stock and admits the entry of no outcrosses to other breeds, although it may operate a controlled 'register' for approved part-bred animals, i.e., Welsh Part-breds, Part-bred Arabs, Part-bred Dartmoor, etc.

Pedigree

This pedigree of a Czech Warmblood covers several generations. It provides incontestable proof of breeding.

This page gives the name, parents, date and place of birth, and is officially authenticated.

This page shows the parents' breeding and, in this instance, lines to Nonius and Furioso horses.

The Open Stud Book

The family of warmblood horses in mainland Europe, which suffered massive disruption, dispersal and loss of records in the two world wars, operates differently, relying on an "open" stud book. This allows stock to be registered so long as the parents themselves are recorded, or are among those approved by the breed society and are of pedigree stock, though not necessarily of the same breed. The system allows greater latitude to breeders, who can mix a variety of bloods to achieve a carefully defined objective. There may, however, be some variations in type.

All the Continental warmbloods carry Thoroughbred blood in varying percentage, and in many there is still an Arab background. The Selle Français, for example, is heavily dependent on Thoroughbred, Anglo-Arab and French Trotter blood, while the Dutch Warmblood, originating in the amalgam of Groningen, Gelderlander and Thoroughbred, has corrected the mix by outcrosses to Oldenburg, Trakehner and Hanoverian.

Types

Horse or pony "types" are those that do not qualify as breeds because of a lack of fixed character. Hunters, hacks, polo ponies and cobs are examples, as is the British Riding Pony, which in any other country would certainly be accorded breed status. Indeed, outside of the color types, many of the American cross-breeds claiming to be "breeds" would be routinely classified as types elsewhere. The colored horse (far right) might be termed a type but is really no more than an example of accidental cross-breeding.

Hot, Warm, and Cold Blood

In arbitrary terms, the world's horses can be divided into light, riding and carriage types, heavy draft horses and ponies, but climate and environment may introduce variations on the basic definition. In tropical climates, for instance, small, hardy, very energetic, pony-sized horses are found, which are capable of enduring hardship and surviving on a minimal feed intake.

Ponies
Ponies conserve heat because of their small stature and body surface and have developed special characteristics to cope with inhospitable environments. They differ from horses in size, being deep and short in relation to their height.

In general terms, again, the tall, long-limbed, thin-skinned and fine-coated light horses have their origin in hot, dry climates, while the slow-moving, short-limbed, deep-chested and large-footed heavy horse derives from the primitive Forest Horse of Northern Europe, which lived in lush, damp marshlands. Ponies, which are differently proportioned from either of these, are deep in the body and short in the limb in relation to their height. Because their environment was largely confined to the colder, northern climates and mountainous or high moorland regions they are equipped to grow thick, waterproof coats as protection against cold and wet.

There are also three other important divisions: hotbloods, coldbloods and warmbloods.

The Hotbloods
Hotblood indicates a unique purity of line and blood that is free from all possible outcrosses. The Arab horse, with a genetic purity extending over, perhaps, 5,000 years, epitomizes the hotblood, and is regarded

Hotblood
The Arab horse, originally bred in desert conditions, represents the fundamental hotblood, descending from pure-bred ancestors, not subjected to outcrossing, over a period of perhaps 5,000 years. Unique among horses, the Arab is regarded as the "fountainhead" of all the breeds.

as the "fountainhead" of all the breeds. Also recognized as hotblood is the Arab's direct derivative, the Thoroughbred, developed on scientific lines over 300 years and with a pedigree to match. These two are recognized as the most outstanding and influential examples of the equine species. As well as being termed hotblood, they are sometimes known by the French and German words, *Pur Sang* and *Vollblut*.

There is an argument for including the enduring Barb and the noble Iberian, or Spanish Horse, in the hotblood category. However, the Barb lacks the evidence of a clear origin and genetic background, while the Spanish Horse has a background that must have brought it into contact with the horses introduced by successive waves of Romans, Vandals and others, as well as Barbs brought in by the Moors from North Africa and large numbers of the pervasive Arab horses. It is nonetheless as distinctive as the Arab and is very influential, stamping its progeny with its special character.

The Warmbloods and Coldbloods

Coldblood is the term used for Europe's heavy horse breeds. Warmblood is applied to ponies and all breeds that combine cold and hot blood in varying percentages. The warmblood inclines almost wholly towards the hotblood, being long in the limbs and general

Warmblood

This German competition horse is termed warmblood, being the result of a careful mix of hot and cold blood that attempts to combine the best characteristics of each.

proportions, and narrow in the body. But while it avoids the cold, slow temperament of the heavy horse, it does not have the hotblood's fiery nature. For the competition horse, that is the best of both worlds.

Coldblood

These heavy horses descend from the slow-moving, primitive horses of Europe, conditioned to survive in cold, wet marshlands. Though far removed from that by selective breeding, they form the coldblood element of the world's horses and contribute to the production of warmblood riding horses.

Conformation

Conformation is about the formation of the skeleton and the muscle structure covering it. In particular, it concerns the symmetrical proportion of the component parts.

The shape and proportions of the well-made horse ensure good balance and, all else being equal, result in a good level of performance. Movement, or action, is also the result of conformation, whether good or bad. Conformation can also affect temperament since it dictates the animal's limitations. If the horse is forced into movements that are beyond his physical ability, he becomes resentful and resistant. A well-made horse is a sound horse, with the potential for a long working life.

Naturally, conformation varies between individuals and affects the use to which the horses are put. At one end of the scale is the "strength" structure of the heavy draught horse, at the other the "speed" structure of the Thoroughbred. In between there will be variations that best equip a horse for a particular activity.

Depth and Length

There are some useful, rule of thumb, guidelines on conformation. The first is the depth through the girth (depth allows room for the lungs and their expansion). This measurement should equal that from the elbow to ground. Secondly, the measurement of the back from the rear of the withers should, ideally, be half the length from the point of the shoulder to the last rib (there are eight "true" ribs, then ten "false" ribs, attached only to the vertebrae and not to the sternum bone). Short backs, within reason, conform to the strength structure. Long backs are weak backs, but mares are allowed more length than geldings and stallions.

Finally, the distance between the last rib and the hip bone should not be more than the width of a man's hand,

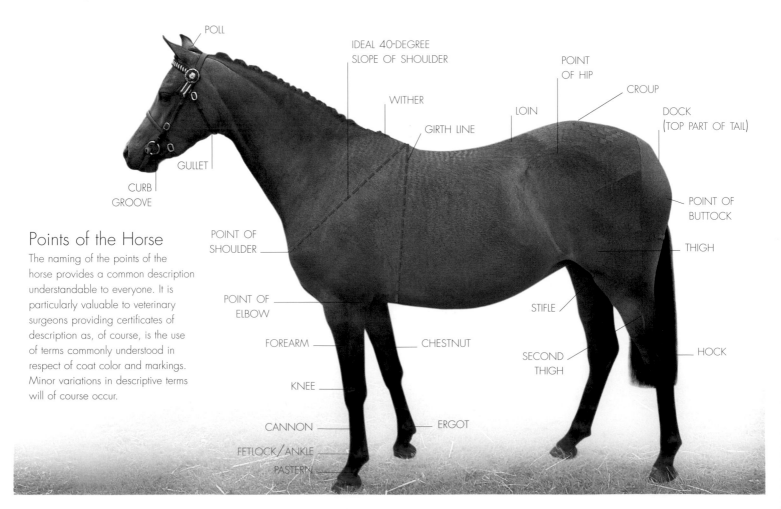

POLL

IDEAL 40-DEGREE SLOPE OF SHOULDER

POINT OF HIP

CROUP

WITHER

DOCK (TOP PART OF TAIL)

LOIN

GIRTH LINE

GULLET

CURB GROOVE

POINT OF BUTTOCK

THIGH

Points of the Horse

The naming of the points of the horse provides a common description understandable to everyone. It is particularly valuable to veterinary surgeons providing certificates of description as, of course, is the use of terms commonly understood in respect of coat color and markings. Minor variations in descriptive terms will of course occur.

POINT OF SHOULDER

POINT OF ELBOW

STIFLE

FOREARM

CHESTNUT

SECOND THIGH

HOCK

KNEE

CANNON

ERGOT

FETLOCK/ANKLE

PASTERN

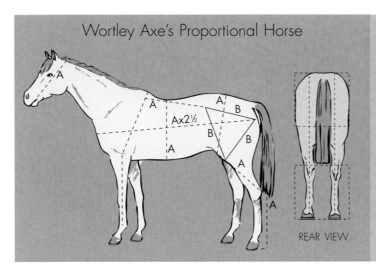

Wortley Axe's Proportional Horse

The most authoritative guide to the proportions of a light horse is that given by Professor Wortley Axe in the late 19th century.

A = length of head
point of hock to ground
point of hock to fold of stifle
chestnut to base of foot
depth of body at girth
fold of stifle to croup
wither to point of hip

Height from fetlock to elbow approximately equals height from elbow to wither

B = seat bone to point of hip seat bone to stifle
stifle to point of hip

A line dropped from the seat bone meets the point of hock and continues down the back of the cannon bone

Hindquarters (rear view)
The side of each square equals the length of the horse's head. The upright line passes through the center of the hocks and fetlocks/ankles

REAR VIEW

otherwise the horse is "short of a rib" and will be slack in this area. It is a serious conformational failing.

The Shoulder

Horsey people are much concerned with the shape of the shoulder, which governs the action. For the stride to be free, long, low and economical, the shoulder (scapula) has to be long and sloped, and the humerus short. The measurements of a good riding shoulder are about 60 degrees from the juncture of neck and withers to the point of the shoulder; 43 degrees from the highest point of wither to point of shoulder; 40 degrees from the rear of the wither to the point. A fairly good assessment can be made with a length of string.

The quarters and forelimbs are best viewed first from behind, then directly in front, and then sideways on.

Conformation Faults

Conformational faults, affecting the horse's action and carriage, and often limiting his performance, occur as a result of poor, incorrect proportions and significant departures from the norm in the structure of the limbs and component parts. Here are some examples of conformational faults in the horse's leg.

Good length from hip to point of buttock

Strong second thigh

GOOD HIND LEG

Hock too high, lack of second thigh

SICKLE HOCK

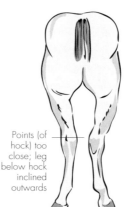

No length from hip to point of buttock and hip to point of hock

HOCKS TOO HIGH

Straight hock results in loss of flexion and propulsion from hind leg

HOCKS TOO STRAIGHT

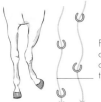

Forelegs raised high and carried outwards in a round, circular action that is inefficient

DISHING/WINGING

The forelegs are crossed with each stride, which is inefficient and may cause the horse to fall

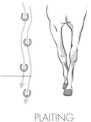

PLAITING

Straight line through buttock, hock, fetlock. Thighs well muscled

GOOD HOCK

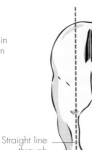

Lack of development in thigh and second thigh

SPLIT UP BEHIND

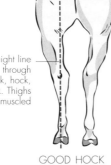

Points (of hock) too close; leg below hock inclined outwards

COW HOCK

GOOD FEET

TURNED OUT TOES

PIGEON TOES

Movement and Paces

In the horse, movement—excepting momentary nervous reactions—is expressed in the four natural paces of walk, trot, canter and gallop. Specialized variations of these paces, however, are found in the gaited American breeds, which have been developed from the old "ambling" or pacing gait seen in the harness-racer.

In school and dressage riding the first three paces (walk, trot and canter) are further divided. Medium walk shows moderate extension, the hind feet touching the ground in front of the prints made by the forefeet. Collected walk, a pace achieved only by the advanced horse, is accompanied by a noticeable shortening of the outline. The steps are higher and shorter, the hind feet touching down behind the prints of the forefeet. In extended walk the horse lengthens his outline, the hind feet touching the ground well in front of the prints of the forefeet. (Free walk is a rest pace, when the outline is lowered, and the head and neck are stretched out.) The pacing gait is a two-beat pace, the legs moving in lateral pairs (*see* Standardbred p.134).

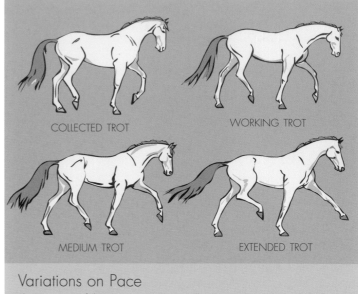

Variations on Pace
The extremes of the trot spectrum are collection and extension. In between are working trot, nearer to collection than otherwise, and medium trot, which is closer to extension. The canter pace is similarly divided and follows the trot spectrum.

Gaited Horses

Most of the specially developed gaits occur in the American breeds, with the exception of the *tølt* of the Icelandic Horse (*see* p.155), and the *revaal* of the Indian Marwari (*see* p.129).

The American gaited horses are the Saddlebred (*see* p.133), the Missouri Foxtrotter and the Tennessee Walker (*see* p.135). In Mexico the Galiceno is also capable of pacing and the slower "ambling," while South America has the amazing Pasos (*see* pp.138–39).

The spectacular Saddlebred is shown as either a three- or five-gaited horse. In both instances, the action is encouraged by special shoeing. The three gaits are all elevated, springy, smooth and rhythmical. The other two specialist gaits are the slow gait, a high-stepping, slow, four-beat gait, and the rack, "a flashy, fast, four-beat gait" with no hint of the lateral pacing movement.

The Foxtrotter gait is unusual. In effect, the horse walks in front and trots behind in a comfortable sliding movement. The Foxtrotter also has a flat foot walk, a four-beat, over-striding, animated gait.

The Tennessee Walker's distinctive feature is the four-beat running walk, in which the hind foot oversteps the prints of the forefeet by between 6in and 15in (15–38cm), according to the speed.

Gallop
The gallop is usually a four-beat pace but it can vary according to the speed. The sequence, if the right fore is the leading leg, is left hind, right hind, left fore, right fore, and then a period of suspension when all four feet are off the ground.

Walk

The walk is a pace of four separate beats made by the footfall of each lateral pair of feet. The walk begins with one or other hind leg, and the sequence of footfall, starting with the left hind leg, is left hind, left fore, right hind, right fore.

Trot

The trot is a two-beat pace. The horse puts down one pair of diagonal legs together and then springs on to the other diagonal after a moment of suspension. One beat is made when left hind and right fore touch the ground and the second when the opposite diagonal pair come down.

Canter

The canter has three beats. If it begins with the left hind leg, the sequence is then the legs of the left diagonal (left fore and right hind simultaneously), and finally the beat of the "leading" leg, the right fore. This is followed by a period of suspension in the air before the next stride is taken.

Colors and Markings

Horses are described by their coat color and can be further identified, as on passports and veterinary certificates, by the white markings that appear mostly on the head and legs.

The main colors are black, brown, bay and chestnut, the last two in a range of shades. Then there is the attractive dun color, either yellow, blue or mouse, which is usually accompanied by a dorsal stripe and black legs, mane and tail. Dun is the color of the early "primitive" horses. Gray is common and becomes whiter with age. Flecked describes a coat with small irregular groups of white hairs; "gray-ticked" is when the coat has sparse gray marks through the body; "flea-bitten" is when gray coats develop small brown or black specks with age. Then there are the roans—blue, red and strawberry—a color caused by white hairs on the primary body color. Creams and Albinos occur due to unpigmented skin. The Palomino has a distinctive golden coat and flaxen mane and tail. Part-colored is a coat of two colors and odd-colored is when the coat has more than two colors. Whole- or solid-colored is the term for a coat containing no hairs of a different color.

American color definitions are different and more picturesque. For example, there is buckskin, a dark cream, either a shade lighter or darker than a pumpkin. Calico refers to a part-colored horse and so, of course, does Pinto, while increasing use is made worldwide of Tobiano and Overo (*see* p.137). (In Europe the terms piebald and skewbald are still used. Piebald is black and white, skewbald is white and any other color except black.)

A Claybank Dun is a horse with a reddish-yellow coat and a darker mane and tail. Sorrel describes a variety of chestnut-red and brown shades.

Color Associations

"A good horse is never a bad color" but horsemen see washy, ill-defined colors as indicating a weak constitution, while strong colors denote the opposite. Duns are thought to be hard and tough; chestnuts, particularly mares, may be fiery in temperament, and black horses are sometimes avoided as being associated with death and the funeral hearse. There used to be a prejudice against colored horses but today

Color Inheritance

Color is determined by a combination of genes, some of which are dominant and some recessive. In horses gray dominates black, bay, and chestnut; bay dominates black; and chestnut is recessive to all colors. So if a bay is mated with a chestnut the foal will be bay, while two chestnuts always produce a chestnut foal.

BAY

BLACK

BROWN

CHESTNUT

Markings

Markings do not always conform exactly to the book definition and variations are bound to occur. The photographs on the right illustrate this. The horse on the left *nearly* has a white face, three quarters perhaps. The one on the right has an "irregular" blaze.

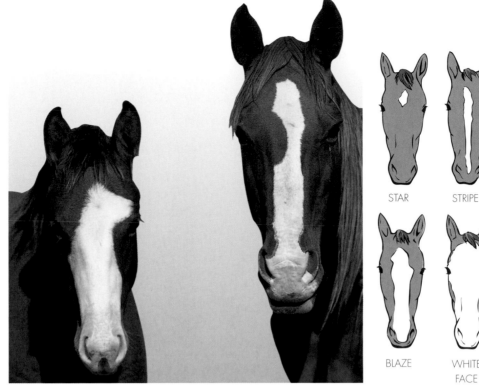

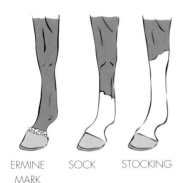

ERMINE MARK   SOCK   STOCKING

STAR   STRIPE   SNIP

BLAZE   WHITE FACE   LIP MARKS

WHITE MUZZE

they are popular in both Europe and America. Gray horses are for rich men—because of the labor involved in keeping them clean!

Markings

Markings are either acquired, such as brand and freeze marks, or natural, taking the form of white hairs on areas of the face and legs.

Whorls can also be considered as identifying marks and in the East have a particular significance. The 14th-century Hindu Asva Sastra lists 117 inauspicious markings, mostly whorls, which should be avoided when purchasing a horse.

More familiar is the indentation on the neck known as "The Prophet's Thumbmark." Legend has it that the Prophet Mohammed placed his hand in blessing on the necks of five superlative mares, the founders of the principal Arab horse families. The mark is said to be inherited by the best of their descendants, regardless of whatever outcrossing may have occurred.

DUN

GRAY

ROAN

PART-COLORED

PALOMINO

Arab

The extraordinarily beautiful Arab is the oldest pure breed in the world and has been the most "prepotent"—the word used to describe the ability to pass on character and type consistently to the subsequent progeny.

The Arab can trace its ancestry back over 5,000 years to the wild horses of the Yemen, which were said to have been first tamed by Baz, the great-great grandson of Noah.

For centuries the Arab was the most important single influence in improving and creating many other breeds, in particular the world's super-horse, the English Thoroughbred. The Thoroughbred is bigger, faster, more valuable and now more important, but cannot approach its progenitor in terms of constitutional soundness and stamina.

The Arab is unmistakable in every way and its floating, elastic action, the arched curve of the neck, and high tail carriage are unique. Its distinctive appearance stems from a structural formation of 17 ribs, 5 lumbar bones, and 16 tail vertebrae. Other breeds have an 18-6-18 formation.

Although spirited and even fiery, the Arab is also gentle and easily managed.

Unique Character

Of all the breeds, the Arab is the most distinctive in appearance. The unmistakable carriage apart, it is the head that is a special feature of the breed.

The arched curve of the neck, giving exceptional all-round mobility to the head, occurs because of the angle at which the head meets the neck. It is termed the *mitbah* and is not found in other breeds. The face is noticeably concave or dished, and the muzzle very small but with exceptionally large nostrils.

The eyes are widely spaced and set low around the *jibbah*, the shield-shaped bulge that is essentially Arabian.

FACT FILE

COLORS	All solid colors
REGION	Middle East, now universal
USES	Riding
HEIGHT	14.2–15hh.

Thoroughbred

The Thoroughbred evolved in England as a racehorse in the 17th to 18th centuries, principally as a result of the import of three Oriental (Arab) stallions: the Byerley Turk, the Darley Arabian and the Godolphin Arabian. These foundation sires, crossed with the native "running" stock, a mix of Barb, Spanish and the indigenous Galloways and Irish Hobbies, founded the four pre-eminent racing lines of Herod, Eclipse, Matchem and Highflyer.

The *General Stud Book*, in which the pedigrees of all Thoroughbreds are recorded, was first published in 1808, and the name Thoroughbred first appeared in Volume II, published in 1821.

FACT FILE	
COLORS	All solid colors
REGION	England, now universal
USES	Racing, competition
HEIGHT	15.2–16.2hh.

Bred for Speed

The Thoroughbred is noted for the long proportions that are associated with speed. The graceful contours of the body give it an extremely refined appearance. The profile of the face is straight, unlike the Arab's. The clean-cut, lean head is covered with thin skin, and the veins are clearly visible. Eyes and nostrils are large; ears, longer than those of the Arab, are alert and mobile, and there is no thickness through the jowl. The modern Thoroughbred matures at a much earlier age than other breeds and can be raced at the age of two and three.

Spanish

Next to the Arab, the predominant influence on the world's horses for the 300 years up to the end of the 18th century was the Spanish Horse or, more correctly, the Iberian Horse, for it includes the Alter-Real and Lusitano breeds of Portugal. Spanish colonists re-introduced horses to the Americas in the 16th century, and their influence is still strong in American breeds, as, indeed, it is in those of Europe.

The Spanish Horse's early origins are possibly with the Barb horses of North Africa crossed with the indigenous

Sorraia and Garrano breeds, but there is otherwise little evidence of significant outcrossing subsequently.

The horse is ideally suited to harness driving and the disciplines of High School riding, and also features in the bull-rings of both Portugal and Spain.

The Noble Horse

The Spanish Horse, wrote William Cavendish, Duke of Newcastle, is "… the noblest horse in the world … and fittest of all for a king in the day of triumph." The proud carriage, enhanced by the luxuriant mane and tail, and the lofty, extravagant action contribute to the breed's essentially heroic character.

FACT FILE	
COLORS	Bay, shades of gray
REGION	Spain, Portugal
USES	Riding, driving
HEIGHT	15.2hh.

Cleveland Bay

This powerful bay horse was developed in the northeast of England, in an area that includes Cleveland. Its ancestor was the Chapman, a pack horse used by travelling salesmen and for carrying ironstone from the hill mines. In the 17th century Barb horses from Tangier were imported to the northeast of England, and in the aftermath of the

Civil War (1640–45) there were many Spanish horses in the area. These added characteristics to the Cleveland. Since then Clevelands have remained pure, although crosses to the Thoroughbred are made to produce a lighter, faster horse. Pure Clevelands are supreme heavyweight hunters and great jumpers, as well as being the most stylish of coach horses.

Strength
The Cleveland Bay is always a rich bay color with well-defined black points, i.e., lower limbs, mane and tail. There is also some evidence of the "hawk- or ram-like" profile inherited from Spanish influence in the 17th and 18th centuries. The powerful back is sometimes a little long, as befits a horse that is equally at home in harness or under saddle. The overall impression is one of great strength combined with active paces.

FACT FILE	
COLORS	Bay with black points
REGION	Northeast England, now universal
USES	Driving, agricultural, riding
HEIGHT	16–16.2hh.

Hackney

In simple terms this very distinctive, high-actioned horse is the most spectacular harness horse in the world. The action is described as "effortless," "electrical" and "snappy." The extravagant, exciting movement is largely inherited, though it can be exaggerated further by skilful training and shoeing. The feet, for instance, are allowed to grow longer than usual to give increased "snap" to the action. The

Hackney (derived from the French *haquenee*, a "nag" or gelding) descends from the famous British trotting "roadsters" of Norfolk and Yorkshire that were so much a feature of 18th-century England. Modern Hackneys are largely confined to the show-ring but are also used in competitive driving.

There is also a Hackney Pony (up to 14hh.), which has its base in the Fell Pony of the English Pennines.

Refined Brilliance

The Hackney is notable for its conformation and, particularly, its brilliant action. The latter, of course, is encouraged by allowing the feet to grow long, but artificial aids such as those used with the show-ring American Saddlebreds, for instance., are never employed. The head is lean and refined, with a straight profile. The graceful neck appears to rise almost vertically from the powerful shoulders. Unlike those of the riding horse, the withers are rounded and low, as is frequently the case in the harness breeds. The body is essentially compact, with great depth through the chest, and the short limbs are notably correct in their conformational detail. The coat, like that of its antecedents the Arab and the Thoroughbred, is fine and silky.

FACT FILE	
COLORS	Brown, black, bay, chestnut
REGION	England
USES	Driving
HEIGHT	14–15.3hh.

Selle Français

Tough, agile and versatile, the French warmblood *Cheval de Selle Français* (French Saddle Horse) is probably as good as any in Europe.

Like all warmbloods, the essential element in the breeding is the Thoroughbred, which gives the progeny the size, speed and courage necessary for competitive sport. However, the base stock for the original French horse was found in fast Norman trotters, derived from

Thoroughbred crosses with the Hackney ancestor, the Norfolk Roadster. Most of today's Selle Français are by Thoroughbred sires.

This is an all-round competition horse with a particular talent for showjumping. A lighter type, with a greater Thoroughbred background, is also bred for races that are limited to non-Thoroughbred horses, and is particularly noted for its ability in jumping races.

A Successful Mix

As is the case with all warmblood horses, there is a variation in type because of the mixed genetic background. Many Selle Français incline towards the Thoroughbred in appearance, but the set of shoulder and neck, which gives the horse a higher and slightly shorter action than the Thoroughbred, derives from the tough trotters that provided the base stock. While the head is not undistinguished, it does not approach the lean refinement of the Thoroughbred head.

FACT FILE	
COLORS	Mostly chestnut; other solid colors
REGION	Normandy, France
USES	Competition riding
HEIGHT	Average 16hh.

Friesian

The existence of this very old breed was recorded by the Romans nearly 2,000 years ago. A coldblood horse, it was improved by both Arab and Spanish Horses and in its turn has been crossed with many other breeds. The Dales and Fell ponies of England were strengthened by crosses with the Friesians when the latter were employed as cavalry by the Roman legions, and there is little doubt that the Friesian is the ancestor of the great Shire horses of England.

A small, very strong horse, it is docile and economical to keep. Today, Friesians work the land, are driven in harness, perform in dressage competitions and still draw funeral hearses.

The Funeral Horse

The small, powerful Friesian is immediately recognizable by the jet-black coat coloring, the full and wavy mane and tail—a relic of the improving blood of the Spanish Horse—and by the considerable feather carried on the lower limbs. The feet, which are of proportionate size to the body and not nearly as large as those of the heavy breeds, are almost always of dense blue horn. While the shoulders, withers and the resultant high action are those of a harness horse, the Friesian, though no great galloper, is also used under saddle, particularly for dressage.

FACT FILE	
COLORS	Black
REGION	Netherlands
USES	Driving, agriculture, riding
HEIGHT	15hh.

Trakehner

This is the "class" horse of mainland Europe, with a history going back to the 1200s, when the Order of Teutonic Knights started a horse-breeding industry in East Prussia. Five hundred years later Friedrich Wilhelm I of Prussia founded the great Royal Trakehner Stud. As well as maintaining a large stallion band, the stud produced elegant, fast coach horses and, later, army remounts and chargers, which were carefully bred and performance tested.

Thoroughbreds and Arabs were used to improve the stock, and by 1913 most Trakehner stallions were Thoroughbred. The most famous stallion was Perfectionist, son of Persimmon, winner of the English

Derby and St. Leger in 1896. His son Tempelhuter is recognized as the foundation sire of the modern breed.

To escape the Russian advance in World War II, the Trakehner mares and their foals trekked 900 miles (1,450km) across Europe to Germany. Only 200 survived to continue the breed. The Trakehner's impressive record as a competition horse exceeds that of any other breed.

FACT FILE	
COLORS	Any solid color
REGION	East Prussia and now Germany
USES	Competition horse
HEIGHT	16–16.2hh.

A Quality Horse

With its background of both Arab and Thoroughbred blood, the Trakehner is a horse of more quality than many other warmbloods. It can almost be considered a stronger version of the Thoroughbred. The head is particularly notable, with wonderfully alert ears and an unmistakable expression that is at once kind and generous. The conformation is good and proportionate, and the feet are hard and well formed. Overall there is a greater uniformity of discernible type than in other warmbloods.

Hanoverian

The Hanoverian is the most numerous and well-known of the European warmbloods and is renowned as an athletic dressage horse and showjumper.

The breed was established at Celle in 1735 as a powerful coach, carriage and farm horse. It was soon crossed with Thoroughbred and Trakehner blood to produce a lighter, more free-moving horse, and the Thoroughbred influence has increased (even in the mid-19th century the Thoroughbred content was reckoned to be 35 percent).

The modern Hanoverian is bred very carefully and undergoes controlled performance testing that takes account of temperament and reliability.

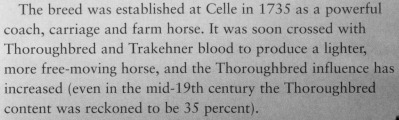

Strength and Agility

While the Hanoverian type is not recognizably fixed, there is usually a characteristic width to the strong quarters and a noticeably flat croup line. The head is sensible and workmanlike, and the body strong and compact. There are few distinguishable features, other than the set of the croup (and that is to be seen in other related warmbloods), but the Hanoverian action is notable. It is always straight, very active and has a particularly elastic quality. Overall, the structure is one of strength, and the Hanoverian has no pretension to speed. It is, nonetheless, a most athletic horse.

FACT FILE	
COLORS	All solid colors
REGION	Germany
USES	Competition
HEIGHT	15.3–16.2hh.

Holstein

Like all the German warmbloods, the Holstein is a mix of breeds refined by the use of Thoroughbred blood. In fact the Holstein Society made more use of Thoroughbreds in the years after World War I than any other. An even more notable earlier outcross was to the Yorkshire Coach Horse (a Cleveland Bay/Thoroughbred cross). This was the cross that established the equable temperament and a characteristic action. Previously Spanish Horses had improved this coarse but tough and reliable coach horse.

Today the Holstein is an all-round competition horse, excelling as a showjumper, dressage horse and particularly as an eventing prospect.

Hunter Type

The modern Holstein is, indubitably, a riding horse. It retains just a little of the knee action inherited from its carriage forebears. Indeed, the quality of the paces is a feature of the breed, the action being very balanced, rhythmical and straight. At its best, the modern Holstein resembles a quality English or Irish hunter. It has the same sensible head, with no trace of the heaviness once associated with the breed. The tail may sometimes be set a little low in the quarter, but is always carried well.

FACT FILE	
COLORS	All solid colors
REGION	Schleswig-Holstein, Germany
USES	Competition, including driving
HEIGHT	16–17hh.

Oldenburg

The heaviest of the German warmbloods, the Oldenburg has an interesting background as the creation of one man, Count Anton Gunther von Oldenburg (1603–1667), who used a half-bred stallion, Kranich, with a strong Spanish background, on a base of Friesian mares. The product was a big, strong, farm/coach horse that could also be ridden. Thereafter, there was the usual influence of half-bred English stallions, Norfolk Roadsters and, after 1897, English Thoroughbreds and Cleveland Bays.

The modern Oldenburg is not fast but is an excellent jumper and dressage horse with very good feet—which is not always the case with other warmbloods.

FACT FILE	
COLORS	Usually brown, black, bay
REGION	Oldenburg, Germany; Friesland
USES	Competition, including harness
HEIGHT	16.2–17.2hh.

Up to Weight

The horse is powerfully built and exceptionally deep-chested, but does not have the galloping Thoroughbred shoulder. The limbs are correspondingly short and strong, to carry the big frame, and are noted for the short cannons and a bone measurement below the knee upwards of 9in (23cm)—a prime requirement of a weight-carrier. The head is best described as plain but honest.

Dutch Warmblood

This is the success story of post World War II warmblood breeding. The Dutch Warmblood, astutely marketed, has become a horse of international repute in a very short space of time.

The Dutch had two native agricultural breeds. There was the Groningen of the north and the Gelderlander of the south. The former was a plain farm horse with especially powerful quarters; the latter had more quality, good stamina and much better shoulders. In essence the Dutch breeders crossed the two and topped off with the ubiquitous Thoroughbred blood and a seasoning of Trakehner, Oldenburg and Hanoverian to produce a world-class competition horse.

FACT FILE	
COLORS	Any solid color
REGION	Netherlands
USES	Competition including driving
HEIGHT	16hh.

A Performer

The clever, controlled amalgam of powerful farm horses and selected Thoroughbreds, and then related warmbloods, has resulted in a most attractive and versatile horse. The Dutch Warmblood is a near-perfect riding type, with an action to match.

Gelderlander

This was the biggest "mongrel" of them all. It was developed a century ago in Gelder province, in the Netherlands, using the common native mares as a base. The aim was to produce a good-actioned carriage horse that could be ridden (at a pinch) and used on the farm. To do so, the Gelder breeders used Cleveland Bay, Norfolk Roadsters, English half-breds, Arabs, Anglo-Arabs, Nonius, Furioso, Oldenburgs, Orlovs, Friesians and Hackneys.

Today's Gelderlander is a superb carriage horse, powerful, with a high, showy action, and is very successful in international driving competitions.

FACT FILE	
COLORS	Predominantly chestnut
REGION	Netherlands
USES	Carriage driving
HEIGHT	16hh.

Elegant Carriage Horse

An upstanding horse, the Gelderlander has a typically short "carriage" neck and inclines towards length in the back. The horse is not built for speed, but the lofty, cadenced action is impressive. There are usually prominent white markings on the legs and on the plain but proportionate head.

Belgian Warmblood

The Belgian Warmblood, produced by breeders usually more concerned with heavy agricultural horses, is a comparatively recent addition to the European family of purpose-bred warmbloods.

In the 1950s lighter Belgian farm horses were crossed with the Gelderlander to give a heavyweight riding horse that was reliable but neither talented nor athletic. Ten years later Holsteins were brought in, along with the gymnastic Selle Français. Inevitably there had to be crosses to the Thoroughbred to improve speed, scope and stamina. Finally, there were more crosses to Anglo-Arabs and Dutch Warmbloods to fix the easy, calm temperament.

The breed is increasingly successful in international showjumping and is making its mark in dressage competition, where the somewhat elevated stride is an advantage.

Sport Horse

A good riding type, by no means without talent, the Belgian Warmblood retains much of the structural strength associated with its farmhorse ancestors. Nonetheless, the proportional correctness of the conformation ensures a sound horse with active, regular paces. There is some elevation in the stride, and there is always conspicuous strength through the broad loin.

FACT FILE	
COLORS	Any solid color
REGION	Belgium
USES	Competition
HEIGHT	16.2hh.

Lipizzaner

The white Lipizzaners of Vienna's Spanish Riding School are world-famous. The School is named after the Spanish Horses that were used there when it opened in 1572. The Lipizzaners take their name from the former Austro-Hungarian court stud at Lipizza (Lipiça), Slovenia, where the breed was founded by nine Spanish stallions and 24 mares imported in 1580 to produce grand, stylish horses for the court stables. Since 1920 the School Lipizzaners have been bred at the Piber Stud in Austria.

During World War II, the stud moved to Hostau in Czechoslovakia, and in 1945, when it might have fallen into German hands, its director succeeded in getting General Patton to rescue the School Lipizzaners from likely extinction and put the stud under the protection of the US army.

The modern Lipizzaner is white, but that was not always so in the early days. Occasionally one finds a bay horse, and traditionally one of this color is kept at the School. Foals are always born black or brown.

Lipizzaners, of the principal lines but usually different in type from the Piber horses, are bred in Hungary, Romania and the former Czechoslovakia. They are, of course, ridden, but many make brilliant harness horses.

FACT FILE	
COLORS	White, occasionally bay
REGION	Former Austro-Hungarian Empire
USES	Riding, harness
HEIGHT	Piber about 15.1hh., others up to 16hh.

The Classical Horse

The Piber Lipizzaners are short, almost cobby sorts, compact and very strong behind, but not without elegance. Variations in type that occur outside Piber include the Hungarian Lipizzaner, which is bigger, lighter built and very free-moving.

Kladruber

The Kladrub Stud in the former Czechoslovakia is one of the oldest in the world. It was founded on Spanish Horses imported in 1572, and its object was to produce carriage horses for ceremonial occasions. Once established, these were always white or black horses, the former derived from Lipizzaner outcrossing.

Originally a heavy specimen with pronounced convex profile and short, high action, it has been a little refined by English half-bred stallions. Today it is a useful heavyweight riding horse, and is still an excellent, showy horse in harness, although not fast in either pursuit.

FACT FILE	
COLORS	White, black
REGION	Kladrub, former Czechoslovakia
USES	Riding, harness
HEIGHT	16–17hh.

Royal Coach Horse

A big, plain horse with very showy action in harness, the Kladruber is nonetheless majestic in appearance and is described as giving an overall impression of "importance." The picture (right) shows a coach being pulled by an impressive 12-horse team, which is unusual by any standards.

French Trotter

Trotting races were popular in France 200 years ago, and the sport remains firmly established today. As a result we have the superlative French Trotter (using the diagonal gait), which was bred in Normandy on a base of Norfolk Roadster, English half-breds, and later, to give extra speed, the Thoroughbred and some Standardbred imports. It is an exceptionally tough horse, which is raced—uniquely—under saddle as well as in harness. It has played a significant part in the development of France's Selle Français, as accomplished a competition horse as any in Europe.

Fast and Tough

The French Trotter, famous for its ground-covering action, is notable for its strong, well-sloped shoulder and the enormous propulsive power of the hocks and powerful, sloping quarters. The head is often handsome and always attractive.

FACT FILE	
COLORS	All solid, mainly chestnut, bay, brown
REGION	Normandy, France
USES	Harness racing
HEIGHT	About 16.2hh.

Asses and Zebras

Unlike horses, asses and zebras originated in the Old World. The domestic ass or donkey was native to North Africa, the zebra family now inhabits southern Africa, and the hemionids, sometimes called onagers, are found in western and central Asia, particularly in Mongolia, India and the Middle East. Asses, hemionids and zebras all belong to *Equus*, but there are significant differences.

Chestnuts, the horny callosities on the lower limbs, are found only on the forelegs of asses, hemionids and zebras, not—as in the case of horses—all four legs. There are five lumbar vertebrae (not six), the ears are long, the back straight, and the feet narrow and straight-sided. The tail is tufted like a cow's, and the mane is short and upright. The period of gestation in the horse is 11 months; that of the ass is 12 (370 days). And, of course, there is the unmistakable bray, instead of a neigh or whinny.

Hemionids

The word hemionid derives from the Greek and means half-ass, the

Burchell's Zebra

The "tiger horse" (*Equus hippotigris burchelli*) as Burchell's Zebra is sometimes called, is the most numerous of African zebras, and always seems to be in good, plump condition.

zoological term for the Asiatic ass being *Equus hemionus onager*. But it would be wrong to think of it as a cross between an ass and something else. Hemionid describes an animal that combines characteristics of both horse and ass with some other distinctive features.

The lower leg bones, for instance, are much longer than in any other form of equid. The other branches, or sub-genera, of hemionid, found in Asia, are the Mongolian Kulan, *Equus hemionus hemionus*; the Tibetan Kiang, *Equus hemionus kiang*; and, in the deserts of north-west India, the Indian Onager or Ghoor-khur, *Equus hemionus khur*—it means wild mule, which it is not. The Persian Onager is extinct in the wild but is preserved in zoos and reserves.

Hemionid Varieties

All these hemionids are closely related but, like all living creatures, each has developed according to its environment. While differing in detail, they all have the long-legged, high-crouped conformation (rather like that of the greyhound) that allows them to move at great speed, sometimes up to 35–40mph (56–64 km/h). Of the hemionids, the Kulan has more horse-related features than the others, particularly in respect of the feet, voice and ears, but its nostrils are much larger than either horse or domestic ass, enabling it to cope with the rarefied atmosphere in which it lives.

Domestic Ass

The domestic ass or donkey, *Equus asinus*, is to be found in almost every part of the world, although it is physically best suited to hot climates. The male is called a "jack" and the female a "jennet." Both have an average height of 40in (1.02m) at the withers, but there are donkeys that are both far bigger and far smaller. The Andalucian jack donkey may stand 15hh., or 60in (1.52m), while the Baudet de Poitou can be a full hand higher—16hh., or 64in (1.63m). At the other end of the scale are the dwarfs of Sicily and India, as small as 24in (61cm). The dorsal eel-stripe and the "shoulder cross" over the withers are a common feature, but the color range is wide, including black, white, gray, part-colored and even spotted coats.

Zebras

Of the teeming herds of zebra once found in Africa, only three species survive. The biggest, at 13.2hh., or 52in (1.32m), is Grevy's Zebra, *Equus dolichohippus*. It differs in proportion and coloring from the others and is more closely related to the primitive horses. The most numerous is Burchell's Zebra (*hippotigris*—"tiger horse"). In smaller numbers, there is the Cape Mountain Zebra. There was, up to the 19th century, another species, called the Quagga. It was fast, graceful, and the stripes were less apparent. Unlike the zebra, which is naturally savage, the Quagga was reputed to be tame and manageable. Projects in back-breeding to produce a "replica" Quagga are under way at Karoo National Park, South Africa and seem to be successful. The "new" Quagga is certainly an attractive and graceful little animal, distinctively marked and likely to be manageable and able to be trained.

Cape Mountain Zebra

The Mountain Zebra is not as numerous as Burchell's. Like the other varieties, it is distinguishable by the different arrangement of the stripes on the head and body. Zebras are usually savage and very few can be trained satisfactorily.

Quagga Replica

The Quagga, reputed to be tame and manageable, was once abundant in Cape Province and the Orange Free State in Africa, but was hunted to extinction by about 1870. Back-breeding to animals closely resembling the Quagga has produced the modern version.

Domestic Ass

The well-loved domestic ass or donkey is found all over the world and there are thriving donkey societies in both Europe and America. At one time, donkeys' milk was a highly sought-after commodity, considered to be health-giving in all sorts of respects.

Wurttemberg

One of the lesser-known German warmbloods, the Wurttemberg is a product of Marbach, the oldest of the German state-owned studs, where it has been bred in evolving forms for over 300 years. Initially, a general-purpose horse was produced from a mix of Spanish, Barb, Friesian and, significantly, Arab outcrosses. When the demand changed to competition prospects, the Trakehner stallion Julmond was introduced in 1960. He is the foundation sire of the modern breed, now much improved again by Thoroughbred infusions to give a hardy, easy-tempered horse sufficiently athletic to compete at international level.

FACT FILE	
COLORS	Brown, black, bay, chestnut
REGION	Germany
USES	Showjumping and other competition
HEIGHT	16.2hh.

Middle-of-the-Road

A good sort of riding horse without any distinctive features, the Wurttemberg is stocky and not unattractive. However, there is some consistency of type. It is reputed to be hardy, long-lived, quiet in temperament, and very economical to keep. The best are athletic animals with a talent for showjumping.

Nonius

The Nonius is an important element in breeding the Hungarian Warmblood, but is also a useful horse in its own right. The breed was originally developed at the great Hungarian state stud at Mezohegyes. Its foundation sire was the unlikely (for he was very ugly) Nonius Senior, by a half-bred English stallion, Orion. He was captured from the French in 1813–14 and went to Mezohegyes in 1816. Despite his conformational failings, he was a prolific sire, producing good stock from all sorts of mares as well as siring the influential Nonius IX. Crossed with Thoroughbreds, Nonius mares produced riding horses of substance with jumping ability. The smaller Nonius, carrying more Arab blood, is an all-round riding and harness horse.

FACT FILE	
COLORS	Predominantly bay
REGION	Hungary
USES	Riding, harness
HEIGHT	Large 15.3–16.2hh., small 14.3–15.3hh.

Fit for Both

A good workman but not especially attractive, the Nonius would make either a useful riding or a driving horse. The neck is not exemplary, the head can be somewhat coarse, and the quarters slope away from the croup. Nonetheless, the Nonius appears in the pedigrees of many of the lesser-known warmbloods.

Furioso

The Furioso (or Furioso-North Star) breed was developed at the Mezohegyes stud in Hungary from Nonius mares put to the English Thoroughbred stallion Furioso (who sired some 95 influential stallions) and North Star, an impeccably bred horse with a line to Eclipse, the greatest racehorse of all. North Star sired many good harness-racers, but the two lines combined in 1885 to become Furioso. Furioso is a good all-round riding horse with Thoroughbred characteristics and some competition potential. It can also be used successfully in harness.

During World War I, in the early years of the 20th century, Furioso and North Star stock were used as cavalry remounts throughout Europe.

Strength and Beauty

Bred all the way from Austria to Poland, the Furioso is more attractive than the Nonius and just as hardy. It has a very intelligent head, derived from its Thoroughbred ancestry, with prominent ears and often a peculiarly squared muzzle. Only rarely are white markings seen on the solid coat colors.

FACT FILE	
COLORS	Any solid color
REGION	Hungary
USES	Riding, harness
HEIGHT	16hh.

Knabstrup

There are few pure-bred Knabstrups today, most of the breed resembling the modern Appaloosa. In the past, however, this old Danish breed was much sought after, particularly for circus work.

The breed descends from a spotted Spanish mare bought by a butcher named Flaebe and sold to a Judge Lunn, who bred from her on his Knabstrup estate. Crossed to a Frederiksborg stallion in 1808, she founded a family of tough, plain, but fast horses who all had the sought-after spotted coats.

Coarse But Colorful

The coat color is that of the Appaloosa and, like the Appaloosa, it owes its distinctive pattern to a spotted strain of the Spanish Horse. The Knabstrup illustrated is a quality horse, but the old breed was usually heavier and coarser in appearance than this, with a straight or convex profile.

FACT FILE	
COLORS	White with brown or black spots
REGION	Denmark
USES	Riding, circus work
HEIGHT	15.2hh–16hh.

Akhal-Teke

The Akhal-Teke breed of Turkmenistan, north of Iran and east of the Caspian Sea, is the mystery horse in the equine jigsaw and an ongoing subject of controversy. The capital city of Ashkhabad was a center for racing—a passion with the Turkmene people—3,000 years ago, and is still a center for Akhal-Teke breeding. Five hundred years later the 30,000 strong Bactrian guard of Darius, king of Persia 521–486BC, was mounted on horses from this region. The argument today revolves around whether the Akhal-Teke preceded the Arab or was influenced by it. It is, of course, a desert horse, thin-skinned and fine-coated, heat-resistant, and capable of extraordinary endurance. Moreover, it closely resembles the Munaghi racing strain of the Arab horse, so far as we are able to tell.

The Akhal-Teke is distinctive, but it is not—at least by Western standards—exemplary in its conformation.

The Akhal-Teke is still raced with enthusiasm; it is unbeatable over long distances (say 2,000 miles/3218km) on its own desert ground and, increasingly, it is a mount for competitive sports—for example, an Akhal-Teke won a dressage gold medal at the Rome Olympics in 1960. Whether it is still pure-bred is a matter for debate, as is its relationship to the Arab.

Unique Coloring

There is nothing quite like this desert horse, although by Western standards there are many conformational failings. It is lean and long-legged, and frequently has a long, tube-like body, but the rib-cage appears shallow. The limbs, too, are not ideal. The hindleg is often sickle-shaped and cow-hocked, and the forelegs are usually set too close together. The long, thin neck rises almost vertically from the shoulder, but the straight-profiled head is fine and arresting. Colors vary; the most striking is the dun, with either a gold or silver metallic bloom to the coat that is both unique and beautiful.

FACT FILE	
COLORS	Bay to dun, often with metallic sheen
REGION	Turkmenistan
USES	Riding, endurance, competition, racing
HEIGHT	15.2hh.

Orlov

The Orlov is Russia's original harness-racer and was developed for that purpose by Count Alexis Grigorievich Orlov, a favorite of the Empress Catherine, in about 1780.

Count Orlov had obtained a white Arab stallion, Smetanka, from the Sultan of Turkey and by using him and his son and grandson, Polkan and Bars I, with Dutch and Danish mares principally, a fixed type was produced. The Orlov was never as fast as the American Standardbred, but by crossing the two, the faster Russian Trotter was produced, while the Orlov was used to upgrade other breeds such as the Don.

FACT FILE	
COLORS	Predominantly gray, also black, bay
REGION	Russia
USES	Carriage and harness racing
HEIGHT	16hh.

Made in Russia

The Orlov is one of Russia's most important breeds. There are five basic types within the breed which, overall is well proportioned. Despite the Arab background, the head, though small, can be coarse. However, the long, swan neck, set high on the shoulders, is a characteristic of the breed.

Don

The Don horse, bred on the Don steppes in southeast Russia, was the traditional mount of the Don Cossacks, the hard-riding cavalry of the Russian armies, who in 1812–14 helped to drive Napoleon's forces out of Russia. Its ancestors were the horses of the nomadic steppe tribes and in particular the Mongolian Nagai. Turkmenes, desert horses related to the Akhal-Teke and mountain horses from the Karabakh Mountains were turned onto the steppe in the 18th century and the herds were later improved with crosses to the Orlov and Anglo-Arabs.

By the beginning of the 20th century the Don was a fixed type. As a cavalry horse, it was hardy and easily kept, and it could also be used in harness.

FACT FILE	
COLORS	Chestnut, brown, often golden sheen
REGION	Don Steppes, Russia
USES	Cavalry remount, riding, harness
HEIGHT	15.3–16.2hh.

The Remount

The Don is described as being "massively built" with a strong constitution. The latter cannot be denied, but the conformational weaknesses result in a restricted and sometimes rough action: it has low withers, a straight shoulder, and deficiencies in the limbs that extend to noticeably upright pasterns. The paces may be neither elastic nor very comfortable, but they are regular. However, the short, constricted structure of the poll makes it difficult to obtain flexion and an acceptable head carriage. Nonetheless, this is a serviceable horse, a practical army remount and can be used in harness or under saddle.

Alter-Real

Portugal's Alter-Real was first bred at the royal Vila de Portel stud at Alter do Chao in 1748. *Real* is Portuguese for royal, and the object of the stud was to provide the royal stables with spectacular carriage horses as well, most importantly, as a horse purpose-bred for the art of classical equitation. The modern Alter, after many disastrous attempts at outcrossing, is now to all intents a wing of the great Andalucian family on which it was originally founded.

The Portuguese School of Equestrian Art use only the Alter-Real, appreciating the high, extravagant action and the noble presence of the breed. The Alter is also seen in the Portuguese bull-rings, where the performance is an art form and the bull is not killed.

FACT FILE	
COLORS	Bay, brown
REGION	Portugal
USES	High School riding, carriage
HEIGHT	15–16hh.

High School Horse

While the Alter is recognizably Iberian, it differs in detail from the other Iberian breeds. This is particularly so in the formation of the back. The result is the showy, elevated movement, short striding with fairly high knee action, and the natural, high-arched carriage of the short, powerful neck. The head is small and intelligent, with the profile frequently concave. Both mane and tail are typically luxuriant.

Lusitano

This spirited, extraordinarily agile horse is the Portuguese version of Spain's Andalucian, with which it shares a common genetic background, although it varies a little in conformational detail. It is nonetheless all-Iberian and enjoys a reputation as the mount of the *campinos* (the herders of Portugal's wild cattle) that is second to none. Nor would the enormously accomplished *cavaleiros*, who display their art in contest with the fighting bulls of the *corrida*, choose any other horse.

It is also an all-round riding horse, now increasingly successful in international competition, and a very showy carriage horse. The breed, although fiery, is innately gentle and quite without vice.

Hero of the Corrida

The Lusitano is an altogether more refined horse than the Alter-Real. It is just as agile, but quicker in its movement, while retaining the characteristic elevated and extravagant action of the Iberian breeds. The head is fine and intelligent, with a neat muzzle and small, alert ears. The neck is naturally short and is carried high and proudly arched. There is particular and exceptional strength over the loin, which allows for pronounced power in the quarters and contributes to the extraordinary agility of this highly responsive and courageous horse.

FACT FILE	
COLORS	Gray, bay, mulberry
REGION	Portugal
USES	High School, general riding
HEIGHT	15.2hh.

Hispano-Arab

The Hispano horse represents an effort to combine the qualities of the Iberian Horse with those of the Arab or Anglo-Arab. Judicious cross-breeding is designed to produce a refined, spirited horse and on the whole it is very successful, although, of course, there will be individuals who incline more or less to the Iberian or Arab character.

Naturally, the Arab influence is evident in the conformation of this horse, particularly about the head and in some cases in the movement also. But

the substance of the Spanish Horse is retained in the powerful back, loins and quarters.

FACT FILE	
COLORS	Most solid colors
REGION	Spain, Portugal
USES	Riding
HEIGHT	15–16hh.

Elegant Cross

Not surprisingly, the prepotent Arab influence is noticeable in this very elegant riding horse. It is especially apparent in the head and, to a degree, in the movement. The Spanish input shows in the back and quarters, and in the hindleg, which is superior to the Arab's.

Barb

The North African Barb is a major influence in the breeds of the world but not much found or used outside North Africa. It can be argued that it is the second of the foundation breeds, and some would hold that it is older than the Arab. Its ancestry cannot be established conclusively and, indeed, it is most probable that Arabs and Barbs were cross-bred during the Muslim conquests of Spain in the 7th and 8th centuries. The Barb stallion has long been the traditional mount of France's famous *Spahi* cavalry.

Today the Barb does not show much sign of Arab blood and is certainly not a beautiful horse. However, it is a true desert horse—tough, enduring and agile—albeit with an uncertain temper.

Primitive Reminder

The true Barb is lightly built, with a flat and upright shoulder that is unusual for a horse of such agility. There is a primitive vigor about the breed, which is reinforced by the narrow skull and convex profile that is not unlike that of the early horses. The Barb is, nonetheless, very fast over short distances.

FACT FILE	
COLORS	Usually gray, also bay, black
REGION	North Africa
USES	General riding
HEIGHT	14.2–15.2hh.

Caspian

In terms of academic research, the Caspian is the most important horse in the world, and the most fascinating. While it is called a pony on account of its size, it is really a horse, with horse characteristics and proportions. Research at the turn of the 19th century suggested the existence, prior to domestication, of four types of *Equus* (*see* pp.10–13). Type Four was a small, very refined horse, like a miniature Arab, and it was considered that this type might be the prototype Arabian, preceding that illustrious breed by 3,000 years.

In the 1960s the American traveller Louise L. Firouz discovered these miniature horses on the shores of the Caspian Sea and founded a stud at Norouzabad. Subsequently studs were formed in the UK and the US.

Renewed scientific interest revealed unique physical characteristics: a notable difference in the shape of the scapula, a different formation of the parietal bones of the head, and an extra molar in the upper jaw.

It was suggested that the miniature horses that were depicted on a cylindrical seal (dated *c*. 548–486BC) as drawing the chariot of King Darius could be forebears of the Caspian. If all the suppositions are correct, the Caspian is the oldest equine breed in existence, apart from the Asiatic Wild Horse.

The modern Caspian, improved by good management, is fast with a long, low, free action, and is a fine jumper. It is excellent in harness, easily handled, and a great mount for children.

Miniature Horse

The modern Caspian is called a pony but is to all intents a small, well-proportioned horse with horse characteristics. These are apparent particularly in the shoulder, which is responsible for the length of stride. A peculiarly vaulted forehead makes the head quite distinctive. The head is short, and has a fine skin covering and a small, tapered muzzle. The eyes are large and have been described as gazelle-like. The breed standard calls for very short ears, stipulating the length as no more than 4.5in (11.4cm).

FACT FILE	
COLORS	Bay, gray, chestnut
REGION	Northern Iran
USES	Driving, riding
HEIGHT	11–12hh.

Marwari

Rajasthan's Marwari is the most distinctive horse of the Indian subcontinent, along with its neighbor and near-relation, the Kathiawari of Gujerat. Bred by the Rathores, traditional rulers of Marwar (Jodhpur), the Marwari horse enjoyed a reputation equal to that of its owners, who were the embodiment of the Rajput warrior.

It is likely that the Marwari originated in the breeds of Turkmenistan, with Arab additions. A true desert horse, it is distinguished by the mobile and remarkable-looking, inward-curving ears. The breed paces naturally in a style called *revaal*—a comfortable, fast, lateral pacing gait. It is also capable of performing the High School airs that are traditional to Rajput horse culture. Today there is a great revival of interest in the Marwari.

FACT FILE	
COLORS	All colors, and part-colored
REGION	Rajasthan, India
USES	Riding
HEIGHT	14.3–15hh.

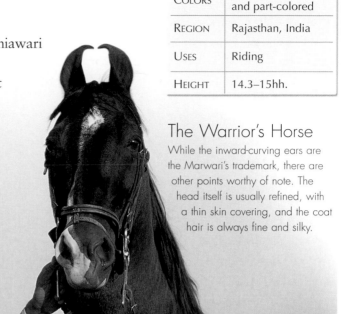

The Warrior's Horse
While the inward-curving ears are the Marwari's trademark, there are other points worthy of note. The head itself is usually refined, with a thin skin covering, and the coat hair is always fine and silky.

Mongolian Pony

In Outer Mongolia there are more ponies than people. These tough examples of "primitive" Mongolian blood are not attractive, but they have inherited the character of their ancestor, the Asiatic Wild Horse, as well as all his prepotent vigor. Indeed, their influence is evident from the Gobi Desert to the Arctic Circle and the Equator.

The ponies survive on minimal feed, in the hardest of climatic conditions and have prodigious stamina. They are quite able to travel 50–60 miles (80–95km) a day and on occasions will go 120 miles (190km) even on rough ground.

Horse-racing is traditional to the people of Mongolia, who often run their races over distances of anything between 20 and 40 miles (30–65km).

FACT FILE	
COLORS	All solid colors
REGION	Mongolia
USES	Riding
HEIGHT	12–13hh.

Handsome is …
This picture is of a Tibetan pony, i.e., a Mongolian in Tibet. The head is large and common, and the neck short and straight. Usually they are also cow-hocked and without withers. Indeed, sometimes the croup is higher than the wither—but it makes no difference to the capacity for work.

Quarter Horse

The Quarter Horse is an all-American product and probably, as it is claimed, "the most popular horse in the world," for there are well over a million registrations.

It was first bred in the 17th century from a base of Spanish, Barb and Arab blood crossed with English imports to Virginia and the Seaboard Settlements.

The horse, a chunky 15hh. that developed exceptional quarters, was used for all purposes. It worked on the farm, hauled goods and lumber, and was put in harness and ridden.

The name derives from the practice of racing over a quarter-mile (0.4km) track cut through the scrub or on the plantations, which, of course, demanded a sprint from an explosive start. Today organized Quarter Horse racing is very popular and offers big prize money.

In the West, the Quarter Horse became the quintessential cow pony on account of its speed, balance and agility, and it excels as a trail-riding mount.

Symmetry in Action

The overall impression here is of a heavily muscled frame, with particularly developed quarters and second thighs, yet entirely proportionate. The neck is, of course, muscular, but it is long and flexible. An arched or crested neck would be an undesirable feature in view of the Quarter Horse's work. It is said of the Quarter Horse that "he can turn on a dime and toss you back ten cents change."

FACT FILE	
COLORS	Chestnut or a solid color
REGION	Virginia, USA
USES	Riding, driving
HEIGHT	15–15.3hh.

Morgan

The Morgan story begins with a phenomenal little horse who founded the first-documented American breed. Originally called Figure, he was later renamed after his owner Justin Morgan, a schoolmaster-cum-innkeeper who acquired him as a two-year-old in about 1795 as payment of a debt.

Figure, no more than 14hh., had a succession of owners and, once it was found that he could outrun and out-haul anything in the locality, he was worked excessively hard for almost 30 years. He drew the plough, cleared woodlands, and undertook every sort of draft work. He was entered in hauling competitions and wagers throughout his life, and regularly raced in harness and under saddle, never being beaten.

As a sire, he stamped his progeny with his special character, and all modern Morgans trace to one of his three famous sons, Sherman, Woodbury and Bullrush.

His antecedents are obscure, but it is generally accepted that he was foaled in West Springfield, Massachusetts. Some claim a part Thoroughbred descent from either Wildair or True Briton; others suggest a Friesian connection; and still more claim him as the son of a Welsh Cob, which is not unlikely.

Whatever the truth, Morgan blood is the underpinning influence for many of the American breeds. Today's versatile Morgans compete in every sort of activity and for many years were the chosen mount of the US cavalry.

FACT FILE	
COLORS	Bay, black, brown, chestnut
REGION	Massachusetts, USA
USES	Riding, harness
HEIGHT	14.1–15.2hh.

Versatility

The Morgan is a compact, well-muscled horse, with exceptionally correct quarters and hindlegs. The body is well rounded, with a short, broad back and wide, deep chest. It is extremely symmetrical in outline and its clean-cut head tapers to a neat muzzle. The eye is large and bright, and the pointed ears are set far apart.

Saddlebred

The show-ring Saddlebred is shown either in three-gaited classes—at a lofty walk, trot and canter—or as a five-gaited horse, which performs in addition the prancing "slow gait" and the full speed "rack," a flashy, four-beat gait. Many regard the classes and the horse as brilliant but unacceptably artificial, the latter on account of the long, heavily shod feet, the nicked tails and so on.

In fact, it is also a fine carriage horse and (with normal feet) an excellent jumper and saddle horse.

It was, indeed, developed in the southern states of the USA as a practical, versatile horse able to carry a rider comfortably during a long working day and over rough terrain.

It derives from the Canadian and Narragansett Pacers, both of which were plantation horses, with Morgan and Thoroughbred blood.

Brilliance
The Saddlebred outline is similar to that of the Hackney, but is unmistakably that of a riding horse. Good limbs and feet are usual, with rather longer than normal pasterns, which ensure a smooth, springy ride.

FACT FILE	
COLORS	Most solid colors
REGION	Kentucky, USA
USES	Riding, harness
HEIGHT	16hh.

Morab

The Morab is one of the more recent examples of an American "invented" breed. It is essentially a Morgan/Arab cross, something that has been known and appreciated for more than 100 years. The claim of breed status would not be recognized outside America, nor, perhaps, outside the societies that are seeking to foster their version of the Morab "breed."

Nonetheless, the Morab Horse Association, one of these societies, operates a detailed registry system and is seeking acceptance of a 25–75 percent (Morgan/Arab) breed standard for registerable Morabs.

There is for the moment no consistency of type, but there are some attractive registered Morabs.

The name Morab was coined by the newspaper magnate William Randolph Hearst long before the Morab Horse societies existed. Hearst had used Arab stallions on his Morgan mares to create a band of work horses for the rough terrain of his California ranch.

FACT FILE	
COLORS	All solid colors
REGION	USA
USES	Riding
HEIGHT	15–16hh.

Inconsistent
This example emphasizes the lack of type in the Morab, making it difficult to appreciate attempts to create a breed. Some Arab features are apparent, particularly about the head; otherwise the animal is unexceptional and shows "too much daylight" between the body and the ground.

Standardbred

Today the American Standardbred is the fastest and most popular harness-racer in the world.

The term Standardbred, first used in 1879, originated in the practice of establishing a speed standard as a qualification for entry into the *American Trotting Register*. The standard was eventually fixed at 2 minutes 30 seconds for the mile (1.6km).

Standardbreds either trot diagonally or pace. The latter, which is usually the faster of the two, is the preferred gait. The first sub-2-minute mile was run in 1897 by a pacer, Star Pointer.

In fact, the story of the Standardbred begins more than 100 years before that date, when an early English "Thoroughbred" called Messenger was imported into America to stand at stud in Pennsylvania, New York and New Jersey.

Messenger, a successful racehorse in England, never raced in harness, but his sire, Mambrino, did trot and was once backed by his owner, Lord Grosvenor, to trot 14 miles (24.4km) to the hour. Messenger was crossed successfully with Morgans and the now extinct Canadian and Narragansett Pacers, but it was his descendant Hambletonian 10, foaled in 1849, who is regarded as the foundation of the breed. Not a handsome horse, he was higher at the croup than the wither, allowing enormous thrust from the quarters.

FACT FILE	
COLORS	All solid colors
REGION	Eastern states, USA
USES	Harness racing
HEIGHT	15.3–16hh.

Purpose-built

The Standardbred is not beautiful, but it has phenomenal power in the limbs and a nearly perfect hindleg and hock joint. The breed is lower and longer in the body than the Thoroughbred, and the croup is often higher than the wither, a factor that contributes to the powerful thrust of the hindleg. The balance is completed by the perfect relationship between the strong shoulders and the neck. The head might be called robust, since in comparison with the Thoroughbred it is plain, though honest in its outlook. Of necessity, the feet have to be good and the action absolutely straight.

Missouri Foxtrotter

The Foxtrotter is perhaps the oldest of the American gaited breeds, having evolved over 170 years ago with the settlers in the Ozark Hills of Missouri. They took with them Morgans, Arabs and Thoroughbreds, and began to develop a new horse to suit their needs, outcrossing to Saddlebreds and Tennessee Walkers.

The result was the unique foxtrot gait: the horse more or less walks in front and trots behind, sliding the hindfeet well under the body, to give the smoothest of rides over all kinds of terrain.

In show classes, artificial aids and weighting of the feet, which could be used to enhance the gait, are not allowed.

FACT FILE	
COLORS	Usually chestnut with white markings
REGION	Missouri, USA
USES	Pleasure/trail riding
HEIGHT	14–16hh.

The Smooth Ride

This is a strong, plain horse, deep-bodied and well muscled throughout. Its hindlegs appear to be more heavily developed than the fore-limbs. The walking movement comes from the depth of the chest and the strong, sloped shoulder, and is without exaggerated knee action. Overall, the outline is lower than that of other gaited breeds.

Tennessee Walker

"Ride one today and you'll own one tomorrow" is the sales pitch of the very successful Tennessee Walking Horse Breeders' Association.

The breed originated as comfortable plantation horses, which were often called Turn-Rows because of the ability they had to turn easily between rows of young plants.

As is the case with all gaited breeds, the foundation was with the old Narragansett Pacer. Thereafter there was an input of Thoroughbred, Morgan, Saddlebred and Standardbred, one of the latter, Black Allan, being the breed's foundation sire. Black Allan was a failure on the track but he consistently passed on his peculiar walking pace.

The modern Tennessee Walker has three gaits: flat walk, running walk (the predominant feature) and a rocking-chair canter. The walk is described as "bounce-free," very relaxing and a great confidence booster. In action the head nods, the ears swing and at top speed, the teeth click!

FACT FILE	
COLORS	Black, chestnut often with white markings
REGION	Tennessee, USA
USES	Pleasure riding
HEIGHT	15–16hh.

The Bounce-free Walk

The Tennessee Walker is large-boned and deep, so lacks the glamour of the Saddlebred, but enthusiasts of the breed are more concerned with the equable temperament and unique gaits than the looks. Special shoes are needed to give the necessary lift to the action, and the feet are grown long.

Palomino

America's Palomino Horse Association produces a "breed standard" that provides useful guidelines on this horse, but it does not confer world breed status on what, however carefully bred, is a color type occurring in horses all over the world.

The Palomino coloring is nonetheless exceptionally attractive. The ideal coat color is that of a newly minted gold coin, but it may be three shades lighter or darker, with a striking white mane and tail.

The American Palomino Association allows Quarter Horse, Arab or Thoroughbred blood for inclusion in the register. The crossings to produce Palomino coloring include the Albino, but the favored one is Palomino crossed with chestnut.

The origin of the name is unclear, but it is suggested that it might be traced to the Spanish word *palomilla*, one meaning of which is a cream-colored horse with white mane and tail. The color does not appear in the pure-bred Arab or in the Thoroughbred.

American Standard

Palomino color is immediately recognizable and may occur in horses of varied breeds and types, both good and bad. However, the height was set by America's Palomino Horse Association Inc. at between 14.1hh. and 16hh., and its breed standard is a guide to the desirable conformation of its registered horses. It acknowledges that conformation will incline towards that of the predominant cross. The emphasis, however, is very much on quality and good conformation. No horse is considered if it "shows coarse, draft horse, Shetland or Paint [Pinto] breeding."

FACT FILE	
COLORS	As above
REGION	Universal
USES	Riding
HEIGHT	USA 14.1–16hh., otherwise any height

Pinto

The name comes from the Spanish *pintado*, painted. In America the Pinto, or Paint Horse, is promoted by two societies. The Pinto Horse Association registers horses, ponies and miniatures in four sections: *stock-type*, mainly Quarter Horse background; *hunter*, largely Thoroughbred; *pleasure*, Arab or Morgan; *saddle*, to include Saddlebred, Hackney or Tennessee Walker. The Paint Horse Association registers stock-type horses, emphasizing bloodlines rather than color.

The distinctive color was always popular in the West among Plains Indians and cowhands alike.

The two recognized American coat patterns are Tobiano, a dominant color, and Overo, which is recessive. There is no fixed Pinto type, but many are well-made, attractive horses.

FACT FILE	
COLORS	See right
REGION	Universal
USES	Riding
HEIGHT	Variable

American Color

The Tobiano coat pattern has a white base overlaid with large colored patches. White crosses over the back, rump, and legs. The Overo has a colored coat splashed with white, which almost never crosses over the back. Conformation varies according to the predominant cross.

Appaloosa

The name is that of the American breed, but spotted coat patterns occur on horses of many breeds throughout the world and are of ancient origin. The Spanish introduced the spotted gene to America and the Nez Percé Indians developed the breed in the mid-18th century. Appaloosa is a corruption of Palouse, the name of a river that flowed through their lands in Oregon.

In the modern Appaloosa, five coat patterns are recognized: *leopard*, white with dark spots over all or part of the body; *snowflake*, white spotting, particularly over hips; *blanket*, hips white or spotted; *marble*, all-over mottle pattern; *frost*, white specks on a dark ground.

American Breed

Type varies, but there are common characteristics: the white sclera round the eye; mottled skin on nose and genitalia; black and white vertical stripes on feet and thin, sparse mane and tail.

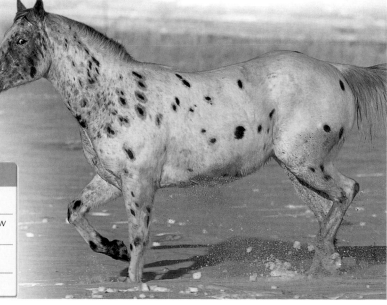

FACT FILE	
COLORS	As above
REGION	Oregon, USA, now universal
USES	Riding
HEIGHT	14.2–15.2hh.

Criollo

Although the name Criollo is applied to a number of South American horses, it is the Argentine Criollo that is most important. It descends from early Spanish stock, with a strong Barb element. A short, stocky horse, it developed a phenomenal degree of toughness, virtually by natural selection, in the feral herds that lived on the *pampas*. It is able to withstand extremes of climate and has even adapted the coat coloring to its surroundings—most Criollos being a shade of dun.

Criollos are used as pack and riding horses, and are the indispensable partner of the *gaucho*, the cowboy of the *pampas*. They are also an essential element in the production of the Argentine polo pony, probably the best in the world. Argentinian breeders put small Thoroughbreds to native Criollos and then put back the Thoroughbred to the subsequent progeny. The result is a distinctive, wiry pony with exceptional hocks and quarters.

FACT FILE	
COLORS	Shades of dun, some part-colors
REGION	Argentina, South America
USES	Pack, riding
HEIGHT	14–15hh.

The Gaucho's Horse

The appearance is of a strong, no-nonsense horse. The build is stocky but not without elegance, and the structure's component parts are usually excellently formed, the limbs being exemplary. The horse is exceptionally well balanced.

The Pasos

Paso means step, and it is the steps or gaits of the Paso horses that are so remarkable and distinctive.

Both horses, the Peruvian and the Paso Fino of Puerto Rico and Colombia, are of Spanish origin. They are, indeed, a careful, skilful mix of Spanish and Spanish Barb strains, accenting the character of the Spanish Jennet, the supreme pacing and ambling horse of 15th- and 16th-century Europe.

Their specialized lateral gaits are natural to both breeds and are only refined and made more brilliant by training.

The hind legs and pasterns are usually long and the joints are capable of extreme flexion. The hock is of exceptional strength. Characteristically, bone and feet are faultless and, as with all Criollo stock, lungs and heart are large.

FACT FILE	
COLORS	Any, mostly bay or chestnut
REGION	South America
USES	Riding
HEIGHT	14–15hh.

Specialist Gaits

The Peruvian Paso moves with a level back in a four-beat, lateral gait (*paso*), swinging the forelegs outwards in the dishing (winging) action called *termino*. The Paso Fino has three gaits: *paso fino*, slow, collected and elevated; *paso corto*, a more extended travelling gait; and the very fast, 16mph (26km/h) *paso largo*.

Falabella

The Falabella was the first notable miniature horse. Miniatures are now popular in many countries but are not necessarily Falabellas.

Originally the Falabella was developed as a miniature horse, not a pony, by a family called Falabella, on their Recreo de Roca Ranch, outside Buenos Aires in Argentina.

Following an accepted breeding technique, the family used the smallest Thoroughbred stallions on small Shetland mares and then in-bred (i.e., father to daughter, sister to brother, etc.) to reduce the size to a maximum of 30in (76cm) at the wither.

Falabellas have no use other than as pets or curiosities, and because of in-breeding they will sometimes have deficiencies in conformation, as well as being disproportionate—for example, big heads, excessively weak quarters, incorrectly shaped lower limbs. This is not always the case, however, with the new wave of non-Falabella miniatures.

FACT FILE	
COLORS	Any
REGION	South America
USES	Pets
HEIGHT	30in (76cm) at wither

Improving Cult
There are resemblances to the Shetland, which formed the base stock. This is particularly noticeable about the sometimes large and heavy head. Nonetheless, conformation in the miniature horse classes improves continually, and some exhibits are proportionate specimens in miniature.

Galiceno

The Spanish province of Galicia was famous for a breed of smooth-gaited horses distinguished by a swift running walk. They were much sought after as a comfortable travelling horse throughout 16th century Europe. The little horses still exist in Galicia, while the modern Galiceno is to be found in considerable numbers in Mexico.

Galiceno stock were among the earliest horses brought by the Spanish to the Americas, and it is almost certain they were descendants of the hardy indigenous ponies of Iberia, the Sorraia and Garrano, which stemmed from primitive stock such as the Tarpan.

The Mexican Galiceno is used as a riding horse, retaining the specialist gait. It is also worked in harness on the land and round the farm. It is acknowledged to be very good-natured and intelligent.

FACT FILE	
COLORS	Dun with black points, Palomino
REGION	Mexico
USES	Riding, agricultural
HEIGHT	14hh.

A Country Horse
A neat, small horse of indeterminate conformation but distinctive character, the Galiceno is noted for its hard feet and inherent soundness as well as for its ability to adapt to varied terrain and changing climatic conditions.

Belgian Heavy Draft

In the Middle Ages the most famous heavy working horse was the Flanders Horse, and it was this horse that later had much to do with the development of the English Shire, Suffolk Punch and Clydesdale. Over the centuries, careful breeding and strict selection produced a unique Belgian heavy horse, which is loosely called the Belgian Heavy Draft. More correctly, it is the Brabant, after one of the principal breeding areas. There were three Brabant groups: the bay *Gros de la Dendre*; the *Gris de Hainaut*, grey dun and red roan horses; and the exceptionally strong *Colosses de la Mehaique*. All had tremendous pulling power, but are not much known or appreciated in Belgium today. On the other hand, the breed has a big following in America, and a number are kept at the Kentucky Horse Park, Lexington, Kentucky, where mammoth mules have been bred from some of the mares.

In its way, and in the context of the heavy horse, the Brabant is just as important in the equine jigsaw as any of the better-known "improving" breeds.

FACT FILE

COLORS	Red roan, chestnut, some bays, duns
REGION	Belgium
USES	Agriculture
HEIGHT	16.2–17hh.

Power

The hallmark of the Belgian is power, and this is evident throughout the short, massive body. The limbs are short, hard and muscled. The huge quarters are massively muscled, with pronounced "double-musculature" over the croup. Neck and shoulders are thick and powerful, but the expressive head is relatively small.

Percheron

The French Percheron is the most elegant of the heavy breeds. Unusually, it owes much to Arab blood, first introduced in the eighth century and made available to breeders in the 18th century by the Royal Stud at Le Pin.

Percherons cross well to produce riding horses, and they were exported all over the world for this purpose. In Australia they were outcrossed to produce tough stock horses, while in the Falklands, crossed with the Criollo, they produced a similar "range" horse.

America was always the biggest market, and in 1910 had no less than 31,900 Percherons.

FACT FILE	
COLORS	Gray and black
REGION	Normandy, France
USES	Broadly agriculture
HEIGHT	16.2–17hh.

Beauty
The Percheron is the most handsome of the heavy breeds and has a low, long-striding action. The head is often beautiful, with a broad, square forehead, straight profile, fine, long ears and prominent, expressive, and alert eyes. The feet are hard, with little feather at the heels.

Clydesdale

Like the Percheron, the Clydesdale has been exported all over the world. Clydesdale teams opened up the prairies of Canada and America, and earned the title "the breed that built Australia."

Because of the breed's "flamboyant" style and action and the excellence of its feet, it was much employed in city draft.

The breed was developed in Scotland's Clyde Valley in the 19th century, so it is not old. The base stock, much influenced by imports of Flemish or Flanders horses, was crossed extensively with the English Shire.

Cow hocks, which turn inwards at the point and are regarded generally as a conformational failing, are acceptable in the breed to ensure "close action."

FACT FILE	
COLORS	Bay, brown, gray, roan, with white
REGION	Scotland
USES	Agriculture, heavy draft
HEIGHT	16.2hh.

Activity
The Clydesdale is a lighter horse and very active in its paces. The legs are longer than in other heavies and terminate in silky feather and hard-wearing feet that are often somewhat flat. The hock joints are strong, but cow hocks are common.

Shire

The English Shire, the supreme heavy horse, gets its name from the English Shire counties of Leicester, Stafford and Derby, which, along with the Fen Country, are the principal breeding areas. It descends from the so-called Great Horse of the 16th century, which was, in fact, not much more than a heavy cob. However, the biggest influence in its evolution was the Flanders Horse, imported into England in the 17th century to work on drainage schemes in the Fens.

Developed as a powerful agricultural horse able to work heavy land, the Shire was also used in heavy city draft. It has many weight-pulling records. Shire classes are a popular feature of every county show.

Gentle Giant

The Shire represents the ultimate "strength structure" combined with impressive weight. The limbs are noticeably clean and hard, with ample bone measurement. The feather on the lower limbs is heavy, but should be straight and silky. Feet are open, solid and well shaped.

FACT FILE	
COLORS	Black, brown, bay, gray
REGION	Midlands of England
USES	Agriculture, heavy draft
HEIGHT	16–19hh.

Suffolk Punch

"A variety of English horse, short-legged and barrel-bodied, a short, fat fellow"—this is one admirable dictionary description of the Suffolk Punch. It is the oldest of the English heavies, and every Suffolk traces its descent to one stallion, Thomas Crisp's Horse of Ufford, foaled in 1768. All Suffolks, like Crisp's Horse, are "chesnut" (spelled that way). Seven shades are recognized, but the most usual is a bright, reddish color. Unlike other heavies, the Suffolk carries little feather on the legs, an advantage on heavy soils.

The Suffolk is exceptionally strong and thrives on smaller rations than do other breeds.

"The Fat Fellow"

The roly-poly, round-bodied Suffolk is among the most attractive of the heavy breeds. Unlike most "heavies," it is clean-legged. A feature is the low shoulder, which contributes to the tractive power.

FACT FILE	
COLORS	Chesnut (*sic*)
REGION	Suffolk, England
USES	Agriculture, heavy draft
HEIGHT	16–16.3hh.

Poitevin

This is the ugly duckling of the heavy breeds. It is unattractive, slow-moving, very hairy and has big, flat feet, which served its ancestors well when draining the marshlands of Poitou in the 17th century.

However, it has a very useful purpose. Bred with the big (16hh.) Baudet de Poitou jackass, it produces the renowned Poitevin mules, the biggest in Europe. There is still a good demand for these mules in those countries where heavy horses cannot be used because the terrain is unsuitable.

FACT FILE	
COLORS	Mostly dun
REGION	Poitou, France
USES	Mule breeding
HEIGHT	16–16.2hh.

Exploited
Everything about the Poitevin is unattractive. It is coarse, the joints are fleshy, the coat hair and feather harsh. It is ponderous and slow in its reactions. It has been put to the heaviest of work, used as a platform for mule breeding, and then sent to the meat market.

Jutland

Horses have been raised on Denmark's Jutland Peninsula for over 1,000 years. In the 12th century, the chunky Jutland was a war-horse with strength enough to carry an armored knight.

Until the 1950s, there were 405 studs in Jutland, with 14,416 mares and 2,563 stallions. Today, Jutlands no longer work the land and are fewer in number, but they are used for city draft and are popular at horse shows.

A big influence in the development of the Jutland was a Suffolk Punch—Oppenheimer LXII—imported in the 1860s, while the Jutland was the foundation for the neighbouring Schleswig-Holstein breed.

FACT FILE	
COLORS	Chestnut
REGION	Denmark
USES	Agriculture, draft
HEIGHT	15.2–16hh.

A Suffolk Cousin
The Jutland is noted for its very tractable nature, and its structure reflects the influence of the Suffolk Punch. However, the lower legs carry heavy feather, which disposes the animal to greasy heels and mud fever. The joints are sometimes insufficiently clean and well-made, being inclined to puffiness.

Mules

The mule is one of the world's most remarkable animals and among the most hard-working. It is probably, also, much misunderstood, although at many points in the world's history it was highly esteemed, and to the Hittites (*see* pp.22–23) was three times more valuable than a chariot horse.

Baby Mule
This appealing baby will not be broken for work until it is about three years old, although it would be wise to get it used to being handled from an early age.

The kings of Israel, as well as the Prophet Mohammed and the great prelates of the medieval church, all rode mules, appreciating the comfort of the ambling pace and the innate sure-footedness.

Jackass Cross
A mule is the product of a cross between a jackass and a horse mare and can vary in size according to the animals selected. As a hybrid it cannot reproduce itself, possibly because of the difference in the gestation period between horse and ass, but the hybrid vigor asserts itself in the mule's bodily strength, which is greater than that of a horse, and the sustained hard work of which it is capable. It adapts more easily to climatic conditions, it is constitutionally as hard as nails and it is economical to keep.

Mule Characteristics
The mule is a highly intelligent animal, given proper treatment, but it has an independent turn of mind that gives it a reputation for stubbornness, when in fact it may be no more than a reflection of the mule's sagacity and highly developed sense of self-preservation.

In appearance the mule resembles the jackass in its extremities—the ears, feet and tail. It might be described as having a horse's body on donkey legs and more like a donkey in front and a horse behind.

Spotted Donkey
This colorful jenny (donkey mare) might well produce an unusually colored hinny foal if put to a small horse stallion. Colored hinnies are popular in the USA.

Kirghiz Trio
This is a small mule by most standards but it will be strong enough to carry a man in the rough Kirghistan country and quite capable of leading this pack camel. Travelling in such a trio is very effective in this difficult terrain.

Mules are used in agriculture, in harness and to carry pack loads up to 380lb (170kg). They are also ridden in Mediterranean countries, which are often too steep and rough for horses—animals that are more expensive and difficult to keep.

Mammoth Mules
In America, mules still retain their popularity, although they are no longer used in transport and agriculture. The huge "mammoth" mules have a considerable following and are used for riding. They are excellent mounts on rough trails, such as those of the Grand Canyon, they are driven in smart turnouts and they also compete in dressage competitions confined to mules!

Mule Transport
Mule transport featured prominently in both world wars, and the modern Indian Army still maintains very large numbers of mules, finding them invaluable in the mountainous terrain of Kashmir and Jammu, where they are often the only practical means of transport.

The legendary Indian Mounted Artillery also uses mules to deliver dismantled screw guns to country inaccessible to motorized vehicles. The Indian Army uses the smaller, agile mule of about 56in (1.42m), or 14hh., usually produced by Indian or Maltese jackasses.

Hinnies
A hinny, male or female, is a cross between a horse and a "jenny," a donkey mare. It resembles the horse in its extremities but has a donkey-shaped body. It is smaller, less versatile and much inferior to the mule in terms of strength and work capacity. Mules are usually uniformly colored, whereas hinnies are gray and also turn up as part-colored, white or even spotted.

Hinnies, in any event, are very difficult to breed and perhaps only one in seven donkeys will conceive if mated with a horse. The colors can be attractive, but the work potential of the hinny is limited.

Mammoth Mule
A splendid pair of mammoth mules that would not be found outside the USA. Indeed, they are something of an American speciality and have a large following.

Dressage Too
Who would have thought it? A mule performing a recognizable dressage movement and making a good job of it. Competitions are, of course, confined to mules.

BREEDS

Eriskay

Despite an active Eriskay Pony Society, and an increased number of 300 (it was 20 in the 1970s), the status of these ponies is still listed as critical by the Rare Breeds Survival Trust. It is the original survivor of the Western Isles breed, and in the 19th century was used for work on the croft farms. While the men earned their living from the sea, the women, children and ponies worked the land. The ponies performed all kinds of tasks, from carrying peat and seaweed in baskets fitted to either side of their backs to pulling carts, harrowing fields and even taking children to school. Eriskays had to be—and generally are—good-natured and friendly in temperament. It is an ideal children's mount.

A Hardy Breed

The lovable Eriskay ponies are true survivors, having lived for centuries in the harsh Scottish climate, which is often cold, wet and windy. They have adapted to these intemperate conditions by growing very dense, waterproof coats and thick, protective manes and tails.

FACT FILE	
COLORS	All
REGION	Eriskay, Scotland
USES	Riding
HEIGHT	12–12.2hh.

Exmoor

The Exmoor is probably as old as any breed, and herds have run out on the moor from which they take their name since before the Ice Age. The pony is virtually weatherproof: it has a double-textured coat to give protection against cold and wet; a thick "ice" tail with extra growth at the top; "toad" eyes, hooded to give more protection; and long nasal passages allowing the air to be warmed before inhalation. It also has a seventh molar tooth that is not present in other *equidae*.

Old as the Hills

The head is of especial interest. The muzzle is mealy colored, the nostrils very wide and the ears short and thick. The forehead is broad, and the "toad" eyes are large and prominent. There are no white markings on the coat.

FACT FILE	
COLORS	Bay, brown, dun. Mealy muzzle
REGION	Exmoor, southwest England
USES	Harness, riding
HEIGHT	12.2–12.3hh.

Dartmoor

This is the Exmoor's nextdoor neighbor but, unlike the Exmoor, it has been crossed with a variety of breeds. Most of the modern Dartmoors are bred on studs away from the moor. Nonetheless, with the help of Arab and Welsh Mountain Pony blood, today's Dartmoor is one of the most elegant riding ponies in the world. It jumps very well and is in great demand all over Europe.

Riding Action

The Dartmoor has a wonderfully sloped shoulder, which, with the length of neck, ensures a riding action not found in other native breeds. It is low, economical and without knee lift—"typical hack or riding action." Nonetheless, the head is all pony, small and full of quality, well set on, with very alert little ears.

FACT FILE	
COLORS	All except part-colors
REGION	Dartmoor, southwest England
USES	Riding
HEIGHT	12.2hh.

New Forest

Originating in what in the 11th century was the royal hunting ground of King William Rufus, the New Forest pony is an extraordinary amalgam of diverse breeds: Welsh, Thoroughbred, Arab, Highland, Dales, Fell, Exmoor, Dartmoor and even a Basuto pony introduced by Lord Lucas at turn of the 19th century. For all that, the modern pony, now stud-bred, is a great performer, able to gallop and jump with the best.

FACT FILE	
COLORS	Any except part-colors
REGION	New Forest, England
USES	Riding
HEIGHT	12.2–14.2hh.

Star Performer

Possibly as a result of an infusion of polo pony blood, the New Forest excels at the canter. Otherwise, the action is free, long and low. The type may vary, and the head sometimes lacks pony quality, but the breed is intelligent, quick to learn and good across country.

Welsh Mountain Pony

The Welsh Mountain Pony is the most numerous of the British Mountain and Moorland breeds. It is also the most beautiful and most perfectly proportioned of them all.

As good in harness as under saddle, it has been used extensively to improve other native pony breeds. Bred on the hills and uplands of Wales for centuries, it shows much evidence of the improving Arab blood, but that has had no effect on the remarkably robust constitution and the super-efficient feed-conversion ability that derive from living in such a harsh environment. The terrain is also responsible for the unmistakable action, the bent knee in front, and the tremendously powerful leverage given by the hocks, as well as an instinct for self-preservation and an inbred, knowing intelligence.

The Welsh Mountain is the foundation of the remaining three Welsh breeds: the Welsh Pony of Riding Type; the Welsh Pony of Cob Type; and the brilliant, awe-inspiring Welsh Cob.

The Perfect Pony

The glory of the Welsh Mountain Pony is the head, dominated as it is by the large, luminous eyes. They, along with the wide, open nostrils, the small muzzle and the dished face, reveal the strong influence over centuries of the pervasive eastern blood. The body is notable for the depth through the girth, which allows ample room for the powerful lungs and a heart that is large in comparison to the pony's size. The action originates in the powerful hind leg, with its exceptionally strong hock joint engaged well under the body.

FACT FILE	
COLORS	Any except part-colors
REGION	Wales
USES	Driving, riding
HEIGHT	Not exceeding 12hh.

Welsh Cob

BREEDS

There are two Welsh Cobs, both of which evolve from crosses with the Mountain Pony. They are, indeed, larger versions of the latter and display all the character and fire of that splendid pony.

Welsh Cobs were firmly established in Wales in the 15th century, when they were ridden to battle, worked on the farms, and both ridden and driven in harness. Until recent times these cobs were an essential element in Welsh rural life.

The Pony of Cob Type, which does not exceed 13.2hh., was and is a "farm" pony. It makes a great hunter for young people and an excellent harness pony. The Welsh Cob proper stands at 15hh. It is a good hunter and jumper and, quite simply, the best harness horse in the business.

Supreme Trotter

Ideally, the Welsh Cob is a larger version of the base provided by the Welsh Mountain Pony. Nothing can be more exciting than "Cob Day" at the Royal Welsh Show, when the Welsh Cob (Section D), the bigger cob, is run out in the main ring at a breathtaking trot, led by trainer-shod runners. No other horse can equal the trotting action of the Cob. The movement is free and forceful in the extreme, driving from the hindlegs with the foreleg being lifted and then fully extended.

FACT FILE	
COLORS	All except part-colors
REGION	Wales
USES	Riding, driving, farm
HEIGHT	Cob Type 13.2hh., Welsh Cob 15hh.

Lundy Pony

The Lundy Pony was founded in 1928 when New Forest stock was put on Lundy Island by its owner, Martin Coles Harman. Lundy is a small island that rises 400ft (122m) out of the sea off the coast of Devon, exposed to the Atlantic southwesterly gales.

Crosses to Thoroughbred stallions turned out to be disastrous. Far more successful, however, were subsequent Welsh and Connemara crosses. It is the Connemara that is responsible for the distinctive present-day Lundy, which is very hardy, tough and full of real pony character.

The Lundy Pony Preservation Society is responsible for the herd and is active in promoting the breed as an all-round children's pony.

FACT FILE	
COLORS	Mainly shades of dun and bay
REGION	Lundy Island, UK
USES	Riding
HEIGHT	Up to 13.2hh.

Talented Ancestry

It is the Connemara cross that contributes so much to the character and appearance of the Lundy Pony. There is a difference in type between the island and the mainland herds, but in essence the conformation, the legacy of the talented Connemara, is that of a top-class competition pony,

Connemara

The Connemara Pony originates from the rugged west coast of Ireland and is the country's only indigenous breed. Its history goes back to the sixth century BC, and there was always a strong Oriental influence, the result of Ireland's trading links. The modern Connemara Pony, agile and inherently sound and hardy, is the world's best performance pony and an excellent cross to produce eventers and showjumpers.

The Connemara's most colorful influence came through the stallion Cannon Ball (born in 1904). The night before the Oughterard Farmers' Race, he was fed half a barrel of oats—and won, 16 years running!

The Best Performer

The Connemara, a brilliant performance pony, has an exceptional length of rein (the measurement over the top of the neck) and riding shoulders that result in "a marked natural proclivity for jumping." The pony is in great demand all through Europe.

FACT FILE	
COLORS	Grey, dun, bay, brown
REGION	West coast of Ireland
USES	Riding
HEIGHT	13–14.2hh.

Dales

The Dales and Fell ponies of northern England are found on the east and west sides of the Pennine hills respectively. They have a common ancestor in the Friesian horse of Roman times, but thereafter the bigger Dales Pony was much influenced by the Welsh Cob Comet, a great trotting horse. Very strong and even-tempered, the Dales Pony made up the pack trains carrying lead ore from the hill mines to the coast. It was always noted as a great trotting pony.

Hardy and economical, the Dales makes a willing, clever hunter, well able to carry adults.

Strength with Action

The Dales Pony is strong enough to carry an adult and is a great harness pony, too. It carries silky feather on the lower limbs and is renowned for the excellence of its feet. The compact, powerful body results in an enormously active movement, but it is a comfortable ride.

FACT FILE	
COLORS	Predominantly black
REGION	Northeast England
USES	Riding, driving
HEIGHT	Up to 14.2hh.

Fell Pony

Like its neighbor the Dales, the lighter Fell Pony was used as a pack pony to carry lead ore and was also much used on farms, particularly for shepherding.

The Fell is noted for its speed, surefootedness and good riding shoulder—qualities inherited from its ancestors, the swift Galloway ponies that were the mounts of border raiders and were possibly part of the Thoroughbred foundation. Through the Wilson ponies (named after a famous 19th-century breeder from Cumbria, in northern England), the Fell was at the base of the modern Hackney Pony.

An illustrious ancestor was Lingcropper, who was found during the 1745 Jacobite rising "cropping ling" (eating heather) at Stainmore, Westmorland, still carrying his saddle.

FACT FILE	
COLORS	Black, brown, gray
REGION	Cumbria, northern England
USES	Riding, driving
HEIGHT	Not over 14hh.

All-rounder
The Fell is lighter than the Dales and has an even better all-round riding action, although in recent years it has made its mark as a quick, courageous pony in competitive driving teams. It carries fine hair at the heels and has hard, sound feet of blue horn. The official breed standard stipulates a bone measurement of 8in (20cm).

Highland

Ponies have probably inhabited northern Scotland from the Ice Age, since when they have been improved by Percheron strains, Spanish horses, Hackney, Arab and Clydesdale. Until fairly recently, there were two distinct types: the heavier mainland, influenced by Clydesdale blood; and the lighter Western Isles, such as the Eriskay. However, that difference is no longer recognized.

The Highland can undertake any type of work in its native environment, but is particularly noted as a very strong and sure-footed pony. Unflappable when deer-stalking, it will carry the dead stag down from the hill. It has been a particular favorite of the British royal family from the time of Queen Victoria.

FACT FILE	
COLORS	Shades of brown, gray, dun, black
REGION	Scottish Highlands and Islands
USES	Agriculture, riding, driving
HEIGHT	14.2hh.

Sure-footed
The Highland is a first-rate riding pony, able to carry a large amount of weight, and notably sure-footed over any terrain. Many Highlands, particularly the duns, have a pronounced dorsal stripe, often with zebra marks round the lower limbs—a characteristic "primitive" marking.

Camargue

Known as "the horses of the sea," these distinctive white horses live in the salty, windswept marshes of the Rhône delta in southern France. They are the traditional mounts of the Camargue cowboys, and work the powerful, black fighting bulls of that region as instinctively as a sheepdog controls a flock of sheep.

Although it is not a model of conformation, the breed is strong and enduring, and is brave and fiery under saddle. It is also hardy, and survives on the sparse food that is provided by the reed beds. The breed is renowned for its exceptional longevity, and frequently lives beyond the age of 25.

Horse of the Sea

A Camargue horse wading through the shallow waters of the Rhone Delta is a magical sight. Their white color gives these animals a certain romantic appeal.

FACT FILE	
COLORS	Gray
REGION	France
USES	Riding
HEIGHT	14.2hh.

Haflinger

The original home of this attractive pony is around the village of Hafling, in the Etschlander Mountains of the Austrian Tyrol, where it has been bred for hundreds of years. Unusually, the foundation and the breed's bloodlines are based solely on an Arab, El Bedavi, who was imported in the 19th century and to whom all Haflingers can be traced.

The principal stud is at Jenesian, and stock are raised on alpine pastures. The mountain environment contributes to the hardiness of the breed and develops heart and lungs. The Haflinger brand is an edelweiss—Austria's native flower—with a letter "H" in the center.

Mountain-bred

The pony is strongly made and muscular throughout the frame. There is length in the back, but this is not unusual in an animal that works under pack as well as in harness. Feet are excellent, and work on the mountain slopes makes the breed naturally sure-footed. The action is free, and the ponies work at a long-striding walk even on rough, steep ground.

FACT FILE	
COLORS	Palomino, chestnut; flaxen mane and tail
REGION	Southern Austrian Tyrol
USES	Agriculture, pack, riding, driving
HEIGHT	13.3hh.

Icelandic

The Icelandic Horse (it is never called a pony) came to this volcanic island in the longboats of the Norsemen between AD860 and 935. It has remained a pure breed since the *Althing*, the Icelandic parliament, prohibited horse imports in AD930.

Selective breeding used to be practiced by stallion fights, but since 1879 has been based on the ability to perform the five traditional gaits: *fetgangur* (walk), used under pack; *brokk* (trot), for crossing rough country; *skeid* (pacing gait), for short distances at speed; *stökk* (fast gallop); and the running walk, the *tølt*.

FACT FILE	
COLORS	15 recognized colors (see right)
REGION	Iceland
USES	Agriculture, pack, riding
HEIGHT	12.3–13.2hh.

Five-gaited Racehorse
Color is one of the main features of the breed, and the 15 recognized colors range from chestnut, through duns, bays and blacks to pie- and skewbalds. Very strong in relation to its size and spirited, it is, nonetheless, a plain animal with a head heavy in proportion to the body.

Shetland

Bleak and inhospitable, with poor, acid soil and no trees, the Shetland Islands are a harsh environment. Not surprisingly, the famous little ponies, which probably came from Scandinavia as much as 10,000 years ago, are the smallest British native breed. Conversely, in relation to their size, they are among the most powerful of the world's horses.

On Shetland—kept on the poorest feed—they carried heavy panniers of seaweed and peat, and were the only means of transport. Once in demand as pit-ponies, they have been exported all over the world. There is a large population in the Netherlands.

A Good Little 'Un
The breed is thickset, deep and muscular, with the tail set well in the quarters. The action is straight, with lift in knees and hocks. The coat changes from a smooth one in summer to a double growth in winter.

FACT FILE	
COLORS	Black (preferably), and most others
REGION	Shetland Islands, now universal
USES	Riding, driving, circus work
HEIGHT	Average 40in at the wither

BREEDS

Cob

The Welsh Cob and Norman Cob are documented breeds, but the Irish and English cobs are types, not recognized breeds, with no set breeding pattern, although entirely distinctive. Some of the best are Irish Draught crosses; others are bred from heavy horses.

The cob is big-bodied, very compact and stands four-square on strong, short legs. Intelligent, with a knowing character, the cob is regarded with affection. The ideal mount for older, heavier riders, being steady and safe while able to gallop and jump, he is often described as the perfect "gentleman's gentleman."

FACT FILE	
COLORS	All colors
REGION	UK, Eire
USES	All-round riding horse
HEIGHT	15–15.1hh.

Comfortable Mount

Although it is heavily built and its structure inclines to strength rather than speed, the Cob should never appear coarse. Ideally, the action is low, avoiding any excessive lift in the knee that might give a jarring ride.

Polo Pony

FACT FILE	
COLORS	All colors
REGION	Argentina, also US, UK
USES	Polo
HEIGHT	Average 15.1hh.

Like the cob, this is a horse type, not a breed. The best are Argentinian ponies (they are never called horses), bred from native Criollos crossed with the quality Thoroughbreds. Indeed, the modern, lean, wiry polo pony—with exceptional hocks—is very Thoroughbred in appearance.

Argentina has the advantage of a traditional horse culture, based on the *gauchos* (cowboys), who are among the world's greatest natural horsemen. Polo, supported by an unlimited supply of horses, has become a way of life.

Polo ponies are courageous, fast, very agile and able to twist and turn at speed. The Argentine ponies will follow the ball instinctively.

The Game of Kings

The polo pony has to be conspicuously strong in the quarters and hocks if it is to accelerate at speed from a halt, make sudden stops and tight turns at speed. The over-riding essential is a lively and courageous disposition.

Hunter

A hunter is simply a type of horse (not a breed) used for the purpose of hunting, and it will vary according to the terrain of the area hunted. Over the big, grass pastures of the English Shires a big, galloping, near-Thoroughbred horse is the best choice; whereas in more enclosed countries, which are hilly or with much land under the plough, a sensible, short-legged sort, a half-bred or even a good cob, will be more suitable.

The best hunters are bred in countries with a long hunting tradition, that is, the UK, US and, above all, Ireland, which produces the supreme Irish Hunter.

The Paragon

A good hunter has to be sound and possessed of a robust constitution if he is to hunt two days a week throughout the season. He has to be a comfortable ride, fast enough to keep up with hounds, and clever enough to jump a variety of obstacles. He also needs courage, stamina and a temperate, well-mannered outlook.

FACT FILE	
COLORS	All colors
REGION	Ireland, UK, US
USES	Hunting
HEIGHT	Variable

Riding Pony

The English Riding Pony was developed specifically for the show-ring and, after the Thoroughbred, is the most notable achievement in the annals of selective breeding. Developed over about 50 years, it is probably the most perfectly proportional equine specimen in the world, and the most elegant. Nonetheless, it remains a type, not a breed.

In three height divisions, 12.2hh., 13.2hh. and 14.2hh., the pony evolved from the skilful mix of British native ponies, Welsh and some Dartmoor, blended with Arab and small Thoroughbred.

The action is free, long, low and in perfect balance, but remains uniquely pony in character.

Perfection of Form

While the Riding Pony inherits the long, low action, perfect balance and presence of the Thoroughbred, it is ridden by children and on that account has to retain the bone, substance and good sense of its native pony ancestors and also have impeccably good manners.

FACT FILE	
COLORS	All except part-colors
REGION	England
USES	Riding
HEIGHT	12.2–14.2hh.

BREEDS

Sable Island

Sable Island lies 100 miles (160km) off the east coast of Nova Scotia and up to the 19th century was nothing more than a sandbank. The Portuguese put cattle and pigs on the island in the 16th century, and horses of Norman or Norman-Breton stock were introduced by the French in the 18th century. A hundred years later, when Nova Scotia was under British rule, English and Spanish-based stock was added. Today, there are probably between 200 and 300 horses on the island, which are said to resemble the Barb of North Africa. The horses are naturally hardy and are claimed to be fast, agile and enduring.

Versatility
Over 100 years ago, an observer wrote of the Sable Island stock: "The horses trot, jump, gallop, paddle, rack, prance, shuffle and waltz," and he remarked particularly on their jumping ability. Sable Island horses retain all that prowess.

FACT FILE	
COLORS	Chestnut, bay, brown, black, gray
REGION	Sable Island, Nova Scotia
USES	Semi-feral
HEIGHT	14–15hh.

Asiatic Wild Horse

The Asiatic Wild Horse, or "Przewalski's Horse," is accepted as one of the prehistoric ancestors of the domestic horse and is the only one surviving in its original form. It was discovered on the edge of Mongolia's Gobi Desert by the Russian Colonel Nikolai Przewalski in 1879 and was named after him.

There are captive populations in zoos and parks across the world, and it is these that have preserved the breed since it became extinct in its native habitat. A few have now been re-introduced to Mongolia, where they are called *Taki*. It is aggressive and fierce in the wild, and its "primitive" appearance is distinctive.

FACT FILE	
COLORS	Sand dun with black mane and tail
REGION	Mongolia, world zoos
USES	Not domesticated
HEIGHT	13hh.

Primitive Foundation
The Asiatic Wild Horse is the only one of the horse's primitive ancestors (Asiatic, Tarpan, Forest) that survives in its original form. It is unmistakable in appearance, with a long, heavy head, a convex profile and eyes set high on the face. Although it is a horse, it has some asinine features.

Tarpan

The Tarpan, which means wild horse, is, with the Asiatic Wild Horse, the accepted primitive ancestor of the domestic light horse. It once inhabited Eastern Europe and the Ukranian steppes. Its scientific name is *Equus caballus gmelini Antonius*. S. G. Gmelin captured wild specimens in 1768, and Helmut Antonius was responsible for the Tarpan's cataloging. The horse is described as having a coat like a deer's in texture, a large, convex head and a straight back. It was lighter and faster than Przewalski's horse, but still fiercely independent. The Tarpan became extinct in 1880 but there are herds bred from Tarpan-related stock in Poland.

Back-breeding

The Tarpan had been hunted to extinction by the late 18th century, but it exists in the "reconstituted" Polish herds at Popielno and Bialowieza, which were created by skilful back-breeding to the undisputed descendants of the Tarpan, the Hucal and Konik ponies of the Ukraine. The pony on the left is a Konik.

FACT FILE	
COLORS	Mouse dun
REGION	Formerly Ukranian steppes
USES	Not domesticated
HEIGHT	13hh.

Batak

The Batak tribes of Sumatra, part of Indonesia, are renowned horse-people. Traditionally, they traded horses, ate horse flesh (still considered a delicacy), raced horses for sport, and even sacrificed horses to placate their gods. Each clan of one tribe, the Toba, kept three sacred horses, allowed to wander at will. Today, the Batak is a working pony, widely used for riding. It is a well-proportioned creature, with a definite Arabian character. It has a fine chiselled head, with a distinctively straight profile. Although good-natured, it is spirited, agile and extremely fast.

FACT FILE	
COLORS	All
REGION	Indonesia
USES	Riding
HEIGHT	Up to 13hh.

A Working Pony
The Batak is native to Central Sumatra. This Batak tribesman is wearing the traditional tribal dress in its striking gold and red cloth. He rides bareback, which is the tradition among Batak people.

Chincoteague

Two herds of "wild" ponies, descendants of stock abandoned in the 17th century, inhabit the islands of Chincoteague and Assateague off the coast of Virginia. The ponies are called Chincoteague but live on Assateague, the larger of the two islands, some under the (surprising) management of the Chincoteague Fire Department. Each year in July, on Pony Penning Day, the ponies swim across the narrow channel to Chincoteague, where young stock are sold. The marshland habitat provides only poor-quality feed, but the ponies are tough and hardy, if undistinguished other than by the evidence of Pinto blood. They are said to make good riding ponies if properly handled.

America's Native Pony
The Chincoteague ponies have the distinction of being America's sole indigenous pony group. Many in fact lack "pony quality," and there is a preponderance of heavy, "horsey" heads—possibly the legacy of the Pinto outcross. On the whole, there are still signs of degeneration in the conformational failings: light bone, poorly developed joints, weak hind legs and narrow chests.

FACT FILE	
COLORS	Various, including part-colored
REGION	Chincoteague and Assateague, USA
USES	Riding
HEIGHT	12hh.

Timor

Ponies are numerous on Timor, Indonesia, where the extensive savannah provides wiry but nutritious feed. At one time the ratio was estimated at one pony to every six people.

The ponies were improved in the 16th and 17th centuries by Arabs imported first by the Portuguese and then by the Dutch colonists. Though small, the ponies are agile, fast, and well able to carry grown men and heavy loads. They are used by the Timor "cowboys," who employ lassos, in the same way as their Western counterparts, to work their herds of *anoa*, the world's smallest buffalo.

Some Timor ponies are sent to Australia, and are said to be good children's ponies.

A Sturdy Build

Despite good grazing, the Timor ponies are small. A possible Mongolian influence may account for the common head, but there are compensations. The back may be straight, but the tail is set high in the quarters and, although the mane and tail are full, the coat is fine.

FACT FILE	
COLORS	Mostly bay
REGION	Timor, Indonesia
USES	Riding, pack
HEIGHT	12hh.

Sumba

The Sumba ponies—found all over Indonesia—are small, and the head is often large and coarse, a legacy of Mongolian ancestry. But, like the Timor, they are strong out of proportion to their size and very agile. They excel as mounts for the popular sport of lance-throwing, in which two sides ride against each other with blunted lances until all the riders of one side have been struck by their opponents' lances.

Selected Sumba ponies are also trained in the traditional dance routines, when, decked with tinkling bells, they dance to the rhythmic beat of the drums. These dancing ponies are highly prized and valuable.

The Dancing Pony

Once more the head is frequently common and heavy, but the ponies have great strength in the back. In many there is a marked resemblance to the Mongolian Pony and even to the Asiatic Wild Horse. This is noticeable particularly in the dun colouring and pronounced dorsal stripe.

FACT FILE	
COLORS	Dun with dorsal eel-stripe
REGION	Sumba and Sumatra, Indonesia
USES	Riding, pack
HEIGHT	12.2hh.

Mustang

The American Mustang (from the Spanish *mestana*, a herd or group of horses) is the descendant of the Spanish Horses that formed feral herds after the Spanish conquests of America in the 16th century. It is America's wild horse and is now, after a period when it was slaughtered indiscriminately for meat, protected by law as an endangered species. There are, however, a variety of organizations devoted to preserving, improving and promoting the Mustang stock. Particular emphasis is given to the encouragement of the Spanish Barb strains that are at the root of the Indian Cayuse and Chickasaw ponies. The Spanish Barb Breeders' Association (formed in 1972) promotes selective breeding and has set up a breed standard.

FACT FILE	
COLORS	Roan, dun, cream, gray, and others
REGION	Western USA
USES	Riding
HEIGHT	13.2–15hh.

Tough Customer

The modern Mustang displays many of the features of its Spanish ancestors, particularly in the range of coat colors and in its constitutional hardiness. There is also evidence of the Spanish Horse in the head, which retains something of the convex profile, and in the typically hard and strong feet.

LEARN TO RIDE

The Right Way

This young rider has had the benefit of an experienced teacher.
She is safe and secure and rides the pony with great confidence.

1 Mounting and Dismounting

Before you can begin learning to ride you have to get into the saddle, safely and without upsetting the pony. First, you must check that the saddle and bridle are fitted properly, with nothing twisted or pulled up too tight (*see* pp.232–33). When your pony stands quietly to be mounted and dismounted, practice getting on and off from both sides—a useful skill for gymkhana games.

MOUNTING

Use right hand to turn stirrup

Turning the Stirrup
Turn the stirrup clockwise towards you so the leather lies correctly against the horse once it is mounted.

SITTING POSITION

Make head, shoulder, hip, and heel form a vertical line

Keep shoulders open and chest out

1 Stand at the near-side shoulder facing the tail, the reins held in the left hand at the wither. The inside rein should be a little shorter so that if the pony moves it will go around you and not away from you. Shift the left hand to the pommel and place your left foot in the stirrup.

Use your left arm to help balance body

Hold off-side of saddle just above and behind flap. Avoid pulling on cantle

Swing right leg well clear of pony's rump

Place ball of foot on tread of stirrup with toe raised a little

2 Hop on the right foot and spring upwards. Swing your leg over; move your right hand forward for support; and lower your seat gently into the saddle.

3 Take up the reins. Let your thighs lie flat on the saddle with the knees held as far down as they will go. Don't grip with the knees, which causes the seat to rise out of the saddle. Instead, wrap your legs around the pony as if you were sitting on a barrel.

Length of Leather

Difficulties are created if the leather is too long or too short. As a guide, take the foot out of the stirrup and let it hang down. The tread of the stirrup should then be in line with your ankle bones. Check that the length of your leathers is equal on both sides. You can test this by putting two fingers of the right hand under the pommel and standing in your stirrups, when you will be better able to feel any inequality.

DISMOUNTING

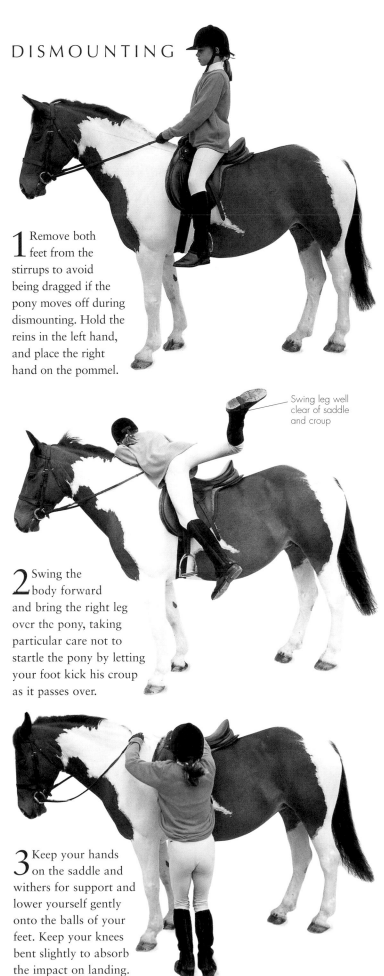

1 Remove both feet from the stirrups to avoid being dragged if the pony moves off during dismounting. Hold the reins in the left hand, and place the right hand on the pommel.

Swing leg well clear of saddle and croup

2 Swing the body forward and bring the right leg over the pony, taking particular care not to startle the pony by letting your foot kick his croup as it passes over.

Hold arms lightly to sides, elbows bent, forearms relaxed

Keep a straight line from elbow to bit

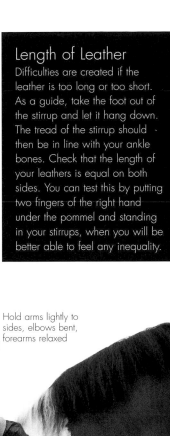

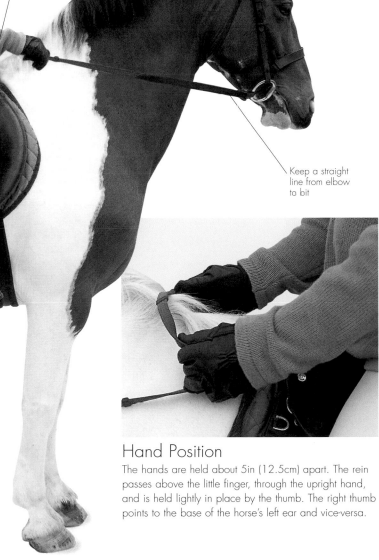

Hand Position

The hands are held about 5in (12.5cm) apart. The rein passes above the little finger, through the upright hand, and is held lightly in place by the thumb. The right thumb points to the base of the horse's left ear and vice-versa.

3 Keep your hands on the saddle and withers for support and lower yourself gently onto the balls of your feet. Keep your knees bent slightly to absorb the impact on landing.

2 Aids and Transitions

To sit centrally and correctly, without conscious effort, is very important but it won't make the pony go. To do that we have to use the aids, a set of physical signals through which we communicate with the pony. They are the language of riding that both we and the pony must learn. The more fluent we are, the better the result—for both pony and rider.

There are two kinds of aids: natural and artificial. The natural aids are your voice, legs, hands, seat, and body weight. The artificial aids are the whip and spurs. Artificial aids are used to support or strengthen the natural aids; they should never be used in place of the natural aids and certainly never to punish the pony. Spurs should not be worn until the rider is sufficiently experienced to be able to ride with

a still, steady leg—and that takes time. The voice can be used to calm a frightened pony, to encourage the lazy and to correct the naughty one. Otherwise speak with your legs and hands.

The legs are the most important of the aids since they control the quarters and create movement, pushing the pony forward to the rider's hands. The legs always act before the hands so that the pony is

UPWARD TRANSITION: HALT TO WALK

Shorten rein slightly, keeping the straight line from elbow to bit

Keep upright

Squeeze on rear of girth in a brushing movement from back to front

Push tummy forward from small of back in time with stride

Follow movement of mouth with fingers

1 First, obtain the pony's full attention by giving a short squeeze with both legs and momentarily closing the fingers on a slightly shortened rein (*see box*).

2 Almost immediately, give a firm, short squeeze with the legs (don't kick); at the same time open the fingers slightly to allow the pony to obey the legs and walk on.

3 To increase the speed of the walk, use the legs alternately in time with the pace. Ideally, apply your left leg as the pony's left hind leg is brought forward, and vice-versa.

ridden from the back to the front. The hands receive the impulsion created by the legs, acting in conjunction with the legs as a sort of combined steering wheel and brake.

The seat and body weight are powerful aids to be used carefully. The seat-bones, pushing up towards the pony's ears from the small of the back, assist the action of the legs to send the pony forwards. Also, weighting one or other seat-bone (by pressing downwards on the appropriate stirrup iron) helps when you are making turns—when the inside bone is the heavier of the two. If the weight is placed a little to the rear—by placing the shoulders slightly behind the hips—the pony slows down, and can be made to halt when the aid is used with the legs and hands.

Changes in pace are called transitions: upward transitions are from one pace to a faster one, while downward transitions are to a slower pace or to halt. Always prepare the pony first (step 1, below).

Opening and Closing Hands

It is never necessary to pull. The hands may move forwards, upwards, downwards, and to the side, but never backwards. The hand *closes*, to restrain the horse, by squeezing the rein as though it were a rubber ball. It *opens*, to release and allow the forward movement, when the fingers relax and stop the squeezing effect. It is absolutely essential that when the legs urge the pony forward the fingers open almost simultaneously to allow him to respond to the leg signal. Think of the hand as a brake, which has to be released when you press the accelerator, the legs.

OPEN HAND

CLOSED HAND

DOWNWARD TRANSITION: WALK TO HALT

Hold hands fractionally higher than usual

Hold legs marginally further back and rest them on pony's sides

Move shoulders back behind line of hips

1 Prepare the pony with a quick squeeze of both legs while closing the fingers for a fraction of a second. When halting, do not let the fingers stay closed and do not pull!

2 Now, apply the legs again and then release them while the hands act, closing and releasing (acting and yielding) until the pony stops.

3 The halt is made more effective by drawing the trunk upwards and inclining the shoulders a little, back behind the line with the hips.

2
CONT.

Aids and Transitions

The aids for trot are virtually the same as they are from halt to walk. Once again, prepare the pony with legs and hands, but, this time, give the leg aid not on the girth but about a hand's breadth behind it. The reason for this slightly different leg position is so that the pony will not confuse the trot signal with that for walk—vital if we ask him to go into a trot directly from halt. As soon as we give the leg aid we must of course open the fingers to allow the horse to pass smoothly into the faster pace without restriction from the hands. Your hands must then remain quite still because unlike in the walk, at trot—a pace in which the pony moves his legs in diagonal pairs (*see* pp.98–99)—the pony's head moves only minimally.

There are two ways of riding the trot: either we sit in the saddle (the sitting trot), or we rise so that the seat is out of the saddle for one beat of the pace (the rising trot). The rising trot is the one that is most often used and the one that is least tiring for the pony.

If you are not very proficient at rising to the trot, try the trot position at walk until you get the hang of it. The beginner's mistake is to push too far up from the knees, rising (usually about 1ft/30cm) out of the saddle and then returning to the saddle with a hefty plonk. Instead, incline the shoulders a little forward, keep the ankle flexible and in line with the hip, then raise the seat-bones 1–2in (2.5–5cm) on the pivot of the knee, keeping the fork in contact with the saddle.

WALK TO TROT

Keep head erect

Shorten rein

Give leg aid
behind girth

1 Prepare the pony with a quick squeeze of both legs while closing the fingers for a fraction of a second. Shorten the rein a little, squeeze strongly with both legs and open the fingers to let the pony go forwards into the new two-beat pace.

2 Establish the speed by giving a series of little squeezes with the fingers if it is too fast, or with the legs if it is too slow. Once you have the speed you want, keep the hands still to conform with the still carriage of the head.

Sitting Trot

Sitting trot is a little more difficult than the rising trot but it has an advantage when schooling of allowing us to make better use of the leg aids. It is important that the ankle holds its position in line with the hip. If it is allowed to move forward so that the toe is in advance of the knee, the whole leg stiffens and the rider just bumps up and down. The knee, lying flat on the saddle, should slide down as far as possible without attempting to grip. Instead, wrap the whole inside leg lightly around the pony's barrel so that you can, indeed, "feel the pony breathe through your boot." Keep the trunk upright with the shoulders open. The small of the back, which connects the top and bottom halves of the body, remains soft and supple. It is the small of the back that absorbs the movement, undulating in time with the stride. It helps to push the tummy out a bit, so that it leads the body. The hips must be carried forward, pushing the fork upwards. If they are allowed to slip back, your bottom will stick out inelegantly and the whole body will stiffen.

Keep seat lightly in contact with saddle throughout

Hips swing upwards and forwards with upward beat

Maintain light, still contact with horse's mouth

Incline back slightly forward, shoulders erect

3 Rise to the trot by inclining the shoulders a little forward, using the knee as the pivot to raise the seat-bones an inch or two (2.5–5cm) from the saddle. Your shoulders and arms should remain still. Don't allow your shoulders to tip forwards.

4 There are three points of contact with the saddle: the two seat-bones and the fork. The fork remains in contact. It is only the seat-bones that need to be raised, and then by only a little. To return to the walk apply the restraining aids as before.

2 CONT.

Aids and Transitions

Once you have thoroughly mastered the trot, the next pace to learn is the canter—a pace of three beats that starts with a hind leg (*see* pp.98–99). Learning to sit at canter is probably easier than learning to rise to the trot, and it is much more enjoyable. The seat remains deep in the saddle, the back is straight and the head is held high. The motion is like that of a rocking horse, and you stay with it by keeping the lower back supple and relaxed.

When asking for canter, the rider gives aids to make the pony "lead" with either his near or off foreleg. To canter on a circle to the right (as shown below) the right foreleg must lead, and vice-versa. The easiest way to strike off on the correct leg is to apply the aids when the horse is entering a circle. This is easy if you are going to canter in an enclosed school, but even in the open the pony needs to be bent in the direction appropriate to whichever leg you want to lead.

It is particularly important that at the moment of striking off you do not look down or, as often happens, allow your body to lean over the leading leg. It is not only ugly but it is also a definite hindrance to the pony because you are overweighting his shoulder just at the moment when it needs the utmost freedom. Similarly, you must allow the pony sufficient rein as he goes into the first stride. If you are too late in opening your fingers they will prevent the pony reaching forward and again restrict his freedom of movement at a crucial point.

TROT TO CANTER

Seat remains deep in saddle

Legs active on girth

Keep back supple

"Open" the inside rein by moving the hand outwards slightly

1 The canter is best approached by riding a corner. Ride energetically at sitting trot for a few strides, checking the pony by using the preparatory aids before reaching the corner. Go into the corner at a strong sitting trot.

2 Stretch the inside leg down to weight the inside seat-bone, place the outside leg flat against the pony behind the girth to control the quarters, and act firmly with the inside leg on the girth. Raise and open the inside hand slightly.

Center of Balance

The center of balance in the horse is at the point of intersection of two imaginary lines, one drawn vertically from just behind the withers, the other drawn horizontally from the point of the shoulder to the rear. This is its position at halt with head and neck held naturally. When moving at speed with head and neck extended, or when jumping, it shifts forwards. In collection, as in *piaffe* (*see* pp.64–65), when the weight is carried more over the hind legs, it moves a little to the rear. When the horse moves sideways it shifts to the side in the direction of the movement.

The head and neck, like a pendulum with a weight on the end, act as the balancing agent for the body. If raised they throw the weight and the center of balance backwards; if stretched forward the opposite occurs. Over broken ground the pony makes constant adjustments to his balance by altering the attitude of head and neck. For the rider to be in balance with the movement her weight has to remain at all times as nearly as possible over the horse's center of balance.

Keep head upright

Push upward from seat

Keep shoulders in line with movement

Body upright

Allow hands to follow movement of head

3 By keeping your head and shoulders in line with the movement, the outside rein will move forward a little to allow the pony to bend to the inside. Apply your inside (in this case right) leg firmly on the girth; place your outside leg behind the girth.

4 Sit up straight: do not lean forward because this puts more weight on the pony's forehand and hinders his movement. The trunk should remain upright, with the small of the back pushing forward in time with the pace.

3 Riding School Figures

Making turns and circles calls for a combination of leg, hand and weight aids. The aim of riding school figures is to make the aids more refined and unobtrusive and to teach the rider to control the pony's posture and movement more effectively.

To be in balance with the pony, the rider's hips and shoulders need to be held in line with the pony's hips.

If, for example, you are turning left, the movement begins with the rider's head turning in that direction. The right shoulder will then be forward of the left and

so will the right hip, both then being in line with the pony's hips. Also, the right hand will be forward of the left and, if the left is then opened, the pony will be able to make the turn without there being any need to pull, which would only put the pony off balance.

RIDING A 5-METER LOOP

Sit centrally with trunk stretched upwards

Allow shoulder to move forward

Allow elbow and hand to move forward

1 Prepare the pony to make the shallow turn by stretching the trunk upwards, applying the legs, briefly, and closing the fingers so as to obtain his attention and bring him together before applying the turning aids. Always warn the pony by using the preparatory aids.

2 Look in the direction you want to go. In turning left, this will cause the right shoulder and hand and the right seat-bone to move forward. Move the left hand outwards to indicate the direction. Act on the girth with the left leg in squeezes; place the right leg on the pony behind the girth to control any swing of the quarters.

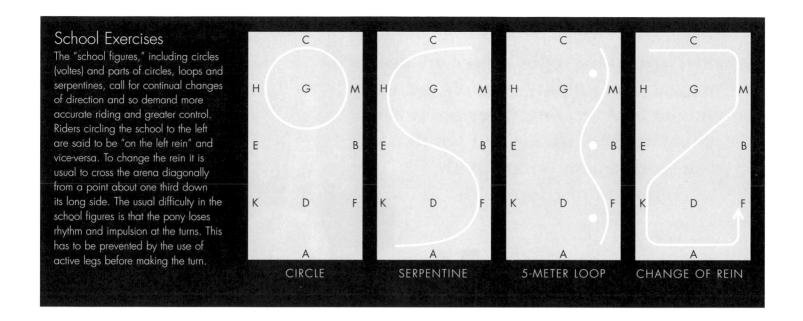

School Exercises

The "school figures," including circles (voltes) and parts of circles, loops and serpentines, call for continual changes of direction and so demand more accurate riding and greater control. Riders circling the school to the left are said to be "on the left rein" and vice-versa. To change the rein it is usual to cross the arena diagonally from a point about one third down its long side. The usual difficulty in the school figures is that the pony loses rhythm and impulsion at the turns. This has to be prevented by the use of active legs before making the turn.

CIRCLE · SERPENTINE · 5-METER LOOP · CHANGE OF REIN

Right hand allows pony to bend

Keep shoulders in line with hips

3 Continue to look in the direction of the movement. Note that the right shoulder and hand are still forward to allow the pony to bend left. Continue to open the left hand outwards, while your left leg acts in squeezes on the girth and your right leg is held in support. We call this Position Left.

4 The pony completes the 5-meter loop with you in Position Left. You must now be thinking about preparing the pony by stretching the trunk upwards, applying the legs and closing the fingers, before reversing your aids and adopting Position Right as you return to the outside track on the arena fence.

4 School Exercises

The exercises ridden in the school are designed to improve the rider's ability to apply the aids effectively and without exaggeration. They are valuable in teaching her how to ride and position the pony more accurately and with the very minimum of effort.

Crossing Stirrups
Lift the stirrups and cross the leathers in front of the pommel.

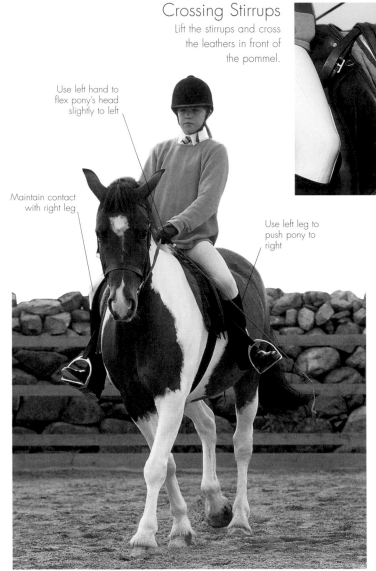

Use left hand to flex pony's head slightly to left

Maintain contact with right leg

Use left leg to push pony to right

STRETCHING THE LEGS

Riding without stirrups at trot is an exercise used to encourage the downward stretch of the leg muscles and to improve the stability of the seat. Most beginners have their stirrups too short and find it difficult to ride with the longer leather that is the most effective for schooling. This exercise is never practiced for anything but short periods because it would cause discomfort and aching in muscles unaccustomed to the work.

LEG YIELD

Leg yielding is a particularly good control exercise that is ridden first at walk, then at trot. The pony, using the inside track—a track made some 6ft (2m) inside the arena fence—is asked to move sideways to the outside track on the rails. Since the outside track is familiar to him he is always more than willing to return to it.

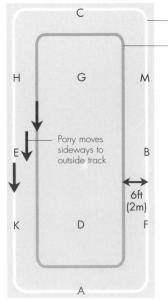

C

Outside track

Inside track

H   G   M

E   B

Pony moves sideways to outside track

6ft (2m)

K   D   F

A

Leg Yield

To obtain a good leg yield we ride the inside track at an active walk on the long side of the arena. If we want to move to the right we raise the hands a little, maintaining a light contact with the mouth while the left hand, pointing to the right hip, bends the pony's head very slightly to the left. It is supported by the right hand opening to make it clear in which direction we want the pony to move. The left leg is applied against the pony to shift him to the right while the right rests in contact as a support.

CANTER EXERCISES

The canter is a pace of three-time, the first beat being made with one or other of the hind legs. The canter on the left circle (the left rein) begins with the right hind leg, followed by the right diagonal (i.e., right fore and left hind) then, after a moment of suspension, the third beat is made with the left fore, the leading leg. To canter on a right-handed circle the sequence is reversed. You are cantering on "the wrong leg" if the pony circles left but is leading with the right fore; he is then in danger of losing his balance altogether. It is all made easier if the pony is asked to canter when approaching a corner of the school, i.e., on an element of a circle.

Ride in active sitting trot

Deepen seat in saddle

Keep body relatively upright

1 Ride actively into the corner at sitting trot, after first preparing the pony, and begin to think about bending the pony to the left, putting him and yourself into Position Left to make the strike-off easier.

2 Sit down deep in the saddle. Stretch the inside left leg by pressing down. Open the left hand a little outwards and support that movement gently with the right rein. You are now ready to canter.

3 Look left. DO NOT tip forward. Keeping the left rein outwards, raise the hand very slightly upward. Now lay the right leg flat just behind the girth and act with the driving left, inside leg.

Keep back straight, supple and upright

Open and close fingers intermittently

Shortening Stride
To shorten the stride sit deep and upright, and act with both legs to push the pony into stronger contact with the hands, which can then be closed and opened intermittently.

Use hands to control impulsion

Sit deep in saddle

Lengthening Stride
To lengthen the stride we use the driving aids. The legs act in firm squeezes, the rider sitting deep, while the hands and fingers open and close to control and limit the impulsion.

5 Learning on the Lunge

Lungeing is the gymnastic exercise where the pony circles the trainer on a web lunge line from the trainer's hand to the nosepiece of the pony's special lunge cavesson. It plays an important part in the early education of the young pony, and it helps to improve the suppleness, balance and carriage.

Advanced work on the lunge, which is limited to the skilled trainer, can take the pony's schooling still further, building on the balanced carriage and acting significantly to improve the jumping style.

However, lunge lessons with an experienced instructor are just as valuable (indeed, essential) to the serious rider wishing to perfect her seat as they are to the young pony.

Significantly, the classical schools of Vienna and Saumur, the homes of the Spanish Riding School and France's black-uniformed *Cadre Noir*, place great emphasis on lunge exercises.

LUNGE EXERCISES

1 Arms outstretched. A difficult position to maintain for more than two circles. It opens the chest and when the trunk is rotated supples the upper body. The seat, however, must remain deep, still, and in contact with the saddle flap. It must not be allowed to rise out of the saddle. A common fault, not seen here, is for the head to sink into stiffening shoulders.

2 The rider and the instructor are concentrating on the seat at walk and are making a good job of it. The vertical line from the rider's head to her heel is excellent. The leg is stretched down the saddle flap and the hand and arm position are relaxed and correct. The next stage will be to ride at sitting trot while keeping the same good seat.

The object of lessons on the lunge is to establish an "independent" seat. That can be defined as one that is not reliant on the reins and in which the body is carried in complete physical freedom and always "in balance" with the movement. When we reach that point we will really be able to influence the horse and communicate with him through our body signals and to listen to what he is saying to us.

Ideally, we need to ride on the lunge every day for 12 months and even then we may not have fulfilled the objective of the independent seat. Clearly, that is not possible, but regular lunge lessons will certainly improve our riding to a remarkable degree.

The general rule is to work a rider who is stiff in the body in active exercises, while those who are slack will do better to concentrate on riding in still positions. In practice it becomes a mix of the two, but in both the instructor has to insist on the exercise being carried out correctly, otherwise it is useless.

At the beginning the rider retains both stirrups and reins and the instructor concentrates on her sitting correctly. Then she dispenses with the rein, holding the saddle front with the fingers of the outside hand while working at walk, trot and even canter. Active exercises are first done with stirrups and then without and to both left and right. The final objective is to have the rider sitting at all three paces, deep and in balance, without stirrups and reins, the hands being held in the riding position. It is more difficult than it sounds, but when you can do it you have really made progress.

3 Swinging the arms backwards and forwards alternately. A difficult exercise, particularly when we start practicing it at trot. The swing forward can cause the seat to lose its 3-point contact and the rider can be tipped off the seat-bones onto the fork. The body has to maintain its upright position. This is, nonetheless, a commendable effort in which the pony also plays a part.

Leg Exercises

Leg suppling, relaxing, and stretching exercises are carried out at the halt, the instructor holding the pony.

The simple exercises being practiced in the pictures below aim to eliminate stiffness in the limbs and joints. They lead to relaxed, supple legs and, importantly, hips too. There are all sorts of variations culminating, perhaps, in the "round the world" movement, when the rider swings around to face the tail and then continues the circle to face the front. The more gymnastic the rider, the better she will be.

6 Jumping

Jumping is fun and can be exciting and very satisfying. Learning to sit over a fence is just as much a part of learning to ride as being able to sit securely and easily at trot and canter, and it is certainly no more difficult or hazardous.

A jump has to be approached energetically and in a regular rhythm. The approach is best made off a preliminary circle and thereafter on a straight line. The rider, in rising trot, needs to incline the shoulders slightly forward, keeping the head up and the back straight. The legs lie close to the pony and squeeze in time with the movement, the hand always following the mouth. The first fence should be low and is usually made up of crossed poles to give every encouragement to horse and rider. To help both to make the right take-off a pole can be laid in front of the fence to enable them to judge the actual moment to jump.

The leathers can be shortened a hole or two so that the weight is on the knee and thigh, while the seat remains lightly in the saddle. The rider's aim is to keep her position and balance in harmony with the pony.

Keep back straight but not stiff

Shorten reins a little and keep light contact

Hold head high, and look forwards

Incline back forwards from the hip

1 Approach the jump in a rising trot and incline your shoulders slightly forwards, keeping your back straight. Keeping your legs close to the pony, squeeze firmly in time with the movement.

2 At take-off, close the angle between body and thigh with a smooth inclination of the shoulders. Move your hands forward to follow the stretch of the pony's neck. The seat will then rise slightly from the saddle.

Crossing Grids

Jumping lessons begin with the rider crossing a grid of poles, carefully spaced at between 4 and 6ft (1.2 and 1.8m) according to the size of the pony. This exercise encourages the rider to keep a good balance and an even length of stride. The poles are crossed at walk and then at trot.

Lightly return weight to saddle

Supple knee and ankle joints absorb shock on landing

As jump is completed, straighten back

Ensure a straight line from elbow to horse's mouth

3 As the pony lands, his head and neck will come up. Keep your head up so that you do not collapse over the pony's neck, and begin to straighten your body to reduce the weight over the pony's forehand.

4 Straighten your shoulders to return the seat to the saddle as the jump is completed. Then incline the shoulders forwards again and, supported by the action of your legs, ride away from the fence.

7 Single-stride Combination

At this stage, the emphasis is shifting to jumping exercises that prepare you to ride a simple jumping track and to cope with the requirements of a cross-country course. Nonetheless, there will be continual returns to the flat work.

Jumping exercises increase the pony's agility and confidence and encourage him to use his initiative in negotiating obstacles calling for a different approach. For the rider the exercises place a premium on accuracy, concentration and determination. The jumping aids, especially those of the leg, will necessarily be stronger than those given on the flat.

However, while the legs need to be firm and decisive, they should never be allowed to become rough.

When the pony is jump-perfect over a small fence, the exercise can be made more demanding by adding another fence at the same height built 18ft (5.4m) from the first. This makes up a single stride combination, allowing the pony to take one

Incline trunk forward on take-off

Let shoulders lead over fence

Keep shoulders open, back flat

Seat just touches saddle

1 Making a controlled approach off a circle, the rider applies the legs in time with the stride, increasing the intensity (without kicking) up to the final take-off stride. Using the knee as a pivot, the body inclines forward, the hands remaining in light contact.

2 As the pony lands, the rider applies her legs, with the trunk still inclined forward but the seat just touching the saddle. The hands move to follow the mouth and allow extension of the neck. The weight is carried over knee and supple ankle joint.

non-jumping canter stride between landing over the first fence and the take-off point for the second fence.

The average canter stride for a horse is between 11 and 12ft (3.3 and 3.6m) and could be shorter for a pony, a fact the instructor takes into account when building the combination fence.

Throughout the jump, it is very important to think about good style, your position over the fence, and the way you apply the leg and hand aids.

Jumping Higher

If rider and pony are able to cope with small fences, easy combinations, bounces and grids, height presents no problem. Jumping a higher fence than you are accustomed to calls only for an extra effort in addition to established techniques. One or two higher fences in a schooling session is sufficient.

NEVER OVER-JUMP the pony— never attempt to make him jump higher than his ability allows, and do not keep him jumping for too long a time.

Keep back flat in line with horse's spine

Keep good contact, allowing pony to arch over fence

Keep head up and look forward

Allow seat to return lightly to saddle

3 The second decisive squeeze of the legs asks for, and obtains, take-off. This position is very good. The rider is focused and in excellent balance. This is a better position than in 1 where she is a little tense and stiff, particularly in the hips.

4 The rider's seat returns to the saddle and the trunk straightens while the legs act firmly to ride *away* from the fence. The rein contact is light and places no restriction on the movement of the pony's head.

8 Grids and Bounces

The introduction to jumping is the single pole laid on the ground.
From that we progress to the grid of up to five carefully spaced
poles (*see* pp.180–81), which not only lead to the first proper
jump but also to the more exciting grid of small fences.

The poles are crossed at walk and trot, energetically
but without the pony becoming excited. It is an
excellent suppling and strengthening exercise for the
pony, while for the rider it improves balance, accuracy
and technique, and is a real help in teaching you to
apply the leg effectively and in rhythm with the stride.

The grid is ridden in rising trot, with the trunk
inclined forward and the head held erect, looking
ahead. The back is flat but not stiff, while the hands

follow the mouth with a very light contact. The
usual faults are for the rider to lean too far forward,
unbalancing the pony by over-weighting the forehand.
The reins then hang loose, all contact with the mouth
is lost, and the leg cannot be used effectively.

The grid of small fences is made up of carefully spaced,
crossed poles. The grid involves a series of "bounce"
jumps, the pony taking off immediately on landing
without there being room for a non-jumping stride.

Hold head erect
and look forward

Excellent, alert
head position

Keep head erect,
while holding
back flat

Ensure contact allows
for rounding of neck

1 The approach is made off a circle in an active trot. The rider
is focused and her position alert but without tension. The
pony's attitude and obvious activity is very good indeed, and so
is the head carriage, which reflects the rider's light, controlling
contact with the mouth.

2 The rider's legs have been applied in rhythm with the stride
and the final, imperative action results in a confident take-
off. Both pony and rider are concentrating on the next jump
but there is no tension in the attitude of either member of
the partnership.

I Trust You

This little exercise is splendid for the rider's balance and confidence over fences and in every other respect; and the pony appreciates it as an expression of the rider's trust in her. Trust in each other is at the very root of successful riding, and it is essential if we are to realize the full potential of our relationship with ponies.

The next step from the single fence is to "fly" through the grid, aiming in the end to do so without stirrups. Indeed, under careful supervision, riders can jump the grid without reins and stirrups and with their eyes shut! It's a wonderful way to teach us the "feel" of riding.

Let hips take seat and trunk forward on pivot of knee

Do not allow hands to restrict pony's neck movement

Ride forward from fence

3 The pony has taken off immediately on landing over the first fence in response to the firm, driving leg aid. The rider acts with the leg again and the pair "bounce" over the third fence. The position of the rider and the attitude of the pony are excellent.

4 Landing after a fluent jump. The rider is in the process of returning to the saddle and will apply the leg aid to "ride away" from the fence. Both partners have obviously enjoyed their experience of the "bounce" grid and are well prepared to jump a course of fences.

9 Jumping a Course

The previous jumping lessons, as well as much of the work on the flat, culminate in a simple practice course, comprising, perhaps, eight fences of different types that are positioned to include changes of direction.

To prepare ourselves and the pony we need first to practice making the directional changes smoothly. A good exercise for this purpose is to ride the Figure 8, bringing the pony back to trot and then asking for canter on the required leg to cross the diagonal and jump the small fences. The Figure 8 at this stage needs to be large so as to avoid making tight turns.

The exercise is not difficult but it does demand accurate riding with plenty of impulsion. In time the complete Figure 8 will be ridden at canter, and if the schooling has been correct you will find that the pony will almost change legs of his own accord.

Another basic jumping exercise is learning how to jump a fence at an angle (*see* box). This is a necessary skill when courses become tighter and more complex.

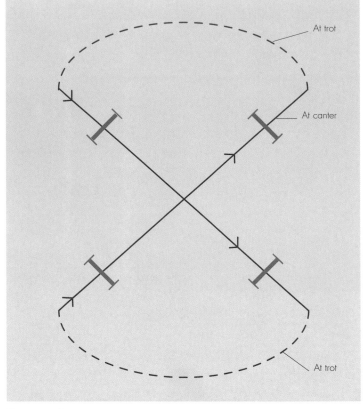

Figure 8
This is a useful exercise but you will need to make full use of the arena to make smooth, accurate approaches. If you cut the corners, allowing the pony to fall inwards, even the smallest fence will become a problem.

Upright
The upright is the most difficult fence because if the take-off is too close the fence will be hit on the ascent, and if it is too far off (when the horse is said to "stand-off") there is a danger of it being hit by the hindlegs. In general terms, the ideal take-off zone is between a distance equal to the height of the fence and up to one and one-third times its height. For the novice pony and rider the fence can be made easier by placing a ground pole in front of it at the appropriate distance and a further pole on the landing side to prevent the descent becoming too steep.

Parallel
Parallel fences have two elements, which in a true parallel are of the same height. This arrangement increases the degree of difficulty and the fence can be made easier if the first element is lowered. The take-off zone needs to be closer to the fence than with an upright since you should concentrate on jumping the second element rather than the first. The landing is further from the fence and the get-away stride longer.

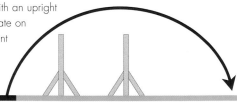

Staircase
The staircase construction is much easier and more encouraging than the upright. It is a fence built with two or three poles set at ascending heights. The landing is well out from the fence and the angle of descent is less steep, allowing for a longer first stride after the landing. The most common type of staircase fence is a triple bar, as illustrated, but it can be made of poles over brush fences.

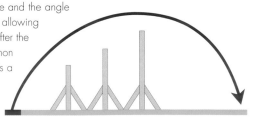

Pyramid
A pyramid arrangement involves three elements, the central one being the highest. It is less commonly seen than other "spread" fences (staircases and parallels), and it is not suitable for novices because of the final element, which cannot be seen until the pony is airborne. In any event it would be unfair to build too big a fence. The landing is far out and the get-away stride is longer.

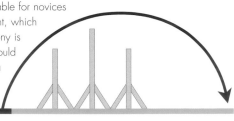

Initially, however, we need to make a straight approach to the fence, concentrating on jumping it exactly at its center.

All fences, whatever the individual difference in appearance made by their presentation, belong to one of four types as illustrated (below left). Each presents its own problem and this has to be taken into account when building and jumping a course of fences.

In jumping courses, fences are said to be "related" when set between 39 and 79ft (11.9 and 24m) apart. Below 38ft (11.7m) they become "combinations", i.e. with one or two non-jumping strides between the two fences. In previous lessons pony and rider have already learned how to cope with simple combinations. Distances between the various fence types vary, however, since they must take into account the angle of descent and the length of get-away stride.

Before jumping the course it is essential that you walk it in company with the instructor, who can point out the problems and the track you should ride. You should also decide on the point of take-off for individual fences, fixing it in your mind, and pay particular attention to the approach for combinations and of the distances involved between elements.

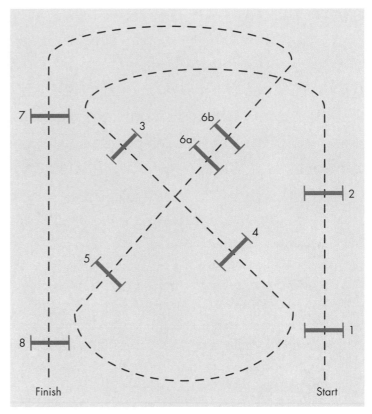

Simple Jumping Course

This straightforward course involves three changes of direction, calling for the rider to make use of all the available space. It also includes a combination, 6a and 6b, which will cause no trouble if jumped from a straight approach.

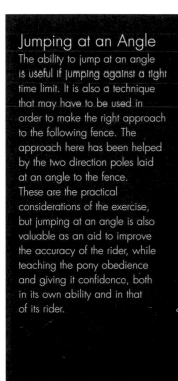

Jumping at an Angle

The ability to jump at an angle is useful if jumping against a tight time limit. It is also a technique that may have to be used in order to make the right approach to the following fence. The approach here has been helped by the two direction poles laid at an angle to the fence. These are the practical considerations of the exercise, but jumping at an angle is also valuable as an aid to improve the accuracy of the rider, while teaching the pony obedience and giving it confidence, both in its own ability and in that of its rider.

10 Riding Cross-country

Riding over a cross-country course has a character of its own, and both horse and rider have to adapt their technique accordingly. It is important to let the horse or pony find his own rhythm and to maintain it even when jumping small natural obstacles such as ditches, streams and banks, which may be found when out hacking.

The essence of cross-country riding is far more free than that of arena jumping and the pony, having found a rhythm, must be allowed to jump out of his stride from a good, swinging canter. The rider, adopting the jumping position, has to place her weight over the continually shifting center of balance while keeping contact with both hands and legs. It is better to ride in a less than absolute forward position over cross-country fences,

while, of course, always being in balance. A common failing is to get too far in advance of the pony's center of balance thus overweighting the forehand, upsetting the stride, and making the leap more physically difficult to accomplish. It is usually better, particularly over drop-fences (see right), to sit somewhat more upright and be prepared to "slip" the rein (allow it to move through the hands) in the spirit of self-preservation.

A VARIETY OF OBSTACLES

Any hesitation must be countered by resolute action

Wonderfully bold jump in just the correct attitude

Returns to more upright position upon landing

1 A cross-country course has all sorts of obstacles, some of them unusual. This rustic chair makes the pony hesitate and in this circumstance the rider must drive on confidently, "attacking" the fence.

2 The confident rider gets a bold, fluent jump which gives the pony confidence. Her easy, balanced seat is as good as it can be and she is presenting no interference to the pony's brave effort.

3 The pony lands well out and the rider, holding the body more upright, adjusts her position at exactly the right moment and is ready to push on and ride away from the fence.

NATURAL GOING

The siting of the fence in relation to the ground governs the approach and makes the jump more or less difficult. This is one of the main problems of cross-country riding.

Hold upper body upright

Keep legs in position on pony

Downhill

This is a drop-fence from a downhill approach and needs to be ridden steadily, with the horse nicely balanced between the rider's hand and leg. Sensibly, the pony looks where she is going, while the rider sits upright and is ready, if necessary, to take the trunk back from the hips and "slip" the rein to keep her seat.

Pyramid

A fence of pyramid construction, sloping away from the ground-line, encourages the horse because it makes it easier to judge the point of take-off, but it is a spread fence and it is necessary for the trajectory of the leap to be longer rather than higher. The ground here makes the rider think about the approach but the jump is well executed and the impression is one of an ongoing combination.

The Shortest Way

Here the rider takes the shortest, boldest way over the corner of the obstacle rather than making two jumps by going in and out of the rail complex. It puts a premium on accuracy and confident forward riding, which this pony and rider find no difficulty in meeting. Importantly, this approach can save precious seconds when the time limit is tight. This is a bold, attacking leap with the rider relaxed and in a good position.

Pole Stockade

An easy, straightforward fence well jumped by a pair whose confidence increases fence by fence. However, there is a possible danger here. The absence of a wing on the right of fence demands accurate presentation of the pony at the obstacle if the risk of a run out on the open side is to be avoided.

Riding Out

Riding out of the confined school environment is just as much a part of learning to ride as the pole grid or the leg-yielding exercise. In the horse world we talk about "hacking" and "going for a hack," words that originate from the French *haquenee*, "a riding horse." Later, the Anglo-Saxons gave the word more specific meaning by creating a Hackney breed (*see* p.107) and the Hack, an elegant type of riding horse.

Riding in the school is about periods of concentrated work (*see* pp.174–77) that are designed to improve the rider's ability to control and position the horse accurately. Riding lessons are also, as a result, confidence building and a means of acquiring a good, firm seat. For the horse or pony the lessons are just as productive. They teach the habit of obedience and the meaning of the rider's aids, encouraging a willing response, while developing the physique, suppleness and balance.

Just as importantly, the lessons create a bond of trust between the horse and rider. They are, in fact, a preparation for riding outside on roads and tracks, and through the open countryside. They are never an end in themselves, unless, perhaps,

Hacking
There is nothing more enjoyable than to ride in the countryside on a nicely mannered horse and with a pleasant companion. It is a relaxing experience that is enjoyed by both horses and riders and a wonderful way of getting to know each other.

Instructional Ride

Riding as a member of a class is part of the learning process and much can be gained from it. Pupils can learn from each other's strengths and weaknesses under the supervision of the instructor, who will always have planned the basis of his or her lesson in advance.

we are concerned with serious, high-level dressage competition. Indeed, if horses and riders did nothing but ride within the boundaries of an arena—going round in perpetual circles, as it were—both would soon become very fed up and disillusioned. And that is where trouble can start.

Gaining Confidence

Riding out is a great recreational activity, a wonderful relaxation after the school discipline, and very necessary to both members of the partnership. At first, the novice rider should go out in company—preferably with the instructor—rather than attempt to venture on to roads, tracks or trails alone. As confidence and ability grow you will go out unaccompanied, but even then you should observe some common-sense precautions.

Make sure, before leaving the stables, that someone responsible knows where you plan to ride and how long you expect to be. You should take advantage of the ubiquitous mobile phone and always take yours with you.

Maintaining Standards

Although hacking is a relaxation it does not mean that standards are allowed to be dropped. You must still ride correctly and keep the pony attentive, never letting him slop along anyhow. If he is not ridden in a balanced fashion it is all too easy for him to come down on slippery roads and rough ground. The maxim to be observed is to always ride 100 yards (91.5m) in front of you and be aware of what is going on the same distance behind you.

Learning Along the Way

While nothing is more pleasant than going for a ride it is also a way of learning without concentrated effort. Almost unconsciously one learns from the example of the instructor, how she positions her horse and how unobtrusively she applies the aids, always riding easily and without fuss.

Remember that horses enjoy riding with others, too. They always go better with a companion, the two enjoying each other's company and drawing confidence from it.

Australia

The Pony Club is well supported throughout Australia. Individual branches arrange instructional rallies that encourage young riders to ride effectively across country. This young lady, sitting well on her attractive pony, is enjoying her ride over a well-built Pony Club course.

Hong Kong

The Pony Club also functions strongly in Hong Kong, staging rallies and organizing all sorts of events and competitions. Riding, indeed, has always been a popular pastime in Hong Kong.

Riding Alone

Riding on one's own is part of owning a horse, and companions are not always available. But this young lady is clearly very competent and has learnt how to control and position her horse well.

OWNING A HORSE

New Partnership

To share your life with a horse, being responsible for his welfare,
is a rewarding experience—as well as being hard work!

Buying the Right Horse

Millions of words have been written about this subject—from full-sized books to the succinct if cynical advice given by John Warde, a famous foxhunter in the 18th and 19th centuries: "Never believe a word any man says about a horse he wishes to sell—not even a bishop." Even more uncompromising are the words *caveat emptor* (let the buyer beware).

Despite all kinds of well-meaning guidance, it is still an unhappy fact that many people buy the wrong horse. What is more, it is usually their own fault.

Of course, buying a horse is not like buying a car or a basket of groceries, simply because we are dealing not with a disposable commodity but with a living animal, whose characteristics are motivated by instinct and habit rather than reason.

However, with a little rational forethought, some old-fashioned common sense, and a modicum of relevant knowledge, it is possible to find just the right horse.

First Considerations

At the outset, there are four factors to be considered:
1 The purpose for which the horse is required.
2 The rider's experience and level of competence.
3 The facilities available for keeping the horse and the circumstances under which he will be kept.
4 The price.

Clearly, it would not be sensible to buy an expensive competition horse if your ambitions do not go further than weekend hacking in the countryside. Nor, indeed, would it be a good choice for a novice rider. It is a fact that most people prefer to think of themselves as competent riders, while parents can be hopelessly optimistic about the equestrian capability of their children. You need to make a ruthlessly honest appraisal of your competence and experience before you become a horse-owner.

The facilities on offer have an equally important bearing on the choice. If you intend to keep the horse out (in those countries where it is practical to do so), you are limited to animals able to live happily under those conditions. Conversely, if the horse is to be kept stabled—a time-consuming, labor-intensive operation—you must have enough time to clean him and the stable, to exercise the animal and to feed him regularly through the day.

Happiness is a Horse
A young lady and a kind, gentle horse, but in this case they are probably not the best combination: small people are best suited to a pony of appropriate size. A full-grown horse is too much for a lightweight young person with short legs.

The Purchase Price

As a guide, price will generally be governed, other than by what you can afford, by conformation (*see* pp.96–97) and appearance; performance ability and/or record; weight-carrying capacity, where that is applicable; age; and manners.

Soundness does not enter into the assessment, since it would be akin to madness to buy an unsound horse whatever the price. Certainly, it would turn out to be the most expensive in the long run.

It is well to buy a well-made horse because in theory, and usually in practice too, he will be better balanced and more enjoyable to ride than one that is not. Also, the structure is more efficient and therefore less likely to suffer strain and injury. If the price is right, blemishes and old scars can be overlooked, so long as the animal is not unsound as a result of them.

Performance has an obvious effect upon price. The horse with ability and a good track record will naturally be more expensive than a horse without those attributes. If you are very heavy, the horse's weight-carrying ability is a factor to be considered and paid for. Conversely, if you are a lightweight, the choice is that much greater.

Age is a factor, but not a hugely significant one. A horse is mature at six and may increase in price up to the age of ten or eleven, when there could be a levelling-off period. It is well to remember, however, that many class competition horses are at the top of their form well into the early teens and beyond.

"Manners" may be said to include: behavior in the stable and when being groomed, clipped and shod; the ease with which the horse can be caught in the field and can be boxed for travelling; and the animal's deportment on the road and in traffic.

The moral that emerges in any exercise involving horse purchase is that the more experienced and skilful the prospective buyer, the wider is the choice open to him or her. Conversely, the less competent buyer who is seeking the "perfect" horse—a paragon yet to be foaled—is likely to have to pay more to find a suitable mount.

A Good Sort
A useful type of horse, capable of a variety of activities. This horse would be a good choice for a keen teenager who enjoys competition and is ready for a faster, more ongoing horse.

Making Your Choice

An Ongoing Cost

Before you buy a horse or pony, it is well to recognize that the purchase price is only the beginning of a continuing expenditure.

A salutary exercise is to estimate the annual cost of horse-keeping. This includes rents and livery charges (where applicable); shoeing once every five weeks and regular dressing of the foot when the horse is unshod; feed and bedding; equipment; insurance; veterinary and transport costs; and, possibly, the cost of paddock management. It all adds up.

The Mechanics of Buying

The experienced owner may buy horses at a sale; others are better advised to buy privately or from a dealer. In that event, it is always wise to take along a friend, preferably not a family relation, to act, if necessary, as an independent witness to the transaction.

Ask questions about manners and suitability for the purpose. Finish by asking "Has the horse any tricks or failings that we should know about?" In most countries the law requires that the vendor shall answer truthfully.

Ponies to Sell

Horse and pony sales are held as a matter of course in most countries, and many experienced horsemen prefer to buy horses at a public sale. It is, indeed, possible to buy very good horses at auction, but it is not advisable for the novice or first-time buyer to purchase in this way, unless, perhaps, accompanied by a trusted, expert adviser.

Subject to Vetting

It is a wise precaution to have your intended purchase examined by a veterinarian of your choice before becoming committed. No reputable vendor will make any objection to your doing so.

Did you know?

The desert-living Bedouin people have very strongly held beliefs when it comes to buying horses. They say of a white-faced horse with four white legs that he "carries his shroud with him," and they would not buy such a one.

Assessing the Horse

The horse can then be brought out for inspection and trotted out in hand, so that you have a chance to assess your intended purchase.

Next, the horse can be tacked up, in your presence or, preferably, by you. Then the vendor or his nominee can ride the horse. There is no point running the risk of a fireworks display by riding an unknown quantity yourself. The ensuing ride should be watched carefully and then you can try the horse, perhaps jumping him over a little fence.

If you do not like the horse, for whatever reason, say so there and then, apologize for wasting the vendor's time, tip the groom if there is one and be on your way.

Otherwise, buy the horse subject to a satisfactory veterinary certificate. This should be given by your own veterinarian, not the one employed by the vendor.

The First Few Days

When you take delivery of the new purchase, give him a few days to get used to new surroundings and a new owner. It is possible that horses, particularly young ones, will try in these early days to test the authority of the new owner. It is not unreasonable, nor unnatural, and such little rebellions should be dealt with firmly and quietly, understanding the underlying reasons.

Getting Settled In
It is probably better to get to know your new horse in the stable before putting him out in a paddock. Once he is in the paddock, take care to visit him frequently.

Don't Take Risks
Always have the horse ridden by the vendor, and watch how he goes for her before you get on him yourself.

Feeding

In the natural state, horses feed on grasses and herbs. These provide the basic life requirements so long as the grazing area is large enough and water supplies are adequate and accessible.

In the domestic state, when horses are expected to carry weight on their backs, often at speed and sometimes over obstacles, the natural food is insufficient and so artificial feeding methods are necessary. The system of feeding and the constituents of the diet will vary in different parts of the world. However, the objective remains the same: the feed, when given in the correct balance and quantity, should provide the necessary strength and energy for the work required, without any serious loss of condition.

The Natural State

Grass, properly managed, is the natural food for this mare and her foal. However, they will both need to be fed supplements to ensure health and growth.

A Balanced Diet

There are three elements constituting a balanced feed intake: food that provides bulk; food that supplies energy; and supplements, such as minerals and vitamins, which meet particular needs.

While feeding for a purpose remains an art, it is, in the 21st century, an art adequately supported by science. Indeed, the modern horse-feed industry is so developed that it is relatively easy to plan suitable rations for various levels of activity. There is a wide variety of mixes and pellet feeds, all conveniently bagged, with details of the content, recommended quantities, and so on, printed on the packaging. In addition, natural feedstuffs such as fresh grass and root crops, including carrots and mangels (sugar-beet), may be given where

they are available. They are valuable in themselves and introduce a succulent variation to the diet.

Grass provides bulk, but the domestic horse in work is reliant on a generous hay ration, made from a variety of grasses. Although hay and grass are both bulk foods, the nutrient value of the latter varies according to the time of year. Also, grass produces a soft, fat condition, not conducive to work. (The exception is alfalfa grass, which is highly nutritious and has a good protein content.)

Energy and body-building foods are a compound of grains. The modern practice is to give them in one of the carefully balanced and graded proprietary mixes or pellet feeds, all of which, along with hay, provide the fibrous roughage on which the digestive system depends.

The proportion of bulk feed to concentrate is accepted as being: two-thirds bulk to one-third concentrates for horses in light work; half and half for horses in moderate work. For horses in hard, fast work the bulk ration may be reduced to a third of the total intake, but never less.

The total food requirement per day is estimated as between 2 and 2.5 percent of the bodyweight of a mature horse. There are formulae for calculating weight, but today it is more usual to use a marked tape placed round the girth, which gives the weight at a glance.

The Rules of Feeding

The basic rules of feeding are: feed little and often, and do not work immediately after feeding.

Both rules arise from the limitations of the horse's digestive system and the position of the relatively small stomach. The bowel (large and small) is capacious, but the system is designed for the slow and almost continuous absorption of food. To meet the requirements

Fresh Water

A supply of fresh water, readily accessible at all times, whether the horse is stabled or at pasture, is an essential element in feeding and management and must never be withheld.

of nature, therefore, the domestic, stabled horse should be fed small amounts every ten minutes, which is clearly impractical. The best that can be done is to feed little and often, dividing the total ration into three, or preferably four, small feeds a day. Given the size of the stomach, no individual feed should exceed 4lb (1.8kg) in weight.

The stomach lies behind the diaphragm, and after feeding it becomes distended and presses up against the latter. Should the horse be ridden in this condition, when the lungs would naturally expand as a result of exertion, both breathing and digestive processes would be impaired. Indigestion would occur, which could lead to colic; if the work was fast the lungs could choke with blood and the stomach could rupture.

Therefore, do not work after feeding—at least not for an hour or so.

Winter Feed

Horses kept out in the cold, winter weather expend energy in simply maintaining body temperature. In winter, the nutrient value of grass is low, only increasing with the first flush of spring grass. It is necessary, therefore, to provide supplementary feeding which can, in part, be provided by a generous ration of good hay. Feeding hay off the ground as shown here is really a wasteful practice because a proportion of the ration may be trodden underfoot.

Grooming

The second factor in the management of the domestic horse that contributes materially to the animal's well-being, as well as being an essential part of any conditioning program, is grooming and strapping/wisping (massage with a hard hay pad), and they are not the same thing. It is reasonable to spend 45 minutes or more cleaning the stabled horse that is in work.

Grooming is absolutely necessary for the stabled horse consuming quantities of artificial food. It is also necessary for those horses that are in receipt of a full ration but live out in what is termed the "combined system," i.e., put out for the day in a protective New Zealand/turnout rug.

For ponies living out day and night all year round, grooming, beyond the removal of superficial mud, is not to be recommended. In these circumstances vigorous grooming would remove the protective, waterproofing grease in the coat.

Space and Convenience

This beautifully kept barn provides ample space in the wide, center aisle to wash the horse, if necessary, and to groom him thoroughly and in comfort. Since the barn door is kept open in the interests of ventilation, it is probably a wise precaution to tie the horse securely.

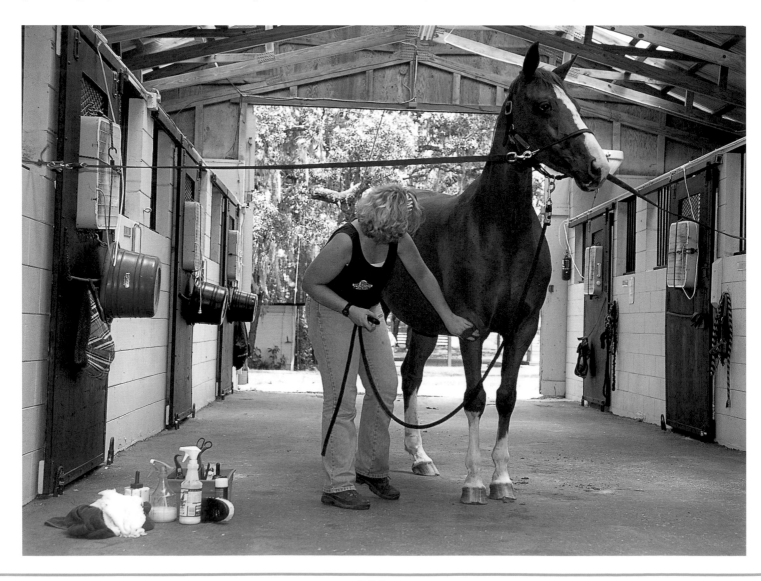

The Grooming Kit

A prerequisite, of course, is a complete grooming kit kept in a convenient container. It should comprise the following:

1. Dandy brush—a stiff-bristled brush to use on muddy legs, etc. It is too harsh to use on the body or the head, or to brush out the tail and mane.
2. Body brush—a soft brush for body, mane and tail.
3. Water brush—a boat-shaped brush, which is used dampened to make the mane and tail hair lie flat or for any other purpose involving water.
4. Metal curry-comb—to clean the brushes not the horse.
5. Rubber or plastic curry-comb—can be used directly on the body and is usually much appreciated because of its gently stimulating action.
6. Hoof-pick—a hooked instrument for cleaning the feet. A strong, curved metal hook is more effective than the ubiquitous folding hoof-pick, and is less easily lost or mislaid.
7. Mane comb—to separate the hair. There are also combs used for shortening and pulling the mane. They are available in both metal and plastic.
8. Sweat-scraper—to remove excess water after bathing.
9. Two sponges—one to clean eyes and nose and one for the dock and possibly the sheath of geldings. These sponges should always be kept separate.
10. Stable rubber—a cloth to give a final polish to the coat. A chamois leather or chamois-leather pad will give an extra fine polish.

The Importance of Grooming

Consumption of concentrate foods makes the horse's body produce large quantities of waste matter. Much is disposed of through the higher respiration rate involved when the horse is exercised and through the natural process of excretion, but a significant amount is dispersed through the pores of the skin. The skin has, therefore, to be kept clean by regular grooming if it is to perform that function.

The act of grooming also contributes to a feeling of well-being in the horse; it creates a comfortable relationship between horse and human; and it encourages circulation and muscle tone.

Grooming, other than the quick rub-over before saddling up for the morning exercise, is best carried out after exercise when the horse is warm and the pores are open. As well as cleaning the horse and stimulating the skin and circulation, the morning grooming session provides an excellent opportunity to carry out a thorough inspection of the animal. We should also look carefully for scratches that may need attention and see that the eyes are clean and not runny.

Picking Out Feet

Before cleaning the body pick out the feet (see right), catching the dirt in a skip. If it is necessary to wash the feet make sure that the heels are well dried. If the heels are left wet, they very easily become chapped and sore and are then liable to contract some infection.

PICKING OUT THE FORE FEET

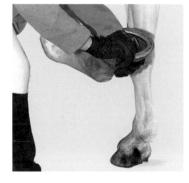

1. Run the hand firmly down the back of the leg along the tendon to the fetlock and lift up the foot.

2. Stand close to the horse. Pass the hand round the hoof and use the hoof-pick in the right hand to clean it.

PICKING OUT THE HIND FEET

1. Stand close. Run the hand from the inside down the back of the leg and pull forward from the fetlock.

2. Hold the foot in the left hand and, with your right hand, clean out from rear to front with the hoof-pick.

The Grooming Procedure

Grooming begins high up on the neck behind the ears using the body brush and working back to the tail. Around the head the brush must be used gently and carefully, ensuring that the wooden back is not banged against the bony projections. On the neck and body the brush can be used vigorously; you can put your whole weight behind each stroke. This can be accomplished only by standing well back from the horse. Use the brush in the right hand while holding the curry-comb in the left (or vice-versa if you are left-handed). After three or four strokes clean the brush on the comb. Work briskly and positively in a good regular rhythm without making sudden movements that might startle the animal. However, care should be exercised when

CLEANING YOUR HORSE

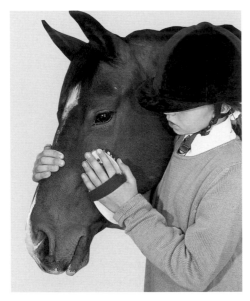

1 Be careful not to let the back of the brush knock against the bony projections on the horse's head. Place right hand as shown.

2 Stand back and get your weight behind the brush with each stroke, using it vigorously from front to rear.

3 Clean the brush every three or four strokes on the curry-comb. You can't clean a horse with a dirty brush.

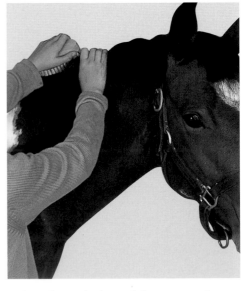

4 Continue brushing over and down the quarters, and right down the leg, taking care how you position your body.

5 Brush the tangles out of the tail and finish it off with the body brush. Take care not to break the hairs.

6 Brush out the hair of the mane and then finish off by laying it with a dampened water brush.

Periodically, geldings need to have their sheaths washed out to remove any accumulated dirt, etc. It is best done wearing a rubber glove and using a thin sponge dipped in warm water. Failure to wash out the sheath can result in discomfort and may stop the horse lowering his penis properly when urinating.

A final, satisfying polish can be put on with a damped stable rubber or chamois leather.

Strapping

Strapping, or wisping, has a more positive purpose in developing and toning the muscles and stimulating the skin and circulation. As a bonus it will also produce a "bloom" on the coat, caused by the release of oil from the glands surrounding each hair in response to the energetic application of the wisp or pad. Properly carried out it is beneficial in all respects to the overall conditioning of the horse. The exercise is best left to the end of the day because it encourages circulation, which naturally slows down in the night hours.

The tool required is a wisp made from a tightly woven rope of hay, about 8ft (2.5m) long, which is, in brief, turned in on itself to make a firm pad. It requires practice to make one satisfactorily but there is a very good alternative. A chamois leather stitched to make a small bag and then stuffed firmly with hay will be just as effective and is less expensive than the smart leather pads sold at the saddler's shop.

To use the wisp it must first be dampened before it is brought down energetically onto the horse following the lay of the coat. It is used rhythmically on the quarters, shoulder and neck, but not on the loins, belly, head or legs.

Most horses enjoy being wisped and quite soon it is possible to see the muscles visibly contract and relax in time to the strokes of the pad. Nonetheless, it should be done gradually, increasing the strength of the pad's application to the body little by little. Begin with 5–10 minutes and work up by degrees to as much as 45 minutes. The exercise will also do wonders for your fitness.

The occasional massage carried out with wet forearms is also a useful technique to use and, though hard work, it is much appreciated by the horse. Indian *saises* (grooms) are expert at grooming and massaging with the forearms. They will rarely use a brush but they achieve excellent results.

Washing

There is no reason why the horse should not be washed after he has worked and got sweaty and dirty. Every so often the horse can be washed to remove any dust from his coat, and it is refreshing for him, too.

brushing the belly and between the hind legs. Many horses, particularly the thin-skinned, well-bred ones, are ticklish in these parts and may try to nip (unless tied up fairly short) or even to cow-kick (kick forwards) with a hind leg at their tormentor.

If the horse is very ticklish it is more sensible to dispense with the brush and use the hand rather than risk an unnecessary upset. Never bang the brush on the body and be especially careful around the loins, where there is a risk of damaging the kidneys.

Brush out the mane and tail carefully so as not to break the hairs and lay them flat with a dampened water brush.

Clean the dock with one sponge; clean the eyes and nostrils with another.

Exercise

Exercise must be carried out to correspond with the food intake. Ideally, the output of energy involved in exercise and work should equal the energy input provided by the feed ration. Too little food and too much work will result in the horse losing condition. Too much food and not enough work, will increase the bodyweight, as well as causing digestive, circulatory, and behavioral problems.

A balanced diet of good quality, fed in sufficient quantity, with the amount being increased to the appropriate level in gradual stages, builds up the body, encourages muscle growth and supplies energy. Grooming makes its contribution, while exercise and work strengthen the body, developing muscle and lung capacity, preventing the horse from becoming fat and hardening the legs and tendons.

There is, however, a real difference between exercise and work. Exercise is not necessarily strenuous, and is given over long periods of time. Work, usually concerned with the school exercises and jumping, is more concentrated and demanding. It is of shorter duration, and is interspersed with periods of rest. The length of the exercise and work sessions is increased gradually, to correspond with the gradual build-up of the feed intake.

Educational Relaxation

Exercise should be enjoyable and a relaxation for the horse, but it can also contain an element of instruction. Opening gates, moving over to one side or the other, and trotting over a piece of broken ground are all educational and contribute to the variety of the exercise program. Nothing is more boring for the horse than trotting round the same route day after day.

Work
The school exercises call for short periods of concentrated work and can be demanding. For this reason, school work is of short duration and is balanced by relaxing exercise.

Hacking Out
To ride out, preferably in company, is an enjoyable relaxation for both horse and rider. Nonetheless, it also has a valuable educational role to play and the horse has still to be ridden actively.

It is helpful in planning exercise routes to coincide with the time available if the average speeds of the paces, walk, trot and canter, are known in their relation to the distance covered. In general, a horse walks one mile (1.6km) in 16 minutes, trots it in eight and canters that distance in five.

Exercise Gaits

Walk and trot are the principal exercise gaits, and those from which the greatest value is derived. However, they will be worse than useless if the horse is not ridden actively. The horse can be encouraged to go in a relaxed, swinging walk, but he has still to work within the frame imposed by leg and hand. The trot, too, must be similarly positive: slow certainly, but active and rhythmical, the horse being held together between hand and leg. Nonetheless, short "rest" periods, when the horse walks on a long rein, are permissible and beneficial.

It is advisable to "change the diagonal" at trot quite frequently, so that the horse develops muscles equally. Trot is a two-time gait, the horse moving the two diagonal pairs of legs alternately with a moment of suspension as he springs from one to the other. The right diagonal is off-fore and near-hind and the left diagonal the opposite pair. At rising trot, the rider is said to be on the right diagonal when her seat touches the saddle as the off-fore and near-hind strike the ground. The rider changes the diagonal by sitting for an extra beat before she rises again, i.e., she bumps once. One can check the diagonal, if in doubt, by

Trotting Uphill

Trotting energetically uphill with the horse framed between the rider's hand and leg is a good exercise in every respect and calls for extra effort. It develops and strengthens the muscles and improves the respiration and lung function.

glancing at the shoulder. When the left shoulder is to the rear as the seat touches down, one is on the right diagonal and vice-versa.

A steady canter (not always on the same stretch of ground) and the occasional gallop help the lungs and respiration. The last mile (1.6km) home should be walked, to allow the horse to cool off, but on rainy days, when the horse is wet, it is better to trot and bring him home warm. He can then be rubbed off and, if a mesh sheet is put on him, he will soon dry out.

"Pipe-openers"

Steady canters and the occasional gallop are excellent "pipe-openers," releasing surplus energy that might otherwise produce too much excitement.

Handling

The keynote to handling horses safely is *quiet confidence*. All your movements should be brisk and deliberate, never hesitant and never sudden. If you tiptoe round the horse, patting him with an outstretched hand, he will sense that you are nervous and quickly become upset and jumpy. But don't overdo the confidence, talking loudly and slapping him heartily—that will just frighten him.

When attending the horse, in the process of grooming and so on, work as close to him as possible and make sure to warn him in advance of your next move with your hand and arm. In particular, stand close when dealing with the hind legs. In the unlikely event of his kicking, the blow will strike you before it has reached maximum force. Moreover, you will be hit by the leg or hock and not by an iron-shod hoof. In fact, very few horses will kick, but never take it for granted.

If you need to move behind him, put your hand on his quarters, stand close and walk round, keeping the hand in place. If you want him to move over, pass round the quarters and ask him to "move over,"

reinforcing the request with a pat from your hand. He will learn to move over from the verbal command alone surprisingly quickly.

To turn the horse in the yard or box, bring the head towards you and tap him on the girth with your free hand, when he will move his quarters away from you.

To approach a horse in the field, do so on an oblique line from the front so that he can see you. Don't creep up behind him or he may be startled and run off.

Leading In-hand

Right from the beginning, teach the horse to lead quietly in-hand. Put him up against a wall, so that he

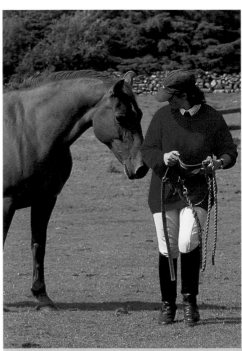

Catching a Horse: Step 1
The horse is wary so the trainer, staying close to him, does not press the point but begins to walk away as though she has lost interest in him.

Step 2
Curious at this tactic, the horse moves up to her as if to say, "Oh, don't be like that, you're my best friend," but still the trainer makes no move.

Step 3
Friends again. The horse allows the trainer to put on his headcollar. Note how the trainer passes the headpiece over his head.

cannot swing his quarters away from you. Stand by his shoulder, not at his head, and hold the lead-rope in the right hand some 18in (45cm) from the mouth or nose. Pass the spare rope across your body and hold the end in the left hand. It helps in the early stages to carry a long whip in the left hand so that you can tap the girth behind your back as you step forward, giving the command "Walk on," or whatever.

Keeping Pace

Stay at the shoulder and keep walking briskly. If he hangs back, tap him with the whip, while keeping your position at the shoulder.

If he goes too fast, lengthen your stride to get a bit in front of his shoulder, say "Whoa" distinctly, check him with the rope, then turn towards him and put the butt end of the whip, held in the left hand, in front of his nose. Make him stand squarely before asking him to move off again.

Feeding Tidbits

When he walks off smartly and halts easily, don't forget to reward him, but not necessarily with a tidbit.

Don't give too many tidbits or the horse comes to expect them all the time. If he doesn't get them then he can become bad-tempered and start to bully you. When you do give a tidbit, put it on the palm of the hand and move the hand towards the muzzle—don't draw the hand backwards, which will encourage the horse to snap.

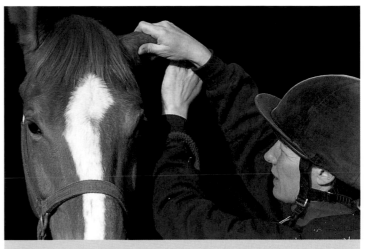

Making Friends
Look at the calm expression on the horse's face as the trainer makes close physical contact with him. He enjoys her stroking and handling his ears and clearly the two have a relationship of trust.

When releasing a horse in the field, always do so keeping his head facing towards you so that if he takes off with an exuberant buck and a kick you will not be in the line of fire.

Leading In-hand
This is how to do it. The stirrup irons have been run up on the saddle so as not to swing against the pony. The leader moves briskly, staying behind the pony's head and holding the rein across her body.

Fairs and Festivals

Fairs and festivals are a deeply rooted tradition in our
civilizations and are to be found in almost every part of
the modern world. Many, particularly those of the East,
have a religious connection and most are involved with
the display and sale of animals: sheep, cattle, camels, and
in India, elephants and almost everywhere, horses.

Many of the great horse shows have
their origin in the medieval fairs,
and Ireland's Royal Dublin Horse
Show, which pioneered the sport
of showjumping, is still at heart a
horse fair, attracting buyers from all
over the world. Indeed, Ireland, a

country forever associated with
horses and horsemen, abounds in
horse fairs. The Clifden Show in
County Galway is a fair for
Connemara ponies (*see* p.152) and so
is Maam Cross in the same county,
while at Buttevant and Ballinasloe

Fair you will find hunters (*see* p.157),
jumpers and youngstock offered by
Ireland's breeders and dealers.

Indian Fairs

Half a world away in India you
can see their entirely recognizable

India

Many of the Indian fairs are brought to vibrant life with
impromptu, but doubtless well-rehearsed, displays of trick
horsemanship, as well as those performing the traditional
dance routines and the high leaps that are inherent to the
traditional horse culture of Rajasthan.

Spanish Fairs

There is a gypsy following for the colorful festivals (*ferias*) of Spain and Portugal, but it is the landed gentry who show off their highly schooled horses, and their beautiful ladies, at the *ferias* of Golega, Santaram, and Jerez. Hundreds of Andalucian, Lusitano and Alter-Real (*see* pp.124–25) horses perform all the brilliant movements of the classical High School in a vibrant colorful spectacle that is uniquely and unforgettably Iberian.

Appleby

On the Wednesday of the Appleby Fair, held annually in June, hundreds of horses are washed in the River Eden in a tradition that extends over 200 years. The fair is held under a Royal Charter of 1685 granted by King James II.

counterparts, wearing turbans and *dhotis* (a long loincloth) instead of the soft cap and tweed jacket of Ballinasloe, making whispered deals over horses in ways that are common to horsey folk the world over.

Most of India's special religious festivals, called *melas*, involve bathing in one or other of the holy rivers or lakes. They are, also, great tourist attractions vigorously exploited by bands of dancers and musicians, and entire communities spring up to enjoy the spectacle.

Pushkar is a little town in Rajasthan, built round the holy waters of the lake formed by the Hindu deity Lord Brahma when the Gods still walked the Earth. During 12 days in the month of *Kartik* (November) thousands of pilgrims come to bathe from the *ghats* (platforms) around the lake. Tourists stay in desert camps, a whole township of stalls selling

craft goods is put up, dancers and musicians arrive in droves, and the dealers in cattle, camels and horses settle in for the duration of the *mela*. Horses are tethered in lines under colorful awnings and the watchful eye of their owners, and are often shown off at breakneck speed in the avenues of sand separating the lines.

Appleby Fair

The English town of Appleby in Cumbria is no bigger than Pushkar. It has no lake but there is the River Eden where on the Wednesday of the annual fair, hundreds of horses are washed traditionally as they have been for over 200 years. The fair is the meeting place of the "travellers," the Romany people for whom horse-dealing is a way of life. After the ritual visit to the river, horses are raced up and down Appleby's streets and the serious trading begins.

Feria at Jerez

The great *feria* at Jerez de la Frontera in Spain, is a spectacle of superb horses, shown off by accomplished horsemen. This multi-horsed team put to a ceremonial carriage bears tribute to the skill of the "whip" (driver).

Ride of the *Rejoneadores*

Dressed in the traditionally severe clothes of the Spanish horseman, the *rejoneadores* (bull-fighters) of Spain parade their highly schooled horses in procession through the streets of Jerez.

Clipping

The heavy winter coat grown by horses in the northern hemisphere, and the accompanying accumulation of grease on the skin, is a natural protection against cold and wet. However, a thick winter coat is not suitable for a stabled horse in work, as it can cause heavy sweating and a subsequent loss in condition.

The removal of the coat by clipping allows the horse to work at varying speeds without distress and makes the management of the horse that much easier. Without the heavy coat the horse dries off quickly and can be kept clean with considerably less effort. Of course, once the coat is clipped off the horse has to be provided with blankets to keep him warm.

In Europe, the horse's winter coat grows through September and is ready to be clipped off in early October. The horse will then need to be clipped again at the end of December.

Hunting Trio
These well-mounted followers of Britain's Ledbury Hunt seem to favor the trace clip, and some variations. The horse on the left sports the traditional trace clip, the others have more individualistic versions.

A blanket clip, sometimes used on thin-skinned Thoroughbreds, is practical and does give a degree of protection to the loins. The trace clip was devised for harness horses but is also a useful clip for hunting ponies kept at grass in New Zealand/turnout blankets.

Clipping Procedure

Modern electrically powered clipping machines are reliable, powerful and, very importantly, quiet and smooth-running. Nonetheless, much depends on the operator and the observance of some common-sense requirements:

- A well-lit stable (daylight is preferable to electricity).
- The horse must be clean and dry. If the coat is wet or dusty the clipper blades will become clogged and the motor overheated.
- Once the clipping has reached the back a blanket should be thrown over the horse to keep him warm.

However clean the coat at the commencement of the clipping session, the skin surface will be covered with grease and dirt at its conclusion. The easiest way to get rid of it is to make the horse sweat by putting on a couple of old blankets and giving him a little sharp exercise; 20 minutes is sufficient. Back in the stable he will begin to sweat when the blankets are taken off. A dampened hay wisp energetically applied will remove all the surplus grease, making the subsequent grooming of the horse that much easier. Grease has to be removed to prevent blockage of the skin pores, which would prevent the excretion of waste matter.

Hunter Clip
The popular hunter clip, which is in general use. It leaves a saddle patch and the hair is also left on the legs, although it can be thinned by using the coarse-toothed clipper blades. In any event, the hair needs to be trimmed.

There are two principal clips and two subsidiary ones, as well as a few variations arising from individual preferences.

Types of Clip

The full clip involves the removal of the whole coat, while the hunter clip leaves a saddle patch on the back and leaves the hair on the legs. The alternatives are the blanket and trace clips. The reasons given in favor of the hunter clip are:

1 The saddle patch helps prevent galls or scalding from the saddle lining when the back is hot and sweaty;
2 The hair on the legs serves as a protection against thorns, cuts, scratches, etc.

Types of Clip
The trace clip is suitable for hunting ponies, although the one illustrated is only a part trace clip. The blanket clip is practical for thin-skinned Thoroughbred sorts. The bib clip is confined to ponies and is really neither one thing or the other.

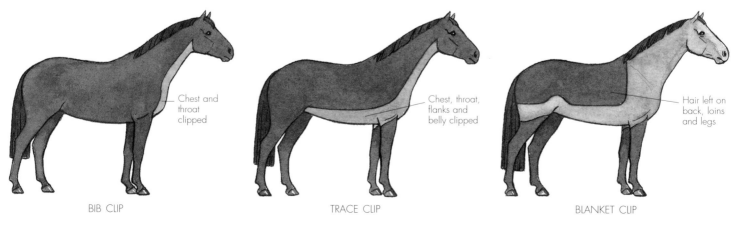

Chest and throat clipped

Chest, throat, flanks and belly clipped

Hair left on back, loins and legs

BIB CLIP   TRACE CLIP   BLANKET CLIP

Braiding and Trimming

Over the centuries horse owners have taken a pride in their horses' appearance. The Mongols (*see* pp.24–25) are an exception, but what could approach the splendidly coiffured horses of the Assyrian Empire? Owners today can scarcely aspire to such elaborate standards, but the mane, tail and legs are trimmed, and for special occasions the mane is braided.

In some instances, and for practical purposes, the mane is removed altogether. This is the case with certain military troop horses, including Britain's King's Troop, Royal Horse Artillery, and also with polo ponies and show-ring cobs. They have their tails and legs trimmed, but their manes are always roached. It is entirely suitable for the thick neck of the cob. It is practical for the troopers and removes any possibility of the driver's whip or the reins being caught in the mane. The same applies to the polo pony, whose rider copes with reins, stick and whip and, like artillery drivers, rides with one hand.

Trimming

Traditionally, manes and tails are thinned by pulling out the hairs little by little, but today thinning knives

Polo Trim
The mane of the polo pony is roached, the hair being clipped. The tail is braided and bound up. Both are precautions against the tail being caught up by a stick or the mane hair interfering with the rider's hand.

Beautiful Braiding
This American pony has a good neck, the appearance of which is improved still more by small, tight braids along its length. However, to braid in this fashion it is first necessary for the mane to be well thinned and trimmed to a length.

claim to be just as efficient and are less likely to make the tail sore. Putting a tail bandage/wrap on for a short period will encourage the shaping of the tail by laying the hair after pulling. The tail can either be left as a "switch," with the end pointed and the hair trimmed down the full length, or it can be "banged," that is, cut off straight at the bottom at a length equalling one hand's breadth below the hock joint.

Thin the mane by pulling the hair from the underside with a short-toothed mane, or trimming, comb (or, of course, a modern mane-trimmer). After thinning, the hairs of the mane should be about 5in (12.5cm) in length. Anything over that is removed with the thumb and a sharp penknife—never with a pair of scissors, which would give the mane a very ragged appearance.

It is customary in both Europe and America to trim the whiskers on the muzzle. It looks tidier but, in fact, takes no notice of their purpose. The whiskers act rather like a radar beam, helping the horse—who cannot see the contents of his manger—to gauge the distance of objects from his mouth. Trim surplus hair on the fetlocks and lower legs with scissors and a comb, in the manner of a hairdresser.

Plaiting

Plaiting, too, is a hairdressing skill, but in fact is not too difficult so long as the mane has been well thinned. If done properly, braiding certainly enhances the appearance of the neck.

It is the neck, or rather its length, that governs the number of braids used. A long neck looks better with fewer braids. Weak necks can be improved by braiding loosely, so as to give the impression of a better top line,

American Style
This coiffure is reminiscent of the splendidly turned out Assyrian horses of long ago, but is in fact, all-American. It is achieved by roaching the top half of the mane and then spending much time styling the remaining hair.

whereas the braids on a strong neck can be small and tight.

The traditional method of braiding involves using a large-eyed needle and strong thread to sew the braids up. This looks neat, but, increasingly, small elastic bands are used to secure the braid— a quicker method. Another fashion trend, particularly popular in the dressage arena, is to finish each braid with a piece of white sticky tape.

Braiding is probably at its most colorful and imaginative on the heavy horse breeds. Manes and tails are braided with cotton braid and are then further ornamented with small, upright ribbons.

Tails on riding horses are often braided as well as the mane, but the growth at the top of the tail has to be left long and untrimmed for this final decorative touch to be accomplished. The manes and tails of Arab horses and the British Mountain and Moorland breeds are brushed but not trimmed or shaped, although that convention may not be observed in America. It is rarely necessary to pull the tail of the Thoroughbred.

Did you know?

The tail hair of horses can be used to make bows for violins and cellos. Rolled into a ball and dampened, horse hair makes a pad that will remove the most obstinate dirt deposits on saddles and bridles. At one time, horse hair was used to stuff furniture.

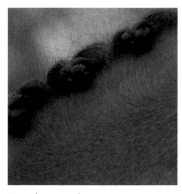

Traditional
Neat, close braids made up in the traditional way and secured by mane thread or small elastic bands.

White Tape
White sticky tape is used to set off the plaits, a fashion followed particularly by dressage riders.

Group Riding

Riding is far from being a solitary exercise. Many riding schools run group rides (through the countryside or along a pleasant stretch of beach, for example), which can last for as little as an hour or as much as a day. There is, too, a trekking industry that allows riders to vacation in the saddle over moorland or hill country for a week or maybe more.

Scotland claims to have invented trekking 50 years ago, organizing accompanied rides on sturdy Highland ponies. The word trekking (i.e., going from place to place) is of Dutch origin and was, it is said, brought back to the UK from the South African (Boer) War by Scotland's Lovat Scouts.

Riding clubs all over Europe feature rides for their members. In the UK for instance, the mounted treasure hunt is popular and so is the "pub ride," when the riders go out to an inn where they can enjoy a leisurely lunch and rest the horses before returning home.

Pony Club Camp

Group riding is, perhaps, epitomized by the traditional annual camp held by branches of the Pony Club, which also holds full-day instructional rallies. The camp is usually held over a week with the children sometimes still living under tents and the ponies tethered in lines, military fashion. The basis of the camp is the instructional ride, but hacking is always included as, of course, are the ever-popular gymkhana games.

Riding Vacations

Riding vacations are now firmly established in the vacation industry worldwide, and there are numerous tour operators in most countries.

British travel firms offer a variety of horse vacations based on rides over the wild uplands and moors of Scotland and

Through the Rockies

Trail riding through the Rocky Mountains is one of the great riding experiences. Sure-footed local horses, saddled Western style, are safe and well used to the country, and there is all the time in the world to admire breathtaking scenery.

Arizona

The American West at its best. Huge areas of desert, scrub and cactus and a dry, warm climate make Arizona a great place to enjoy well-organized ranch vacations. Riders use the comfortable and reassuring Western saddles and the horses are uniformly good.

The Open Moorland

There are wonderful opportunities to ride on the moorlands of Exmoor and Dartmoor in the southwest of Britain. The going is good and the ponies well cared for and reliable.

Wales, for instance, and, of course, on Exmoor, in the southwest of England. Elsewhere in Europe there is hardly a country that does not cater for riders.

Spain, particularly Andalucía, has its own very organized industry, with riding on Andalucian horses, that caters for novice riders as well as the very fit, adventurous and experienced ones. As a bonus there are the colorful, bustling *feria* (*see* p.209) and the displays of classical horsemanship that can be seen at places such as Jerez, home of the Andalucian School of Equestrian Art.

Western Riding

America has possibly the greatest variety of all, and some of the most adventurous trips. Especially popular are the vacations on ranches, where you ride Western style. There are also trail rides through the Rockies and most of the national parks.

Riding in Asia

Further afield, there are superbly organized trips in Rajasthan, India, on the famously curved-eared Marwari horses. Guests can ride through the countryside and villages to get a unique insight into Indian rural life, while the accommodation in desert forts is luxurious and the best way to appreciate Indian living first-hand.

Today, one can even vacation enjoyably in Mongolia. Guests are mounted on the small but tough and spirited Mongolian ponies and ride in the high-peaked saddles that have not changed much since the days of Genghis Khan and his Mongol "hordes" (*see* pp.24–25). Mongolian vacations are not for the faint-hearted or the overly fastidious, but in a group of like-minded companions they can be the unique riding experience.

Whatever the trip, much of the pleasure is obtained through being part of a group of people sharing the same sense of adventure, all enjoying the opportunity to indulge their hobby in a new and sometimes exotic environment. The riding vacation is now sufficiently established to ensure that horses and equipment are of a uniformly good standard.

Australia

The best way to see the Australian outback is from the back of a good Australian stock horse. The rides are relaxed, the climate pleasant, and the country wonderfully varied and full of wildlife.

Blue Danube

There are some unusual and exciting riding tours at various points along one of the greatest of Europe's rivers, and if you want to get to the other side it's possible to make the crossing by boat.

The Foot and the Shoe

One of the oldest horsey sayings, "No foot—no 'oss," is unmistakable in its meaning and quite unarguable. It is also true that the importance of skilful farriery cannot be overstated.

Horses are shod as a result of domestication. In the wild the hoof was hard enough to withstand any wear caused by moving slowly over the grazing grounds. When the horse has to work at speed and carrying weight, and often on hard road surfaces, the horn, without the protection of a shoe, would break and wear away quickly, making the horse footsore and lame.

The craft of farriery is a highly skilled one, and in many countries only qualified practitioners, recognized by law, are permitted to shoe horses.

Anatomy of the Foot

The foot, or pedal joint, is a sensitive structure made up of three bones—the "coffin" or pedal bone, the navicular, and the lower part of the short pastern, also called the coronet bone.

The foot is protected by an outer case of horn, known as the wall, which is insensitive. The underside of the foot is protected by the sole and the V-shaped rubbery frog, which acts as a shock-absorber and an anti-slip device. It carries some of the horse's weight, which is otherwise borne by the edge of the wall and the shoe.

The insensitive horn is separated from the sensitive foot by the "white line" that runs round the wall and is quite visible on the sole of a scrubbed foot. The sensitive part of the foot, inside the wall, is primarily

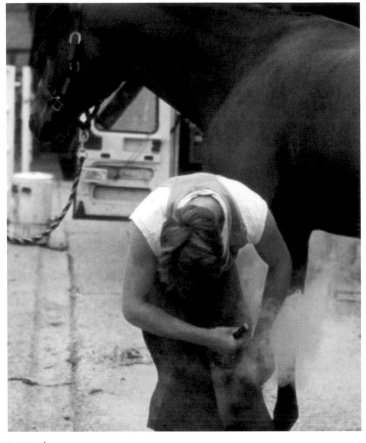

Hot-shoeing

Most farriers prefer hot-shoeing to cold. The hot shoe is placed on the foot, burning a mark where it touches. The fit and the evenness of the surface contact can then be checked and corrected as necessary. Cold-shoeing, when the ready-made shoe is fitted without its being heated, is a much less satisfactory method and limits the corrective measures that can otherwise be taken.

The Foot

The sole of the foot has a hard, insensitive outer covering protecting an inner, sensitive casing known as the fleshy sole. This last provides for the growth of the outer, horny sole. A healthy sole is slightly concave in shape, offering a better foothold and being less prone to bruising. A thin sole, particularly if it is inclined to be flat, is more easily damaged and may have to be protected by special shoeing.

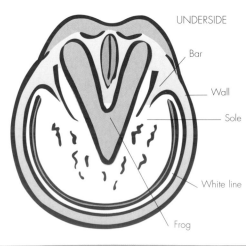

UNDERSIDE

Bar

Wall

Sole

White line

Frog

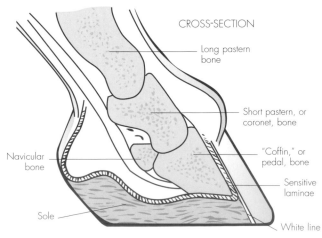

CROSS-SECTION

Long pastern bone

Short pastern, or coronet, bone

"Coffin," or pedal, bone

Sensitive laminae

White line

Navicular bone

Sole

made up of the sensitive laminae, which are the feather-like structures that have a nerve supply and conduct blood to and from the foot.

Fitting the Shoe

The farrier has to place his securing nails outside the white line in the insensitive horn. If the nail, by mistake, enters the sensitive structure, it causes pain and lameness.

Horn grows at the rate of between ¼ and ⅜in (6 10mm) each month and has to be removed by rasping/filing to keep the foot level. In normal conditions new shoes are required on average every five weeks.

The farrier prepares the foot with the object of its meeting the ground exactly level, not favoring one side or the other. If they are uneven, the feet will turn either in or out, placing an unequal strain on the joint and lower leg. The farrier corrects the first condition by rasping back the overgrowth on the inside of the wall, and the second by levelling the outside overgrowth.

He is also concerned to maintain the correct Foot-Pastern Axis (FPA), so that the angles between fetlock, toe and heel correspond to the degree of slope of the shoulder. In a well-made horse, the angle of slope will be between 43 and 45° from the highest point of the wither to the point of the shoulder. The correct FPA ensures the most economical and smooth flightpath of the foot and the minimum of concussion.

The number of nails securing the shoe is usually four on the outside of the wall and three on the inside.

Rasping

Rasping the underside of the foot removes the surplus growth and ensures that the foot is exactly level as it touches the ground. Rasping the wall of the foot is not a recommended practice.

A well-made shoe follows the rim of the wall exactly. It is neither too short, nor too long, nor too wide. In fact, it fits the foot, rather than the foot being rasped to fit the shoe.

Oiling the Feet

Hoof oil is usually applied for its cosmetic effect but it has a more important role in controlling the moisture content of the foot. Moisture is lost by evaporation and this is particularly evident in the stabled horse. The horn then dries, becomes brittle and cracks.

Moisture can be replaced by daily washing and then retained by applying oil.

Oil should be applied after exercise or turning out, otherwise it has the effect of preventing moisture being absorbed. In wet conditions, oil prevents excessive absorption of water and prevents the horn softening. In dry conditions, oil prevents loss of moisture content.

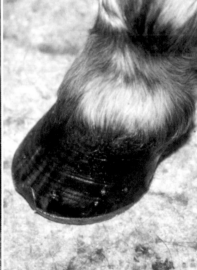

Before and After Shoeing

In the picture of the foot on the left, the clenches have risen away from the wall and the foot appears to have become long in the toe. The foot on the right is shorter in comparison, the surplus growth having been removed from the underside as in the picture of rasping above. The well-made shoe must follow exactly the rim of the wall and be neither too wide, too long, nor too short. Too wide a shoe encourages brushing, too long a shoe, projecting beyond the heels, is easily torn off. Too short a shoe allows bruising of the heels and increases the likelihood of corns.

The Healthy Horse

The horse reveals his state of health in his general appearance—for example, he may appear listless or "tucked-up" (when the flanks look hollow), but more specific pointers are his pulse, temperature, respiration and excreta. As always, the well-being of the horse depends on the owner's powers of observation—a quality developed by experience and deliberate application.

The normal temperature of the horse is 100–101.5°F (37.7–38.6°C). Above this, it is likely he has an infection.

The normal pulse rate of the horse is 35–40 beats per minute. Naturally this rises during exertion, but an increase in the pulse rate at rest is usually symptomatic of a feverish condition. If the pulse rate reaches 50 beats per minute, the animal is experiencing pain. A condition of this severity is usually accompanied by sweating.

Respiration at rest is between 8 and 12 breaths per minute. Again, of course, it will be faster during and immediately after exertion. Faster than this at rest, when the breathing will be laboured, indicates pain and will almost certainly be accompanied by a rise in temperature and possibly by sweating also. The respiration rate can be checked by standing behind the horse and counting the number of times the flanks rise and fall in 60 seconds. Each rise and fall equals one breath.

All horses carry a worm burden and regular dosing is an essential part of stable-management. Modern worming pastes can be administered orally, and are usually given at varying intervals on veterinary advice.

Visible Symptoms

Droppings vary in color and consistency according to the food intake. The lush spring grass, for instance, will result in noticeably loose motions. In health, droppings are otherwise generally well formed, slightly moist, and not strong smelling.

Mucus in the droppings results from some derangement of the digestion. Yellow, foul-smelling droppings are usually a sign of a liver disorder and probably indicate the presence of a heavy red-worm infestation.

Urine should not be excessively colored. Thick, cloudy urine is associated with a kidney problem, and bloody water accompanies a kidney inflammation. Excessive urine flow may be caused by a diabetic

The eye is open, bright and alert

The coat has a sheen and the hairs lie flat

The skin has always to be loose and clean

The Indications of Good Health

It is the overall impression that indicates better than anything else the health of the horse, combined with the owner's ability to detect signs of ill health. The conscientious horse owner develops a good eye in these respects and makes sure he supervises his charges regularly and as frequently as possible.

condition, while a constant dribble is usually caused by an inflamed bladder.

The state of the limbs provides a good indication of general health. They ought to feel cool and free from swelling. Pronounced puffiness indicates sprain damage, poor circulation, irritation, or a possible heart condition.

In health the eye is bright and alert, with the membranes under the lids, as well as those of the nostrils, an even pink color. Redness denotes inflammation; white is a sign of debility; yellow is concerned with disorders of the liver, and bright purple occurs as a result of improper blood aeration, as in pneumonia, etc.

The coat should lie flat and carry a sheen, except in the case of horses wintering out. A staring coat, with the hairs appearing to be upright, can mean malnutrition. When hair is easily pulled from the mane, there will probably be other general symptoms of ill health.

A tight skin may also be due to malnutrition or possibly to the onset of some disease. It should be loose and clean, and should return immediately to normal when pulled. If it does not lie flat again quickly when released, the horse is dehydrated.

Teeth are in need of attention when wet or balled food is left in the manger.

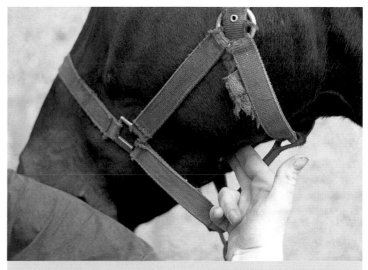

Checking Pulse

You can feel the pulse with your fingers on the inner surface of the lower jaw, just behind the elbow, or just above and behind the eye. The easiest way to work out the pulse rate is to count with a stopwatch the number of beats occurring in 20 seconds and then to multiply by three. Frequent practice will make perfect. Check it every day.

Movement

The horse in good health should appear to be almost literally "bursting with energy." In movement, the horse should display unmistakable vigor. He should move with loose, unrestricted freedom, expressive of supple muscles and complete soundness throughout the skeletal structure.

Common Ailments

No animal is more prone to injury than the horse. He is surprisingly clumsy, and his instinctive defense system, based on swift flight and often violent physical reaction to dangers real or, more often, imagined, can get him into all sorts of trouble. For these reasons he is exceptionally dependent on us and in need of our constant supervision.

The best approach to minor injuries and simple ailments is a combination of common sense and a degree of basic knowledge. Beyond that, it is always advisable to seek veterinary assistance. In fact, a fundamental requirement of good horse management is knowing when to call the veterinarian.

Inoculation and Vaccination

Just like humans, horses and ponies can be protected from serious diseases by inoculation and vaccination. The most serious complaints are tetanus, once known as lockjaw (which was a symptom of the disease). It is caused by the entry of the tetanus bacillus into the body through a wound or scratch, and it is generally fatal.

Equine influenza, whatever the strain of virus, is highly contagious, and the incidence of the disease continues to increase rapidly as improved methods of transport encourage greater

Floating/rasping Teeth
Teeth can become sharp through uneven wear. They need attention every six months.

Good Management
A well-kept stable yard, neat, tidy, and properly maintained. It gives an immediate impression of high standards, happy horses and good management practice.

Worming

All domestic horses harbor parasites, the most dangerous of which is the red worm (strongyle). They can be controlled by regular worming. Administering the paste by syringe makes the job easier.

movement of horses both within national boundaries and throughout the world.

Both these potential killer diseases can be prevented by vaccination and courses of injections. The majority of large horse shows and competitions make immunization a condition of entry.

Wounds

The best horse management manuals categorize wounds as follows: punctures; cuts and tears (lacerations); deep wounds; and bruise wounds.

The most common puncture wounds can be caused by a thorn, which is a reason for regular inspection of the legs, particularly after riding cross-country. Once located, the thorn has to be removed and a simple poultice will then take care of any residual infection. In some cases the veterinarian will recommend an antibiotic. If the thorn cannot be removed, the veterinarian has to cut it out. Serious punctures made by stakes, nails and so on, as well as punctures to the sole of the foot, need veterinary attention and thereafter will usually require poulticing.

Small cuts and tears can be washed clean with a mild disinfectant solution, or one made with salt or Epsom salts, and then treated with a wound powder. More serious injuries, which need to be stitched, will require veterinary attention and antibiotics.

Deep wounds are more troublesome and may bleed profusely. If the bleeding is venous, it will be dull red in colour and can be controlled by generous applications of water from the hosepipe. Arterial bleeding is more frightening, as the bright scarlet blood spurts violently from the wound. In the first place, control the bleeding by applying pressure *on the wound* (a padded, flat pebble or coin) and wrapping tightly over it; but it will need veterinary attention—and quickly.

Bruise wounds may be caused by kicks or blows and are not always easily detected. Cold water or cold packs are the answer, but if the wound occurs where bones are close to the surface it can be dangerous and will need professional examination.

In all these cases, rest is essential to allow time for the healing process. Rest, as well as the immediate removal of the offending piece of saddlery, is also the solution to girth, saddle and bit galls. These injuries are the result of bad management and are unforgivable. The horse should not be worked until the wound has been effectively treated and has properly healed.

POULTICING A WOUND

1 Poulticing a puncture wound in the foot follows drainage of the wound. The poultice, of whatever material, is then packed into the foot and covered with plastic to continue the drawing process. Thereafter it has to be kept in place.

2 The foot has then to be bandaged, a job for an expert, and then fitted with a purpose-made rubber poultice boot, or something similar. Even a strong, plastic bag secured to the leg can be surprisingly effective.

Detection and Prevention

Trotting Out
Trotting the horse to enable the onlooker to detect lameness has to be done on a hard, level surface.

Lameness in a horse, ranging from temporary lameness to some conditions for which there is no certain cure, is a common condition and the causes are numerous. They are usually found in the feet and lower limbs, but the source can also occur in the shoulder, where it is more difficult to detect.

To pinpoint the source of lameness or the general area involved, the horse needs to be trotted out on a loosely held lead-rope, on hard, level ground.

Lameness in the forelegs is detected by watching the head as the horse is trotted towards you. If the horse "nods" and the head rises and falls, the lame leg is the one on which the head is raised.

To detect lameness in the hind limbs, the horse is trotted away from you. Watch the highest part of the quarters, which will rise and fall quite clearly. The lame leg is the one upon which the corresponding hip is raised, i.e., raised left hip shows lameness in left hind leg. Usually, in cases of shoulder lameness, the toe of the affected leg is dragged and the leg is not carried so far forward as the other one. At rest, the horse holds the affected limb, resting on the toe, behind the sound leg. Where there is severe lameness in the foreleg, the horse holds the affected leg pointed out in front. In all cases, there is usually heat in the leg or foot.

Foot Problems
Sprains are, of course, a common cause of lameness, along with bruised soles caused by treading on a sharp stone or something similar; corns are also a factor and occur generally because the shoes have been left on too long. Thrush, another avoidable condition that contributes to lameness, is caused when the horse stands in a dirty stable. There is a foul-smelling discharge from the cleft of the frog, which can be treated with disinfectant, when the feet have been pared, and then with Stockholm tar.

Laminitis, an acute inflammation within the protective wall of the foot, is disabling and very painful. Ponies on lush grazing are particularly susceptible. The dreaded navicular disease appears first as intermittent lameness. It is connected with a degeneration of the navicular bone of the foot (*see* pp.216–17) and, while the condition can be alleviated, there is no real cure.

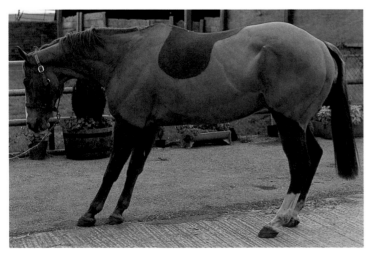

Severe Laminitis
This is a severe case of laminitis that requires expert veterinary supervision. The disease is now better understood than ever before, and treatment can bring some relief from pain. Diet is a major factor, as is expert trimming of the feet.

Bucking
Bucking can be triggered by resentment or just a sense of fun. Conversely, it might signal back pain caused by a pulled muscle or the discomfort of a badly fitting saddle. Persistent bucking should be thoroughly investigated.

Digestive, Skin, and Respiratory Problems

Digestive complaints are centred round colic, the equine equivalent of the human tummy ache. Severe cases need immediate veterinary attention.

Skin diseases, even the distressing sweet itch caused by midges, can usually be contained by drugs and sensible management.

Respiratory diseases are more common than in the past and are usually due to dust allergies. The answer is to feed dust-free, bagged hay and use paper or rubber-mat bedding.

Coughs and colds affect horses as much as humans. Plenty of fresh air, rest, a laxative diet and a cough mixture smeared on the tongue will usually bring relief. There are also modern and very effective antibiotics available.

Soaking Hay

Soaking hay well before feeding helps to reduce the dust spores that can exacerbate respiratory problems.

Did you know?

Epsom salts are one of the most versatile substances. For dietary problems causing a pimply condition of the skin, a large handful of salts in the feed works wonders. They are also good for swollen legs if mixed with glycerine and applied in a paste.

Colic Symptoms

Colic is the equine equivalent of tummy ache but can be far more dangerous. The horse displays uneasiness by continually glancing at the flanks, and in severe cases may roll violently. Veterinary assistance should be sought before the horse reaches this dangerous point.

Natural Healing

In the 21st century an industry has grown up around natural healing treatments for every sort of complaint suffered by humans and, increasingly, horses, too. In some areas, like physiotherapy and to an extent homeopathy, there is acceptance by the medical and veterinary professions, while electronic therapies have long been practiced in the treatment of both humans and horses.

Sometimes, unfortunately, extravagant claims are made by manufacturers of natural products—many of which are of herbal origin—and for the most part there is no scientific proof to support these claims. However, that is no reason to think that they do not work with certain horses, in certain conditions. The same, of course, is true, to a degree, in the human context, where conventional medical treatment is based on carefully monitored synthetic drugs. The latter are characterized by relatively swift reactions, whereas treatment using natural medicine is cumulative, producing slower, long-term results, but without the side-effects of synthetic drugs.

Homeopathy

Foremost in the field of natural medicine is homeopathy. Christian Samuel Hahnemann, the 18th-century pioneer of the science, adopted the phrase *Similia similibus curentur*, "Let like be treated by like," and was concerned to stimulate the body to heal itself. There are very few conditions that cannot be treated by homeopathy. Even when surgical intervention is necessary, homeopathy can play a supportive role. Some of the best-known homeopathic remedies are Arnica, Rhus toxicadendrum and Ruta. The latter two are used to counter the effect of sprains and strains, while the versatile Arnica is used to treat cases of extreme exertion (as occurs during horse trials or racing), and is also very effective when used to alleviate severe bruising, shock and stress.

Herbal Remedies

Less complex are the herbal remedies, many of which, including comfrey, devil's claw and dandelion, are used in the long-term treatment of arthritic inflammation and reduced circulation.

Aromatherapy and Acupuncture

Aromatherapy, based on essential oils and essences, is practiced on horses as well as humans, as is acupuncture, one of the oldest medical therapies in the world. Equine acupuncture, which uses 8in (20cm) needles, is reinforced with herbs, which are either burned briefly on the skin or are inserted under the skin at the acupuncture points.

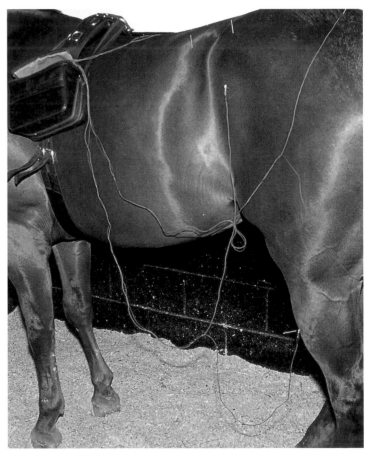

Electronic Therapy

Various forms of electronic therapy are used successfully to treat the effects of muscle strain and bruising caused either by accident or as the result of extreme exertion during competition. Indeed, electronics can be used to assist treatments by acupuncture, intensifying the action of the needles.

Physiotherapy

The *qualified* horse physiotherapist plays an increasingly important role in the treatment of injuries brought about, largely, as a result of the lifestyle of the modern horse. These highly-skilled practitioners have an in-depth knowledge of horse anatomy and physiology and work in conjunction with the veterinarian. However, treatment by unqualified persons can be dangerous.

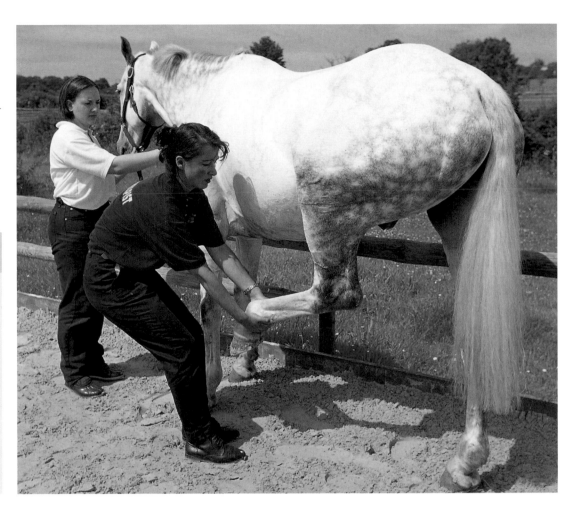

Did you know?

In China, where acupuncture has been practised for over 3,000 years, every country commune has two medical practitioners, one employing Western medicine and the other practicing acupuncture.

Massage and Manipulation

Physiotherapy, which is very much older than conventional medicine, is an accepted and significant complementary therapy in the treatment of humans and animals. A range of machines is now in use, extending the positive effects of hand massage.

Chiropractors are concerned with manipulation of any misplacements of the bone structure, as might occur as the result of a heavy fall or blow or, indeed, from bad riding techniques.

Like physiotherapists, chiropractors are highly skilled practitioners and must hold appropriate qualifications before practicing.

Swimming

Today, a natural therapy that is playing an increasingly significant part in equine convalescence is swimming. Swimming allows the limbs to be exercised without the damaging effects of concussion that can result from conventional exercise. It is widely practiced in the treatment of injuries to competition horses and racehorses and has very good results in these instances.

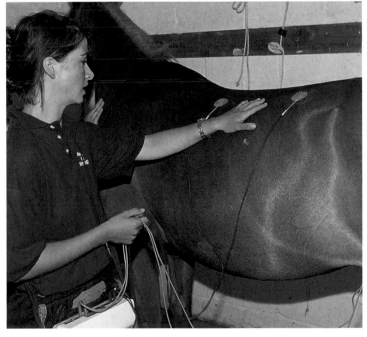

Targeting Pain

Electronics, properly applied by expert and qualified practitioners, can pinpoint the source of pain and be used to monitor the effects of subsequent treatment. Back pain is as common in horses as humans. In horses, it can be caused by excessive effort or exertion or, which is common, by an inexpertly fitted or constructed saddle and an inexperienced or incompetent rider.

TACK AND EQUIPMENT

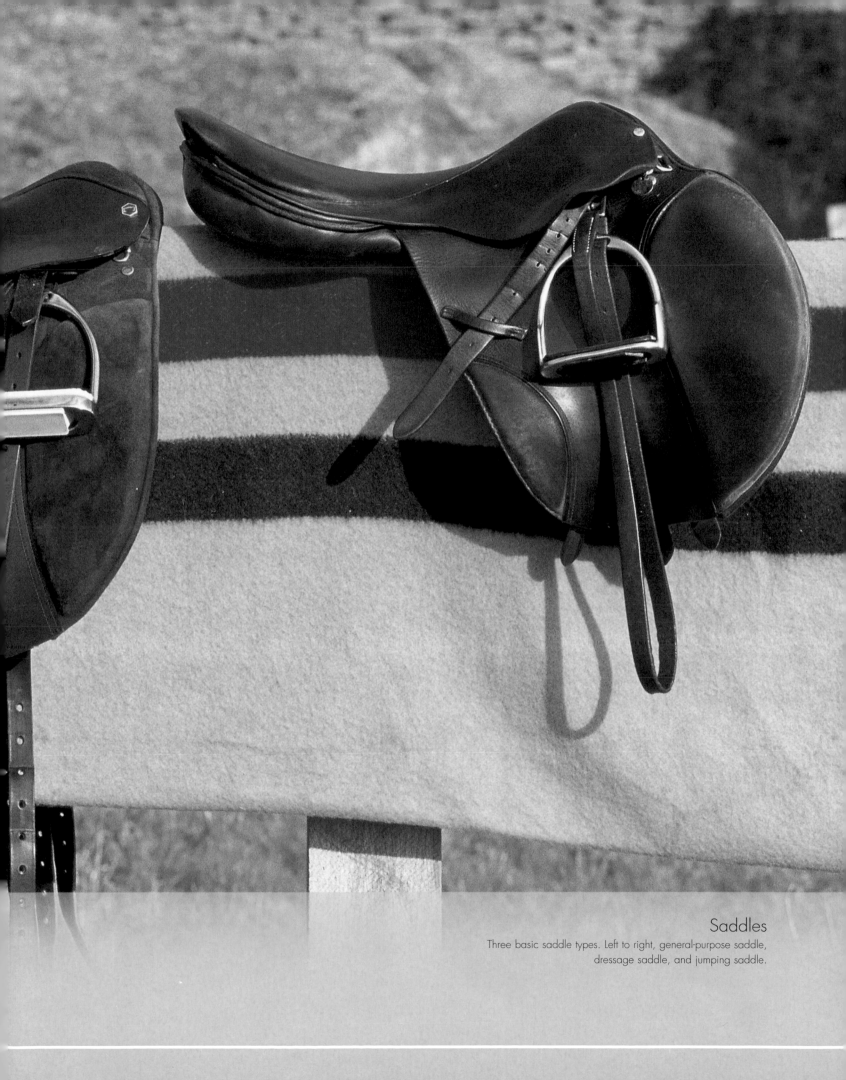

Saddles

Three basic saddle types. Left to right, general-purpose saddle, dressage saddle, and jumping saddle.

The Saddle

Saddles are built on a frame called the "tree," which is made of either laminated wood or molded plastic reinforced with metal. The tree is fitted with the stirrup "bars," to carry the leathers and stirrup irons, and is made in a range of sizes and fittings. The tree is in effect the "skeleton" of the saddle, defining its ultimate size and shape.

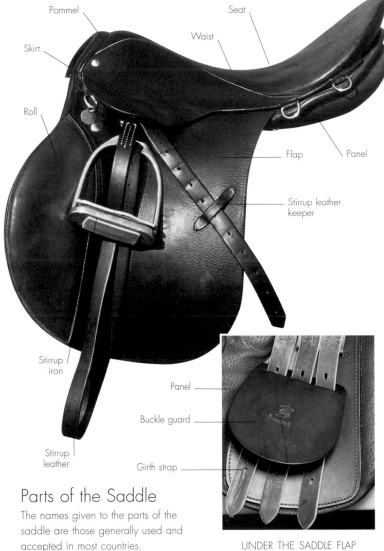

Pommel
Seat
Skirt
Waist
Roll
Flap
Panel
Stirrup leather keeper
Stirrup iron
Stirrup leather

A spring tree, common to most modern saddles, is made when two sections of sprung steel are laid along the wooden frame from the head (or pommel) to the cantle. They give a resilience to the seat, which allows the rider closer contact with the horse and is thought to be more comfortable for both.

The tree is covered with leather or a synthetic material, and the seat itself is padded. Girth straps are attached to webs passed over the arms of the tree and then a "panel" is fitted and stuffed with wool to act as a cushion between the tree and the horse's back.

The design of the saddle is governed by its intended purpose, and the trend is increasingly towards the creation of very specialist designs to meet the requirements of the various disciplines.

Parts of the Saddle

The names given to the parts of the saddle are those generally used and accepted in most countries.

Panel
Buckle guard
Girth strap

UNDER THE SADDLE FLAP

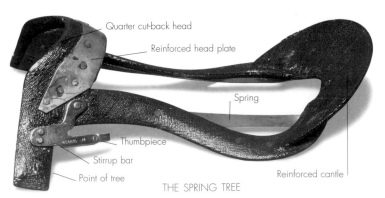

Quarter cut-back head
Reinforced head plate
Spring
Thumbpiece
Stirrup bar
Point of tree
Reinforced cantle

THE SPRING TREE

Quarter cut-back head

General purpose (GP) Saddle

The general purpose saddle is the pattern most suitable for the majority of riders wishing to ride at middle level in a variety of activities. Indeed, it is the middle-of-the-road all-rounder.

Saddle Design

The two extremes of saddle design are represented by the lightweight racing saddle, weighing as little as 1lb (2.2kg) and acting as no more than an anchor for similarly lightweight stirrup irons and leathers, and the highly specialized dressage saddle appropriate to high-level competition. In between there are jumping and event saddles, general-purpose designs, polo saddles, and saddles suitable for endurance riding. The Western saddle and to a lesser degree the Australian stock saddle are entities in their own right.

The purpose of any well-designed modern saddle is to provide maximum comfort, security, and control (all interdependent) while positioning the body in relation to the movement and as near as possible to the horse's center of balance (*see* p.173).

Types of Saddle

The dressage saddle is characterized by a fairly dipped seat, and it is cut straight in front with the bars set to the rear (an extended bar) to allow for the long leg position. It is a saddle for the experienced, educated rider.

The flap of the jumping saddle is cut much further forward to accommodate the shorter leg position. Some patterns are dipped in the seat but many employ the flatter seat and most claim "close contact" as a result.

Synthetic Saddles

The modern range of synthetic saddles is comprehensive and well designed and constructed. The saddles' polymer trees are consistently symmetrical (which is not always the case with the laminated wooden tree), and the material is comfortable, waterproof and easy to maintain. They are also cheaper than their leather counterparts.

There is no definitive design for the endurance saddle but the patterns are built to ensure the spread of the weight over as big an area of the back as possible and to afford maximum comfort to horse and rider.

Polo saddles come closer to the old type of English hunting saddle than others and are often made on a very strong "rigid" tree, i.e., one without "springs." The flap is not inclined too forward, nor is the seat noticeably dipped, and support rolls are not much in evidence. They are very strong throughout to conform to the demanding requirements of the game.

For most riders a general purpose saddle, with a certain dip to the seat, supportive rolls, and not cut too far forward, will be the most practical choice.

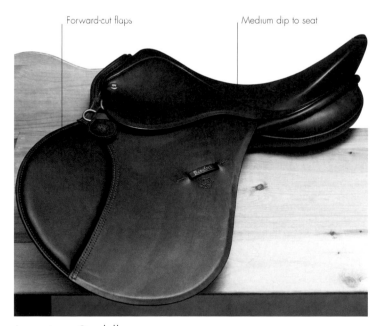

Forward-cut flaps   Medium dip to seat

Jumping Saddle

The jumping saddle is cut forward in the flap to accommodate the rider's shorter leg position. Very often the seat is flatter than that of either the dressage or the general purpose saddle.

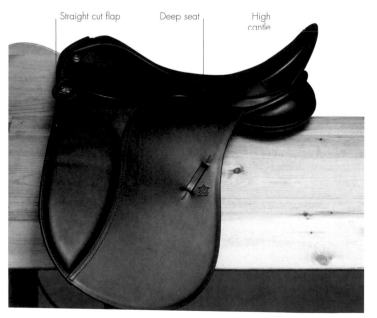

Straight cut flap   Deep seat   High cantle

Dressage Saddle

The dressage saddle is cut to reflect the longer leg position required, and the stirrup bar is set further to the rear. There is usually strong support for the thigh combined with a deep seat.

Saddles and Mountings

Saddle mountings comprise the girth, stirrup leathers, and the stirrup irons. There are numerous patterns of leather girths, and a number made from nylon or cotton covering a center of resilient foam. The most common leather girths are the three-fold, made from soft baghide and folded as the name suggests. A good one will be supplied with a lining of serge in the fold, which can be greased to further soften the leather. The Balding and Atherstone girths are both shaped at the elbow to prevent the risk of galling in that area.

Specialist Girths

Dressage girths are shorter than the conventional ones and are attached to long, extended girth straps. The object is to remove any bulk, caused by the buckles, from under the rider's thigh, and in this they succeed very well.

Many girths are made with elastic inserts and some are made entirely from broad elastic web, so as to allow for the expansion of the lungs at moments of peak effort. These are popular in competitive riding. Racing girths, most often used in pairs, each girth terminating in a single buckle, can be made from elastic or from wool web. They are used in conjunction with a surcingle or over-girth (fitted over the top of a saddle), an item usually fitted for eventers and showjumpers also.

Stirrups

The best stirrup leathers are made from oak-bark tanned, pre-stretched ox-hide, or from the "unbreakable" red buffalo hide. It won't break but it does stretch and goes on stretching.

Stirrup irons are made of stainless steel and are usually used with rubber stirrup treads. There are also some ingenious "safety" irons that will allow the foot to go free in the event of a fall.

The Western Saddle

Western saddles originated from those brought to the New World by the Spanish conquistadores. Over the years, they were adapted to meet local needs but they were all influenced by the practicalities of working cattle. The horn acts as a post to which the lariat (lasso) is tied when roping an animal. It came into general use in the early 19th century and remains a feature common to Western saddles.

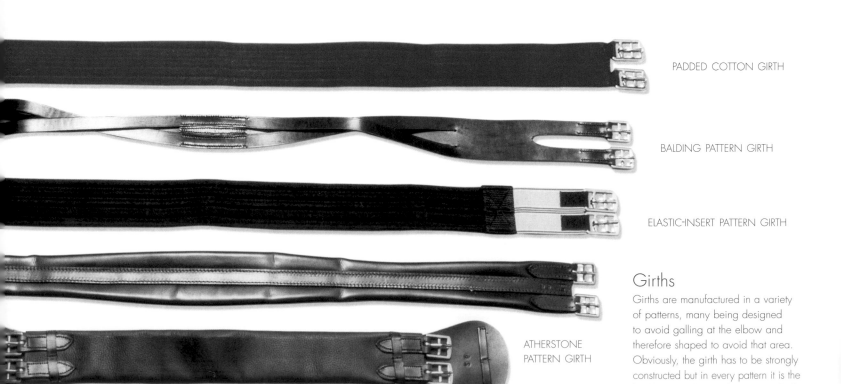

PADDED COTTON GIRTH

BALDING PATTERN GIRTH

ELASTIC-INSERT PATTERN GIRTH

ATHERSTONE PATTERN GIRTH

SHORT DRESSAGE GIRTH

Girths

Girths are manufactured in a variety of patterns, many being designed to avoid galling at the elbow and therefore shaped to avoid that area. Obviously, the girth has to be strongly constructed but in every pattern it is the buckle that is the weakest point. Ideally this should be made of stainless steel.

Essentially, the Western saddle was designed as a work platform for the cowboy who spent long hours on horseback. It is heavy by comparison with European, English seat saddles, but it is comfortable for the rider, whose weight is carried over the largest possible area of the horse's back and, since it is always used with a pad or blanket, it rarely gives rise to back problems. Just as much a working saddle is the Australian stock (or "buckjumping") saddle.

Western Bridle

In the later stages of training the bridle incorporates the long-cheeked bit with a ported mouth. This bridle is secured by two ear-loops and has no throatlatch.

The long-cheeked bit is usual for the schooled Western horse

Strong, supporting cantle increases rider's security

Sometimes horses are bitted in snaffles rather than in the Western curb bit

Wide, wooden stirrup attached to the "fender"

Western Rigging

Western saddles are secured by the cinch (from *cincha*, meaning girth), which fastens to the rigging either on-tree or in-skirt – that is, the ring to which the cinch is attached is either on the rigging straps on the saddle tree or built into the skirt. Western saddles, like European ones, are made in patterns to suit a variety of purposes.

SADDLING UP WESTERN STYLE

1 A thick, folded blanket is first put on the back, care being taken to ensure that it lies flat without being wrinkled.

2 The heavy saddle is then lifted onto the back while ensuring that the blanket is not disturbed in any way.

3 The saddle is secured by the cinch attached to the rigging. It needs to be tight enough to prevent slipping upon mounting.

4 Finally the bridle is fitted and checked over. In this case the throatlatch passes through the loops of the browband.

Saddle Fitting

While the saddle must suit the rider and the purpose, it is even more important that it fits the horse. A badly fitting saddle causes pain and impedes the movement substantially. Additionally, it can lead to resentment and rebellion. Most riders appreciate the importance of the saddle, but the principles of saddle fitting, which were well known 100 and 200 years ago, are not always so well understood today.

The basic saddle requirement is that it should:
- Conform to the shape of the horse's back;
- Avoid the possibility of damaging any part with which it comes in contact;
- Afford complete comfort;
- Not restrict the freedom and potential of the natural movement.

The Saddle Tree

To begin with, the tree itself (*see* p.228) must fit the back and then the finished saddle (so long as it is constructed without error) will also fit. Too broad a tree will press on the wither with obvious results. If it is too narrow, the points (the extensions below the side-bars) will pinch painfully. Too long a tree would put pressure on the loin where it could cause serious damage; too short a tree would concentrate the rider's weight over too small an area.

◄ Check Forearch
When the rider is mounted, she should check that the forearch is sufficiently clear of the wither by inserting three fingers beneath it.

Check that point of tree is not exerting pressure

Saddle must fit rider as well as horse

Flap must not interfere with horse's shoulder

When mounted, tighten girth by a single hole

Check Flap
Check that the saddle flap is not so far forward that it interferes with the movement of the shoulder. It is also very important to check that the points of the tree (*see* p.228) are not exerting pressure.

Fitting Guidelines
Check the points made above, then check the saddle's construction, in particular the width of the channel dividing the panel. Make sure that when the rider is mounted it is possible to see clearance from the cantle to the pommel when viewed from behind. Trot the horse out to observe the freedom of movement.

The Correct Fit Under Saddle

When the rider is in place in the saddle there must be clearance of the spine along its length and across its width. The forearch has to be sufficiently clear of the wither to allow the insertion of three fingers between the two. Similarly, the cantle should not exert any direct pressure. The clearance across the backbone depends on the width of the channel dividing the panel. It needs to be 2.5–3in (6.4–7.6cm), at least, along the whole length of the saddle.

If there is pressure on any part of the spinal complex the horse will try to avoid it by hollowing his back. Apart from the discomfort, which may cause the horse to refuse to jump, the stride will be noticeably shortened.

Panel and Flaps

At no time should the cut of the panel and flaps interfere with the movement of the scapula (shoulder). A saddle cut too far forward so that it lies on the big trapezius muscle, instead of behind it, restricts the movement of the shoulder and shortens the stride.

The panel has to bear evenly over the whole back surface, so that the rider's weight is spread over as large an area as possible. It has also to be "in balance," being flocked evenly so that one side is not higher than the other, for example.

Very obviously, the panel has to be smooth and free from irregularities. A lump in the panel, for instance, would cause a point of pressure, just as a wrinkle

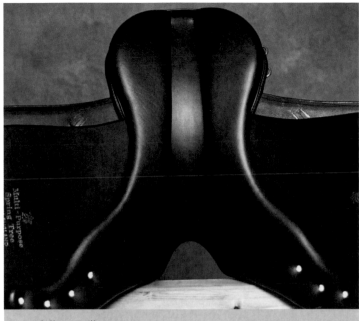

Saddle Gullet

If the saddle is to exert no inhibiting pressure on the horse's spinal complex, the gullet (the channel dividing the panel) must be at least 2.5–3in (6.25–7.5cm) wide along its length. Remember that an ill-fitting saddle can *never* be made to fit simply by placing a thick numnah underneath it.

in your sock would start to cause a blister on a long-distance walk.

Snug Fit

Finally, while the saddle conforms to all those criteria, it should also fit as closely as possible. If it sits too high off the back it will rock and cause friction. That, in turn, is a source of soreness.

PUTTING ON A SADDLE

1 The instructor, approaching from the near side, carries the saddle on her forearm preparatory to placing it on the back in front of the wither.

2 She slides the saddle back into place, then fastens the girth, not too tightly, on the girth straps, making sure that it lies flat and is not pinching.

3 She checks the saddle fit from the off side and makes sure that the girth has not been twisted or is in any other way out of place.

4 This is the saddle in place on the horse's back. A light numnah is also used but this does not affect the fit of this well-made saddle.

Bits and Bridles

To understand the role of the bit, it follows that you need to be familiar with: the parts of the head and mouth involved in bitting and the result of pressures being applied to them; the types of bit available and the effect of variations occurring within a group; the effect of the various types of auxiliaries that may be used with the bit; the conformation of the bit.

The Bridle

A bridle comprises the leather parts: the headpiece which incorporates the throatlatch, spelled that way but pronounced throatlash. To the headpiece are attached the cheekpieces (often simply called cheeks) and the front or browband. In the double bridle (*see* p.236) there is the addition of the sliphead, which carries the bridoon. Then there are the reins and the noseband and, to complete the bridle, the bit or bits.

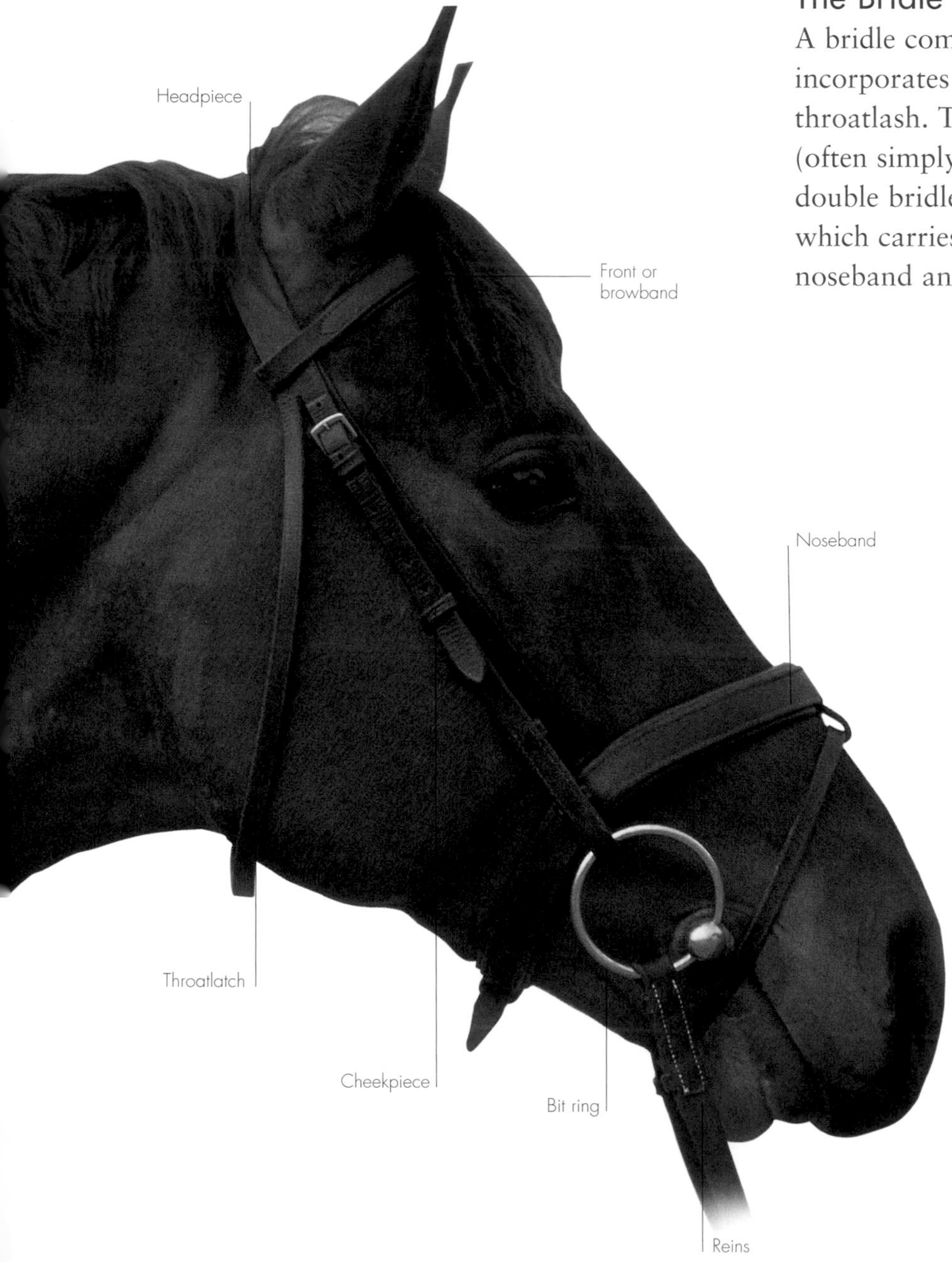

Headpiece

Front or browband

Noseband

Throatlatch

Cheekpiece

Bit ring

Reins

Parts of the Bridle

Just as there are names given to the points of the horse so it is helpful to have names for the various parts that make up the complete bridle.

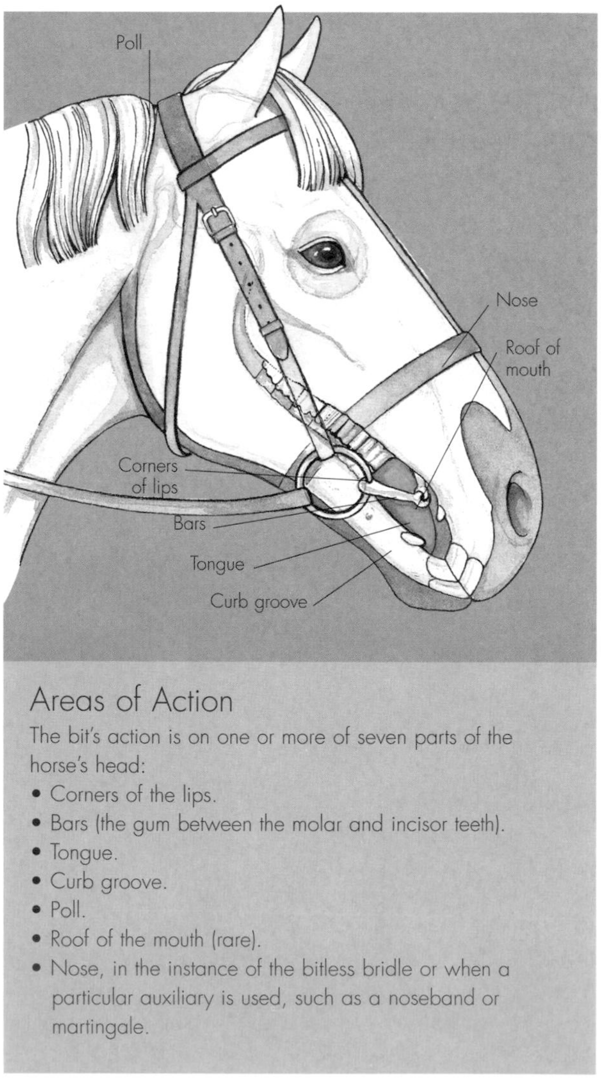

Poll

Nose

Roof of mouth

Corners of lips

Bars

Tongue

Curb groove

Areas of Action

The bit's action is on one or more of seven parts of the horse's head:
- Corners of the lips.
- Bars (the gum between the molar and incisor teeth).
- Tongue.
- Curb groove.
- Poll.
- Roof of the mouth (rare).
- Nose, in the instance of the bitless bridle or when a particular auxiliary is used, such as a noseband or martingale.

The object in fitting the bridle (*see* below) is to safeguard the comfort of the horse. Too tight a throatlatch will, to all intents, throttle him. Too tight a browband will pull the headpiece forward to press on the back of the ears. This is uncomfortable and will cause the horse to shake his head in irritation. The noseband should fit snugly but not tightly (too tight a noseband is a common failing with modern riders).

Fitting the Bit

The snaffle bit, the bridoon of the double bridle, and the Pelham (*see* pp.236–37) should fit just high enough to wrinkle the corners of the mouth. It should be neither too big nor too small, but should correspond to the width of the mouth. The curb bit (which fits below the bridoon on the double bridle) and the Pelham should rest comfortably on the bars. Both, of course, should fit the mouth snugly so that the bit cannot be slid across the mouth to the detriment of its central action.

Action and Pressure

The action of the bit and the degree of pressure applied to the mouth will vary according to the following factors:

- The construction of the bit.
- The conformation of the mouth.
- The angle at which the mouth is carried in relation to the hand.
- The type of any accessory fitted to strengthen the action of the bit or to accentuate a particular characteristic.

What is very certain is that the bit and its action is only as effective as the rider's ability to use the supporting aids of the legs and body. As someone said, "It's not the bit you put in his mouth, but the hands on the end of it." And the hands, of course, depend on the rider having acquired the desirable independent seat, which is the result of having learned to ride properly.

PUTTING ON A BRIDLE

1 With the right hand round the nose and holding the bridle, the left hand holds the bit preparatory to slipping it into the mouth.

2 Sliding a thumb into the side of the mouth encourages it to open. The bit is slipped in—but without banging the teeth.

3 The bit is now in the mouth and held in place by the trainer's right hand and the bridle can be moved back over the ears.

4 The bridle is put gently over the ears, the trainer being careful not to pull the ears and so cause the horse to throw its head.

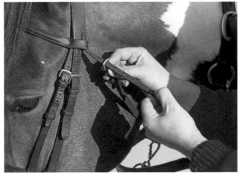

5 The throatlatch can now be fastened sufficiently loosely to allow the insertion of two fingers between it and the throat.

6 The bridle is now in place and all adjustments have been made to the trainer's satisfaction.

Types of Bits

There are five principal bit groups, with a variety of patterns in each, and all are an extension of the hand aid. They are: snaffle; curb, usually used with a bridoon (a light snaffle) as in the double bridle; Pelham; gag; and nose, which is also known as a bitless bridle or, incorrectly, hackamore.

Snaffle

The snaffle group, which has more variations than any other, is still the simplest form of control. The mildest of the snaffles is that with a mullen, or half-moon, mouthpiece, particularly if it is made of soft polyurethane. A little sharper and possibly more effective is the jointed mouthpiece, which can act like a nutcracker across the lower jaw.

It is generally accepted that the snaffle acts upwards against the corners of the lips, but, in fact, a lot depends on the head carriage. If the head is lower than the hand then the action is, indeed, upwards. As the training progresses, the head is carried higher and the face comes nearer to being vertical, the rein forming a straight line with the hand. The action is then increasingly across the lower jaw.

Double

This is the most advanced form of bitting and the most complex in its action. It employs two reins and two bits in the mouth, the bridoon (light snaffle), which raises the head, and the curb bit, which encourages the horse to flex at the poll and in the lower jaw while carrying the head in the near-vertical plane. The mouthpiece of the curb is made with a central "port," allowing room

SNAFFLE

DOUBLE BRIDLE

GAG

PELHAM

for the tongue, and the bit rests on the bars of the mouth. If the port were unusually high it would exert severe pressure on the roof of the mouth.

The curb bit comes into play when the cheeks (*see* above right) take up an angle of 45 degrees in response to pressure on the curb rein. In that position the "eye" of the bit, above the mouthpiece (*see* above right), which is fastened to the bridle head, moves forwards

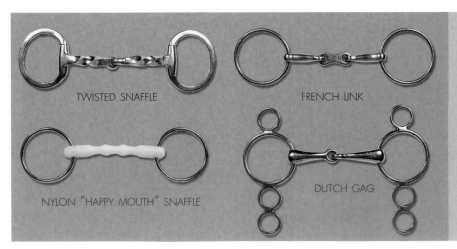
TWISTED SNAFFLE

FRENCH LINK

NYLON "HAPPY MOUTH" SNAFFLE

DUTCH GAG

Snaffle Types

The twisted snaffle is a powerful "stopping" bit that in rough hands can cause pain and bruising. It has no place in educated riding. The French Link or French Bradoon, is softer in its action across the lower jaw because it has the effect of reducing the intensity of the "nutcracker" action of the ordinary centrally jointed snaffle. The link lies comfortably on the tongue. The "Happy Mouth" snaffle of flexible polyurethane conforms to the shape of the mouth and "gives" according to the pressure applied by either hand or horse. It is mild and eminently sensible. The Dutch Gag is, in fact, a multi-ring snaffle that can exert downward pressure on the poll depending upon to which ring the rein is attached.

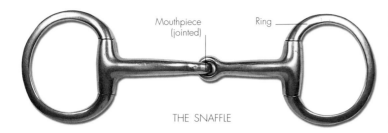

THE SNAFFLE

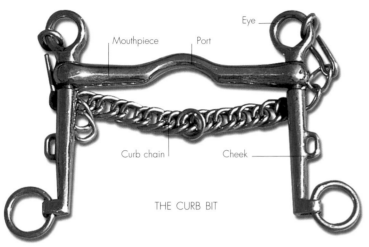

THE CURB BIT

Snaffle and Curb

The jointed snaffle illustrated is fitted with eggbutt cheeks that prevent the bit sliding across the mouth and minimize the risk of pinching the lips. The curb bit has a slide- or turn-cheek previously termed "Ward Union". It is less popular and probably less efficient than a fixed-cheek bit.

and puts downward pressure on the poll. Meanwhile, the curb chain, attached to the eye and lying in the curb groove, tightens to encourage a relaxation of the lower jaw and a retraction of the nose.

Pelham

The Pelham bridle has a single mouthpiece and two reins, and attempts to achieve the same result as the double bridle, which it clearly does not. Nonetheless, it is a useful, kind bit and many horses go well in it, especially when it has a plain, mullen mouthpiece, which spreads pressure over the tongue instead of concentrating it on the bars.

Gag

The gag bridle is really an exaggerated snaffle. It is fitted with bit rings that have a hole top and bottom through which the cheek of the bridle is passed before being attached to the rein. The upward action is consequently increased very considerably and gives a lot of control over a hard-pulling horse. It is very popular as a cross-country bridle.

Hackamore

The hackamore is in reality the Californian system of bitting that begins with a heavy noseband that is gradually replaced by a succession of increasingly lightweight ones; it culminates in the fitting of a long-cheeked curb bit. By that time the horse will go happily and in balance on a loose, looping rein, bit pressure being no more than minimal.

Accessories

The word describes pieces of equipment that support or strengthen the bit, notably nosebands and martingales. Nosebands can be adjusted so that they close the mouth, preventing evasion of the bit's action, and exert pressure on the nose, which helps to keep the head in place.

Martingales prevent the horse from throwing up the head and/or carrying the mouth higher than the hand, so increasing the rider's control. The most common is the running martingale, made with rings through which the rein can be passed. It acts to bring downward pressure on the mouth. In far less general use is the standing martingale, which is attached to the noseband and keeps the head in position by exerting downward pressure directly on the nose.

Nose or Bitless Bridle
The bitless bridle, not necessarily a hackamore, exerts control through pressure applied on the nose, the severity of which depends on the degree of leverage made possible by the length of the cheek. Because there are no bits in the mouth, the nose or bitless bridle is often regarded as being mild in its action. In fact, in the wrong hands, it can be very severe and cause soreness and callousing of the nose.

Boots and Blankets

Boots, and bandages too, are used as a protection against injuries that may result from blows caused by the horse striking into himself when working, loss of balance while travelling, or, perhaps, by slipping up when on roads or tracks. Equestrian clothing in all its variety plays an important part in the overall management of the horse.

The most usual injuries (caused by interfering) are "brushing", "overreaching" and, to a lesser degree, by "speedicutting." Brushing is when the inside of the leg, usually around the fetlock joint, is struck by the opposite foot. Boots, therefore, are cupped round the joint and mostly made from shock-absorbent material. An overreach can be a painful and disabling injury. It occurs when the toes of the hind feet strike into the heels of the forelegs. Rubber, bell-shaped boots fitted over the hoof and covering the heels will provide very adequate protection. Speedicutting is fortunately less common. It occurs when the hind foot strikes the inside of the opposite leg above the joint and just below the hock when the horse is galloping fast. The speedicut boot is, therefore, shaped to provide protection in that area.

Boots and wraps are also used to give support, especially to the tendons of the forelegs. Competition horses are always fitted with protective boots, and the legs may also be wrapped. Polo ponies are always played with strong boots, fitted all round to give protection to the whole lower leg. Polo boots are also very useful when schooling young horses whose co-ordination is not fully developed.

Boots that enclose the whole lower leg are necessary when travelling, and knee-caps or boots are a sensible protection against slipping when riding on roads.

Blankets

Horse blankets, usually called sheets, rugs, or simply "horse clothing" in the UK and Ireland, are available in enormous variety and in every sort of fabric, from the warm duvet-type stable blanket to the thermal and mesh sheets that will prevent sweating after work. The majority are carefully constructed and well shaped, which was not always the case in the past.

New Zealand rugs are indispensable to the well-equipped tack room. They are made from strong waterproof material, often blanket-lined, and offer good protection against wet and cold for horses and ponies turned out in the paddock. They originated in New Zealand but are in use almost universally and, not unreasonably, are often termed "turnout" rugs. They are available in a range of weights, since it can be raining heavily when the temperature is moderate enough.

Very light turnout rugs are used in summer conditions to combat the nuisance of flies. The cotton ones are, indeed, called summer sheets and are not, of course, waterproof.

◄Brushing and Overreach Boots

Easily fitted, Velcro-fastening brushing boots give protection against knocks, while the rubber overreach boots protect the heel from injuries inflicted by a blow from a hind toe.

Knee Boots►

Protection for the knees is a sensible precaution to take when riding horses on potentially slippery roadways or when travelling. Scarred knees are a permanent disfigurement as well as being unsightly.

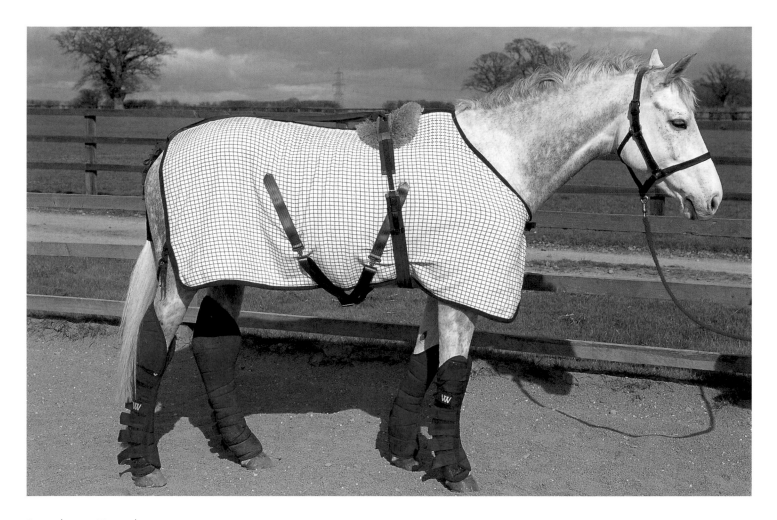

Ready to Travel

Dressed to travel comfortably in the box or trailer, this horse is wearing a light thermal sheet secured with surcingles. His tail is wrapped lest it should be rubbed, and all four legs are protected by full-length boots extending over the joints and down to the coronet.

For travelling and stable use there are "breathable," thermal type sheets; heavy, quilted blankets, often made in polypropylene, which has the advantage of being easily cleaned; and, for "Sunday best" occasions, opulent wool blankets, which can be further enhanced by sewing the owner's initials on the quarters.

Then there are exercise sheets, waterproof or wool, fitted under the saddle of the clipped horse to lie over the back as protection against cold and wet. As with all blankets, it is advisable to fit a fillet-string from the back edges round the quarters to save the blanket being blown up in the wind.

Wool stable blankets and exercise sheets are often made in fawn wool with black, red and blue stripes. Traditionally, the cloth is made at Witney, UK, and was first manufactured for the Hudson Bay Company, which traded it to the native Canadians for furs.

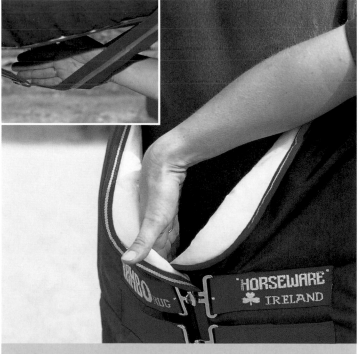

Fitting Tips

The blanket has to be big enough to ensure that it does not rub, particularly in the area of the shoulder. The surcingles keeping it in place should allow for the insertion of a hand between the strap and the body.

Care and Cleaning

Leather is the basic material used in the manufacture of saddlery, and if we are to keep our tack in good order we have to know something about its special properties.

In the first place, good leather has plenty of substance—thickness—so as to absorb and retain the fat content acquired in the dressing process. Secondly, although it may seem an obvious remark, it has two sides, the flesh and the grain. The flesh is the inside and is capable of absorbing, and losing (through the pores in the leather), the grease that keeps it soft and supple. The outside, or grain side, is dressed, printed, and waterproofed, during which process the pores are closed and so are not able to absorb a fat dressing.

Fat Content

The fat content is the "lifeblood" of leather. A percentage of it is lost every day in the course of use and it needs to be replenished, just as our bodies need food to replace our used energy.

The three factors that cause the fat content to be lost and the leather to become hard and brittle are: water, heat and neglect. Water, particularly hot water, melts and removes the fat, whereas heat dries it out. In fact, bridles and girths lose some of the fat content every

Learning the Right Way
To clean tack properly you must first take it to pieces. Then with a damp sponge or cloth you can get rid of the accumulated dirt and sweat deposits.

time they are used because of the heat and sweat from the horse's body. It would not, therefore, be advisable or sensible to wash tack in hot water after use or dry it off in front of a radiator or over the kitchen stove. If you do, the leather dries and becomes both brittle and dangerous.

Soap and Dressing

Before applying a dressing to the flesh side of the leather, where the pores can receive it, the sweat deposits, which block the pores, have to be removed with a damp sponge and warm water.

The grain side, of either saddle or bridle, can be finished off with saddle soap applied with a slightly damp sponge. The surface can then be polished with a chamois leather to give a satisfying sheen. A useful tip is to dip the end of the bar of saddle soap in water and use it with a dry sponge, rather than to wet the sponge itself.

Reserve the leather dressing for the inside of the flaps—the flesh or underside—so that it can work through and keep them soft. If you put too much grease on the outside of the saddle, where it will not be absorbed, your enthusiasm will result in a very stained pair of breeches.

Regular Care

Saddle soap should be used regularly every day and a leather dressing applied perhaps once weekly. It is, nonetheless, quite possible to overfeed leather, being too generous with the dressing used. The leather will then become unpleasantly greasy, it will lose its firm feel and become flabby, just like an over-indulged human body.

Furthermore, be careful with aniline finished products. Many of our soft, instant-comfort leathers are given an aniline finish, which is very good but needs special attention. Aniline does not like soap, particularly that containing glycerine. Instead one must use, sparingly, a gentle cream or wax-based product.

Most saddle-makers put a label on the saddle giving advice on how and with what the leather should be treated. It needs to be read carefully and the advice followed.

Did you know?

"Jockeys" are those annoying little black blobs of grease that accumulate on the panel and sweat flap, as well as on stirrup leathers. They can be removed very easily with a ball of horsehair made up from tail pullings.

CLEANING TACK

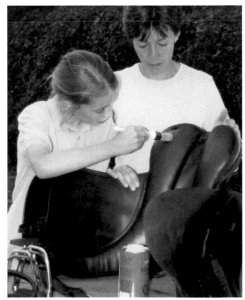

1 Apply saddle soap and work up a lather, but don't use too much water. Wet the soap and use a dry sponge rather than wetting the sponge itself.

2 Get a lovely sheen by rubbing the soaped surface with a soft cloth. Rub vigorously to remove any surplus and you won't get your jodhpurs stained with grease when riding.

3 The leather dressing, which replaces the essential fat content, has to be applied to the underside (the "flesh" side) of the leather where the pores are open to receive it.

What to Wear

Nomadic steppe horsemen wore rough trousers tucked into boots 2,500 years ago, but modern riding dress has its origins in the English hunting field of the 18th and 19th centuries—with, of course, national variations. Essentially, riding clothes were practical, hard-wearing and devoid of frills, but not lacking in style, and that situation remains unaltered in the present day.

Most of the disciplines, jumping, dressage, driving, and so on, lay down rules or recommendations for correct dress, while the sport of hunting follows a traditional and well-understood code of turnout.

Pony Club Rules

The British Pony Club has a comprehensive set of rules for various activities and in every case emphasizes that the wearing of hard hats of an approved pattern and fitted with chinstraps is compulsory. For jumping or riding across country, body protectors of an approved pattern are also compulsory, and the rule is strictly enforced at every level of competition. The Pony Club also states that jewellery, which, of course, includes large or dangling earrings or, indeed, any earrings, "is not allowed." Nor does the Pony Club encourage wearing

flowers or "brightly-colored accessories." Ladies are encouraged to wear hairnets when in riding clothes.

Dressing by Discipline

For rallies and Pony Club events, not including polo, riders wear shirts, ties and tweed coats. They also wear breeches with long boots, half-chaps, or gaiters (which must be of the same color as the footwear), or jodhpurs with jodhpur boots. Jodhpurs originate in the Rajput state of that name in India, where they are a traditional item of clothing.

When permission is given to wear spurs, they must be short, blunt ones and they should be worn on the counter of the boot (i.e., where the foot meets the leg of the boot) and not low down on the heel.

For dressage competitions members can wear navy

Dressage Competitions

This young lady is appropriately dressed for the level at which she is competing. She has chosen to wear a hunting tie and white gloves, which are quite acceptable.

Pony Club

Good, practical turnout for a hot day. Both girls wear properly fitting hard hats and are wearing body protectors of an approved pattern. It is not a smart occasion but the impression is one of neatness and relaxed confidence.

blue or black coats with either a tie or a hunting tie, and they must wear gloves, preferably brown leather or string gloves, but not black or navy ones.

The rules are relaxed for mounted games competitions, when coats and so on would be inappropriate, and, of course, for cross-country events.

Horse Trials

Horse trials follow the accepted hunting attire in general, although, of course, that does not apply to the cross-country phase, and ladies at advanced competitions may wear tail-coats for the dressage test.

Adult Dressage

Adult dressage divides its dress rulings between advanced tests and others. At advanced level the dress is a black tail-coat with top hat, hunting tie, white breeches, black long boots and gloves. No color is specified for gloves in the rules, but brown, or more usually white, leather would be correct. Otherwise black or navy coats are acceptable worn with a tie and a hunting or crash cap. Breeches must be white, cream, or beige. Leather gaiters of the same color as the footwear are now permitted.

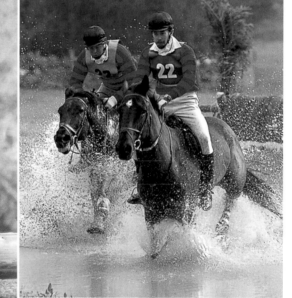

Team Chasing

This popular, down-to-earth sport is about performance rather than appearance, but these riders wear crash hats, body protectors, and shirts in their team colors.

Hunter Trials

There is a sense of style about this competent pair. The rider wears a crash hat with a smart cover matching the jacket, beneath which is the all-important body protector, and she wears the obligatory number cloth.

Hunting and Showing

Hunting Dress

Hunting, on which so many rules of dress are based, is not really as formal in its requirements as it may seem, but it has its conventions.

Members, at the invitation of the Masters, may wear a scarlet coat with the hunt button. The latter may also be worn with a black coat. The correct number of buttons to be worn by members/subscribers is three; the Masters wear four and the hunt servants wear five. White breeches are worn with a scarlet coat and topped boots—these are boots with a differently colored top (or cuff) which can be Melton tan (yellow) or mahogany colored. White garter straps are always worn with topped boots. If a black coat is worn, buff-colored breeches are probably correct worn with a black long boot (sometimes called Butcher boots). Ladies wear black or navy-blue coats with buff breeches and long boots.

Hunt followers carry a hunting whip (it is not called a crop), not a cutting or jumping whip. The hunting whip comprises the stock with a horn handle, and a thong culminating in a cord lash, which is about 4in (10cm) long. However, cracking one's whip is not within the province of the hunt member and is best left to the officials.

Arabian Costume

This Arabian fantasy is indeed "most gorgeously apparelled" and the rider's dress and the horse's extravagant accoutrements bear witness to much thought and careful application. American Parade or Costume classes are always colorful, spectacular and very, very professional. A turnout of this quality, and the overall appearance, makes the job of the judges extremely difficult.

"Ratcatcher" is the turnout for autumn hunting before the season starts properly (in Britain and Ireland) on November 1. It is hunting cap, bowler, or crash hat, worn with a tweed coat, buff breeches and black or brown boots.

Hunting gloves may be knitted string ones or leather and in bad weather it is sensible to carry a spare pair tucked under your girth straps.

Hunting Folk

Mother and daughter, both well mounted and conventionally dressed, make a charming picture. Daughter, sensibly equipped with a hard hat, is very neat indeed, while the knowing pony is a delight. Mother is in every way elegant, and the hunt facing on her coat lends a touch of distinction.

Did you know?

Spurs used to be called "latchfords" after a 19th-century loriner (a maker of metal objects, such as bits and spurs), Benjamin Latchford of St. Martin's Lane, London.

◀Smiling Champion

This smiling championship winner, complete with ribbons worn in the traditional manner, has chosen to wear a teamed shirt and tie in red, matched by her discreet buttonhole. The cap is neat, smart and worn straight on the head, while her elegant coat is well cut.

American Entry▶

This young lady at an American show adds distinction to her black coat and hard hat by wearing a nicely tied and pinned hunting tie. Clearly, the pony, who also wears appropriate headgear, approves of her turnout.

Elegant Hack▶

This competitor in the hack class at a major show turns out in full rig with shining top hat and a red waistcoat, with the color picked up by the flower at her buttonhole. Neatly gloved hands complete a charming picture.

Show-ring Attire

The show-ring also has its conventions. For the county shows, tweed coats are worn and ladies often wear navy coats but with collars and ties and not white breeches. Again, earrings and other visible jewellery are frowned upon. For the big international shows matters become more formal with hunting dress worn for the evening performances.

In the show-ring it is customary for competitors to carry riding canes, usually leather covered. It is very incorrect to carry a whip of any kind.

At the major shows the most formal dress is worn in the evening. Ladies will wear silk top hats while the men adopt what is sometimes called "park" dress. Starting at the top, it comprises the obligatory top hat; stiff-collared white shirt worn, usually, with a gray silk tie or morning dress cravat; a black morning tail-coat with the addition of a buttonhole and pocket handkerchief; a waistcoat, either gray, buff, or of some contrasting color; and close-fitting black riding trousers, or overalls, secured under the instep of a black jodhpur-type boot with dress spurs.

Casual Riding

For casual riding clothing needs to be practical but can obviously be more relaxed. Nonetheless, you should wear a hard hat, and proper jodhpur boots if wearing jeans, and a riding parker is certainly in order.

In Britain all riders are encouraged to wear fluorescent, reflective safety bands when riding on roads so that they can be seen clearly by car and truck drivers. This, of course, is not the case in all countries and in some, indeed, little emphasis is placed even on the wearing of hard hats.

The best guidelines to follow, whatever the activity, are to wear neat, clean, and comfortable clothes and to go easy with the jewellery—it doesn't go with horses. It used to be said that a rider should dress neatly, with boots well polished and a hat worn straight on the head, as a compliment to the horse he rode.

Western Dress

While Western dress is essentially durable and practical, drawing its inspiration from sources as diverse as the Jewish tailor, Levi Strauss, and the Mexican *vaquero*, the West's first cowboy, it is not without style and color, nor without a touch of the dandy. It is, nonetheless, a most comfortable form of riding dress.

Levi Strauss, from New York, was the inventor of the cowboy's low-hipped, narrow-legged denim "pants" (they are always "pants" in the Western idiom) that are still called "Levis." His pants, which were first made in the 1850s, have spawned a whole legion of imitations and created a universal garment.

Hats and Boots

John Betterson Stetson gave his name to one of the best-known hats in the world when he set up shop in Philadelphia in 1865.

His hats, made from beaver felt, were expensive, $30 at a time when the average monthly wage for a cowhand was no more than that, but they lasted a lifetime. They gave protection against wind, rain, or snow and could be used as a water scoop. Today the hat is an all-important element to set off the turnout of the Western rider.

The Western leather boot (*see* far right) is even more expensive than the Stetson hat and frequently elaborately decorated. Spurs are similarly ornamented. They are

Riding High

A comfortable, practical, and colorful outfit and a good, easy Western seat. The hat is smart and gives protection from sun and rain, but the centrepiece, literally, of the turnout is the large ornate belt buckle. The horse, too, looks to be happy with his authentic Western equipment.

Holding the Reins

This is the way the rider holds the reins Western style. These are split reins, unlike the European patterns which are joined with a buckle. Western riders, of course, ride with one hand on the reins.

Footwear

The Western boot is built from the softest leather, often elaborately tooled. The high, forward-sloped heels were made that way to give the wearer greater purchase when holding a roped calf, and the practice is still followed. The heel also prevents the foot from slipping through the stirrup, the Western rider putting the foot home in the iron rather than riding on the ball of the foot. The toes are deliberately pointed so that the foot goes into the stirrup easily.

heavy with large, loose rowels that jangle so as to make cattle aware of the cowboy's presence. Some, indeed, are fitted with extra "jangle bobs," small, independent, metal bobs fitted to the end of the shank. Gloves of stout leather are also part of the dress, originally, of course, to prevent rope burns when using the lasso or *riata*.

Chaps

Chaps (*chaparejos* or *chaperreras*) are, in fact, leather overalls, though in the modern context they are a fashion garment, usually cut to extend over the boot to make the leg look longer and more elegant. Many models are decorated with fringes, which once had a practical purpose. They acted as tiny drainpipes to draw away rain. Modern chaps are made of much lighter leather than the original working chaps and are often coloured to match the outfit.

The original patterns were the "shotgun" with tassels; the lesser known, broad, and tasselled "chinks"; and the heavy-duty "batwing," fastening with snap hooks. There were also "woollies" where the hair was left on the leather. They were warm, but uncomfortable in the wet and very

smelly, too. Modern chaps, especially those for ladies, are shaped to flatter and are closer fitting.

Shirts and Neckwear

Western shirts were usually made up in checked patterns, but modern ones go further than that, and some are extravagant to the point of being garish. They are usually worn with a vest and that, too, can sometimes be of startling design and hue.

Neckwear varies from the smart "bolo" tie, a strip of thin leather or plaited cord secured with an unmistakably Western decorative buckle, to the more workaday bandanna (from the Hindi *bandhnu*). The bandanna of the cowhand was hardly a fashion accessory. It could be used as a face-mask against the dust, a strainer of muddy water, or even, in necessity, a sling or tourniquet.

Surprisingly, dress regulations for Western show-ring riding are more exacting and rigid than the more liberal "recommendations" made for show classes in Europe. All in all, American competitors are, it seems, more concerned with niceties and matters of "correctness" than their European counterparts.

Spurs

The Western spur is large, frequently decorated and always fitted with revolving, jangling rowels. The spur is held in place by a stout strap across the foot and rarely has a strap under the instep.

High Heel

This is the authentic Western boot made from soft leather and hand-tooled. The soles are thin, the toe is pointed to slip easily into the stirrup, and the heel is characteristically high and forward-sloped.

Glossary

*Words or phrases appearing in **bold** have their own entries within the glossary.*

A

ABOVE THE BIT When the horse's mouth is held above the level of the hand.

ACTION Movement of the skeletal frame in locomotion.

AIDS The system of signals employing hand, leg, weight and voice used by the rider to communicate with the horse.

AIRS ABOVE THE GROUND High School movements performed with the forelegs or all the legs off the ground. Also known as "leaps."

ALFALFA Deep-rooting leguminous plant—highly nutritious as grazing or when fed as hay. Also called "lucerne."

AMBLE Lateral pacing gait, slower than pacing.

ARTIFICIAL AIDS The whip and spur used to reinforce the *natural* **aids** made with limbs and voice.

B

BACK AT THE KNEE When the forelegs are curved backwards below the knee. Also called "calf-knee" or "buck-knee."

BACK-BREEDING Breeding back to particular individuals to produce a particular characteristic.

BARREL Horse's body between **forearms** and **loins**.

BARS Area of gum on the lower jaw between the molar and incisor teeth.

BEHIND THE BIT When the nose is brought behind the vertical towards the chest, the bit being dropped in the mouth.

BLEMISH Mark left by injury or disease.

BLOOD HORSE Thoroughbred horse (also *vollblut* or *pur sang*).

BLOODSTOCK Horses bred for racing.

BLUE FEET Dense, blue-black coloring of the horn.

BOATER A canal horse.

BONE Measurement taken around the leg below the knee or hock. "Light of bone" signifies insufficient bone measurement.

BOSAL Plaited noseband used in Western system of bitting.

BOW HOCKS Outward turning hock joints. The opposite of **cow hocks**.

BOXY FEET Upright, narrow feet with closed heel. Also called "donkey," "mule," or "club feet."

BREAKING The early schooling of the horse, i.e., accustoming to saddle or harness.

BREECHING Broad leather band behind the quarters of a harness horse to hold the vehicle when pulling uphill, backing up, or going downhill.

BREED Equine group bred selectively for consistent character over a long period with **pedigrees** entered in a recognized **stud book**.

BROKEN COLORED Term applied to a coat of two colors, usually used to refer to donkey coats. *See also* **whole** (**solid**) color.

BUCK Leap in the air with back arched, all four feet off the ground, or a kick with the hind legs made with the head lowered.

BUFFALO-HIDE Usually from Indian buffalo. Red in color and soft, it is virtually unbreakable but very prone to stretching.

BY Word used when describing breeding, i.e., *by* so-and-so, the sire or **stallion**; *out of* so-and-so, the **mare**.

C

CANNON BONE Bone of the foreleg between knee and fetlock, also called "shin bone." **Shank** and shannon are sometimes used for the same bone of the hind leg.

CANTLE The rear part of the tree or saddle seat.

CAPPED HOCK Swelling on the point of the hock caused by a blow.

CAPRIOLE Classical **air above the ground**. The horse leaps from all four feet, striking out with the hind legs while the body is in mid-air. Literally, "leap of the goat" from the Italian *capra*.

CARRIAGE HORSE Relatively light, elegant horse for carriage use.

CART HORSE Coldblood, heavy draft horse.

CHAPS Leather overalls worn over jeans or something similar. Of Western origin.

CHARGER An officer's horse.

CHESTNUT Horny growth on the inside of all four legs. Also called "castors" and thought to be scent-glands. Also color description for a reddish brown coat.

CHUKKA Polo term for the periods into which the game is divided.

CLASSICS The classic races for three-year-olds held as part of national racing programs.

CLEAN-BRED An animal of any **breed** of pure **pedigree** blood.

CLEAN-LEGGED Without **feather** on the lower limbs, i.e., Cleveland Bay, Suffolk Punch.

CLOSE-COUPLED Short connections between the parts, particularly in relation to the length of the back. No slackness in area of the **loin**. Also called "short-coupled."

COACH HORSE A powerful animal capable of drawing a heavy coach, less refined than a **carriage horse**.

COLDBLOOD Characterized by **heavy horses** descending from the prehistoric Forest Horse of Europe.

COLLECTION When the base line of the horse is shortened, concentrating the forces to the center. The croup is lowered, the weight carried more over the hind legs. The neck is raised and arched, the head is held in the vertical plane. The opposite of **extension**.

COLT Uncastrated male horse up to four years old. Male foals are termed "colt foals."

COMMON Describes an animal of coarse appearance, usually of **coldblood** or non-**pedigree** parentage.

CONCOURS COMPLET French term for "horse trials."

CONFORMATION The formation of the skeleton and the muscle structure covering it; the symmetrical proportion of the component parts.

COUNTRY The area hunted by agreement by a registered hunt.

COURBETTE Classical **air above the ground** following the **levade**. The horse bounds forward in the levade position.

COW HOCKS Hocks turned in at the points like those of a cow.

CRACKED HEELS Inflammation of the heels resulting in a discharge of pus.

CROSS-BREEDING The mating of different **breeds** or **types**. Also called "outcrossing."

CUE American term for the **aids** or signals.

CURB BIT Mouthpiece fitted with cheeks on a system of levers with a chain (attached to the eyes of the bit) that lies in the **curb groove**.

CURB GROOVE The area above the lower lip in which the chain of the **curb bit** lies.

D

DAM The female parent.

DEEP GOING Heavy, wet, or soft ground underfoot. Also described as "heavy going."

DEPTH Refers to the depth of the body between withers and elbow, i.e., "good depth of **girth**."

DESERT HORSE Horse bred in desert conditions or bred from such stock. Desert horses are resistant to heat, fine-skinned, and thin-coated, and able to operate on a sub-normal water intake. *See also* **dry**.

DIAGONAL The diagonal is formed by the foreleg and opposite hind leg, i.e., left fore, right hind is the left diagonal and vice-versa.

DIPPED BACK Pronounced hollow back

usually found in older horses. Also called "sway back."

DISHED FACE Pronounced concave face profile. A distinctive feature of the Arab horse.

DISHING/WINGING When the toe of the foreleg is thrown outwards in a circular movement. Considered to be a faulty **action**.

DOCK The bony part of the tail on which the hair grows.

DOCKING The amputation of the tail for the sake of appearance. It is illegal in some countries, including Britain.

DONKEY FEET *see* **boxy feet**.

DORSAL STRIPE Strip of black or brown hair extending from the neck to the tail. Most usually found in dun-coloured animals. Also called an "eel stripe."

DOUBLE MUSCLING Pronounced muscle growth at the croup, found in some heavy **breeds**.

DRAG HUNT Hunting with hounds following an artificial scent laid previously.

DRAFT Term applied to a horse drawing a vehicle, i.e., "in draft." Usually associated with **heavy horse breeds**, i.e., heavy "draft" horse.

DRY The lean appearance about the head of **desert horses**. There is an absence of fatty tissue and the veins are prominent under the skin.

E

EEL STRIPE *see* **dorsal stripe**.

ENGAGEMENT When the hind legs are brought well under the body and deliver greater propulsion as a result, they are termed "engaged" or "well-engaged."

ENTIRE Describing a **stallion**, an uncastrated male horse.

ERGOT Horny growth on the back of the fetlock.

EWE NECK A weak formation with a concave outline on the top of the neck and pronounced muscling of the underside. Usually accompanies a **dipped back**.

EXERCISE Riding the horse for the purpose of exercise. It is carried out over relatively long periods of time and is not of a strenuous nature. The opposite of **work**.

EXTENSION The noticeable lengthening of the stride and outline. The opposite of **collection**.

EXTRAVAGANT A high knee and hock **action** like that of the Hackney or Saddlebred might be termed "extravagant."

F

FALSE RIB The 10 asternal ribs attached only to the vertebrae and not to the sternum bone, which are to the rear of the eight "true" (sternal) ribs.

FEATHER Long hair on the lower legs and fetlocks usually associated with **heavy horses, coldblood breeds,** or their crosses.

FILLY A female horse under four years old.

FIVE-GAITED Term for the Saddlebred horse exhibited at walk, trot, canter, slow-gait, and **rack**.

FLEHMEN The action, often of **stallions**, of curling back the lips. It can be caused by the presence of in-season **mares** but may also occur in response to strong or unusual tastes and smells, such as garlic or lemon.

FLEXION The horse, in response to the action of the bit, yields the lower jaw when bending at the poll. Flexion also describes the full bending of the hock and fetlock joints.

FLY-BOAT High-speed passenger and light freight canal boat drawn by pairs of horses hitched fore and aft. Capable of 10–12mph (16–19km/h).

FOAL Colt, gelding, or **filly** up to a year old.

FPA Foot-pastern-axis. The angles between fetlock, toe and heel correspond to the slope of the shoulder and ensure the most efficient flight path of the foot. A priority in farriery.

FOREARM Upper part of the foreleg above the knee.

FOREHAND The forepart of the body: head, neck, shoulder, withers and forelegs.

FORELOCK The mane between the ears lying over the forehead.

FOUR-IN-HAND Team of four **harness horses**.

FROG The rubbery horn pad on the sole of the foot, which acts as a shock-absorber and an anti-slip device.

FULL MOUTH A horse at six years with all his permanent teeth is said to have a "full mouth."

G

GAITED HORSE American term for horses displaying artificial as well as natural gaits.

GASKIN "Second thigh" extending upwards from hock to stifle.

GAUCHO South American cowboy.

GELDING A castrated male horse.

GSB General **Stud Book** in which all Thoroughbred **mares** and their progeny foaled in the UK and Ireland are listed. Founded in 1791 and published by Weatherby's.

GIRTH The circumference of the body measured around the **barrel**. Also refers to band securing the saddle.

GOOD FRONT Describes a horse with prominent wither formation, long slope of shoulder, and generous length of neck.

GOOSE-RUMP Pronounced muscular development at the croup, sometimes called the "jumper's bump."

GYMKHANA Anglo-Indian word now used to describe mounted games.

H

HACK A type of elegant riding horse, or to "go for a hack," i.e., go for a ride.

HALF-BRED Cross between a Thoroughbred and any other **breed**.

HALTER A web or rope headcollar. "Halter class" in competition is for animals led **in-hand**.

HAND Unit of measurement used in measuring the horse from highest point of the wither to the ground. One hand equals 4in (10.16cm).

HARNESS The equipment of the driving horse.

HARNESS HORSE A horse used in **harness** or having harness-type **conformation** and **action**.

HAUTE ECOLE The classical art of advanced riding. *See also* **airs above the ground**.

HEAVY HORSE Any type of heavy **draft** breeds.

HEAVYWEIGHT Horse judged to be able to carry a rider of 196lbs (95.2kg).

HEMIONID An animal combining characteristics of both horse and ass, i.e., Mongolian Kulan, Tibetan Kiang. Not a cross between horse and ass.

HIGH SCHOOL *see* **Haute Ecole**.

HIND QUARTERS The body from the back of the flanks to the top of the tail down to the top of the gaskin. Often referred to as "quarters."

HOGGED MANE A mane that has been removed by clipping. American **roached mane**.

HOLLOW BACK *see* **dipped back**.

HORSE KILLER Description given to the heavy American four to five bottom ploughs drawn by eight-horse teams.

HORSE-POWER The power required to raise 550lb (250kg) one foot (30cm) in one second is measured as one "horse-power." This is equivalent to 745.7 watts.

HOT An excitable horse is said to be "hot" or to "hot up."

HOTBLOOD Term used to describe the Arab and Thoroughbred.

HUNT SEAT American term for English or European riding style.

I

IBERIAN HORSE Composite term for the horses of Spain and Portugal: Andalucian (Spanish Horse), Lusitano, Alter-Real, Hispano-Arab.

IN-BREEDING Breeding between close relatives to fix or accentuate particular characteristics, i.e., "incest" breeding, **mare** to its own **sire**, etc.

IN FRONT OF THE BIT A term used to describe a horse pulling hard and becoming out of hand.

IN-HAND A horse controlled from the ground or one competing in led or "in-hand" classes.

J

JIBBAH The unique bulge on the forehead of the Arab horse.

JOG-TROT A short-paced, jogging trot.

L

LEADER Either of the leading pair of horses in a team of four; a single horse harnessed in front of another as in a **tandem**.

LEAN HEAD A fine head, thin skinned without fleshiness. *See* **dry** head.

LENGTH OF REIN A good "length of rein" refers to an adequate measurement over the top of the neck from withers to poll.

LEVADE First of the **airs above the ground**, in which the **forehand**, with forelegs bent, is raised off the ground on deeply bent hind legs. A controlled half-rear.

LIGHT HORSE Horse other than a pony or **heavy horse** suitable for riding and carriage work.

LIGHT OF BONE Insufficient bone below the knee to perform under the rider's weight without risk of strain. See **bone**.

LIGHTWEIGHT A horse that because of its build and **bone** measurement is not considered to be able to carry over 175lbs (79kg) comfortably.

LINE-BREEDING The mating of animals having a common ancestor some generations previously to accentuate a particular feature.

LOADED SHOULDER Excessive muscling over the shoulder region (i.e., "muscle-bound") that inhibits the movement.

LOIN Area either side of the spine lying just behind the saddle.

LOPE The slow Western canter performed with low head carriage.

LUCERNE *see* **alfalfa**.

M

MANEGE Enclosed arena used for schooling exercises.

MARE Female horse aged four years or over.

MEALY MUZZLE Oatmeal-colored muzzle, a feature of the Exmoor pony.

MIDDLEWEIGHT A horse judged capable of carrying a rider of up to 196lbs (89kg).

MITBAH The angle at which the neck of the Arab horse meets with the head. It results in the characteristic arched neck.

N

NARRAGANSETT PACER A pacing **breed** that was developed as a plantation horse around Narragansett Bay, Rhode Island, US, up to the 19th century. None exist today, but the Narragansett Pacer is at the base of many pacing and **gaited** American breeds.

NATIVE PONIES A name for the Mountain and Moorland **breeds** of Great Britain.

NICK The practice of "nicking" and re-setting the muscles under the tail to give an artificially high carriage. Also, a term used to describe successful cross-mating, i.e., "a good nick."

O

ODD-COLORED Coat with patches of more than two colors.

OMNIBUS Passenger vehicle originating in France, originally *voiture omnibus,* meaning "carriage for everyone". Later shortened to "bus".

ONAGER A **hemionid**, the zoological term for the wild ass is *Equus hemionus onager*.

ON THE BIT The horse accepting the bit, with the head carried in a near-vertical plane and the mouth a little below the rider's hand.

ON THE LEG Term describing a horse disproportionately long in the leg probably because of lack of **depth** through the body.

ORIENTAL HORSES Horses of eastern origin, either Arab or Barb, used in the formation of the English Thoroughbred.

OUTCROSS Mating of unrelated horses: the introduction of outside blood to a **breed**.

OVERBENT The horse is **behind the bit**, the mouth tucked into the chest to evade control.

OVER-TOPPED Too heavy a body in respect of the supporting limbs.

OXER Obstacle of parallel poles with a brush fence set between the two to increase the difficulty.

P

PACER Horse employing the lateral **action** at trot rather than the conventional **diagonal** movement.

PACK HORSE Horse used to transport goods carried in packs on either side of the back.

PALFREY Medieval **saddle horse** famed for its comfortable **ambling** pace.

PARIETAL BONES The bones on the top of the skull.

PARROT-MOUTH A condition in which the incisors of the upper jaw project beyond those of the lower, making mastication difficult. The opposite of **undershot**.

PART-BRED Progeny having Thoroughbred blood and that of another **breed** in various percentages.

PEDIGREE Details of ancestry recorded in a **stud book**.

PIEBALD English term for a coat of black and white patches. *See also* **skewbald**.

PIGEON TOES Feet turned inwards, a fault sometimes called "pin-toes."

PLAITING Faulty **action** in which the forefeet cross over each other.

POINTS External features of **conformation**. Also relating to color, e.g., bay with black points, meaning black lower legs, mane and tail.

POMMEL The head or front arch of the saddle.

POSTILLION Rider driving a **harness horse**, or a pair of horses, from the saddle.

PREPOTENT Having the ability consistently to pass on character and type to the progeny.

PRIMITIVE Term used to describe the early sub-species: Asiatic Wild Horse, Tarpan, Forest Horse, Tundra Horse.

PRIMITIVE VIGOR Dominant character and **prepotency** associated with early wild horses.

PURE-BRED Horse of unmixed breeding.

Q

QUALITY Refinement in **breeds** or **types** usually traceable to Arab or Thoroughbred influence.

QUARTERS *see* **hind quarters**.

QUIDDING The dropping of balls of food from the mouth because of abnormalities of the teeth.

R

RACEHORSE A horse bred for racing and so usually a Thoroughbred.

RACK The fifth gait of the American Saddlebred. "A flashy, four-beat gait" unrelated to pacing.

RANGY Description of horse having size combined with **scope** of movement.

REMUDA The herd of broken horses used on a Western ranch.

REVAAL The pacing gait of the Marwari and Kathiawari horses.

RISING A horse approaching say five years is referred to as being "rising five."

ROACH BACK Convex curvature of the back, the opposite of a **dipped back**.

ROACHED MANE American term for clipping off the mane.

ROADSTER The famous Norfolk Roadster, a trotting **saddle horse**, ancestor of the Hackney Horse. Also in the US a light **harness horse**, usually a Standardbred.

ROMAN NOSE A convex profile found in many **heavy horse breeds**.

ROSIN-BACK A broad-backed horse used in the circus. So called because rosin is sprinkled on the horse's bare back to increase the rider's grip.

RUNNING HORSE English racing stock, the "running horses" that provided a base for the Thoroughbred when crossed with **Oriental** sires.

S

SADDLE HORSE A riding horse.

SADDLE MARKS White hair in the saddle area, the result of pressure.

SADDLE SEAT Riding style adopted for gaited horse classes.

SAW HORSE A wooden trestle on which to store saddles.

SCHOOL MOVEMENTS The exercises carried out in the riding school. Also "school figures" involving patterns. *See also* **manege**.

SCOPE Capability for free athletic movement in a high degree.

SECOND THIGH *see* **gaskin**.

SELLE ROYALE The school saddle of classical riding with supportive rolls built at front and back.

SET TAIL Tail that has been **nicked** and set to give a high tail carriage.

SHADOW ROLL A thick sheepskin noseband that blocks the horse's view of the ground immediately beneath him. Used in harness racing to prevent horses shying at shadows, etc. Employed also in racing to encourage concentration.

SHANK BONE Hind **cannon bone**.

SHILLIBEER A horse-drawn **omnibus** named after George Shillibeer who set up a passenger service in London, England, in 1829.

SHORT-COUPLED *see* **close-coupled**.

SHORT OF A RIB A marked space between the last rib and the hip. Found in conjunction with a long back and **slack loins**.

SICKLE HOCKS Weak, bent hocks resembling a sickle in shape.

SIRE The male parent.

SISTEMA *Il sistema*, the practice of forward riding, the forward seat, introduced and taught by Federico Caprilli.

SKEWBALD English term for a coat color of irregular white and colored patches other than black. *See also* **piebald**.

SLAB-SIDED Flat-ribbed.

SLACK LOINS Weakness in the loins, a noticeable gap between the last rib and hip.

SLIP HEAD Head strap and cheekpiece supporting the bradoon of a double bridle.

SNAFFLE-MOUTH Description for a light-mouthed horse that can be ridden in a snaffle bridle under all circumstances.

SOLID A coat of a single color, i.e., bay, chestnut, etc., is called solid-colored. Also called "whole."

SOUND HORSE A sound horse is in perfect physical health with no bodily defects and without impediment to sight or **action**.

SPLIT-UP BEHIND From behind, the thighs divide high up under the dock. It is a fault caused by pronounced weakness of the **gaskins**.

STALLION An uncastrated male horse of four years old or more.

STAMP A **prepotent** horse is said to "stamp" his stock with his own physical character and attributes.

STAMP OF HORSE A recognizable type or pattern of horse.

STOCK SADDLE Western saddle, or a reference to American show classes ridden in Western style.

STUD A breeding establishment—a stud farm. Also used as an alternative to **stallion**.

STUD BOOK A book kept by a **breed** society in which the **pedigrees** of stock eligible for entry are recorded.

SUBSTANCE The physical quality of the body in terms of build and general musculature.

SWAY As in "sway back"; *see* **dipped back**.

T

TACK A general word for saddlery. An abbreviation of "tackle."

TAIL MALE LINE Descent through the male parent line.

TANDEM An arrangement in which two horses are harnessed one behind the other.

THICK-WINDED Congested in the breathing.

THROATLATCH Strap from the headpiece of the bridle passing round the throat.

TIED-IN BELOW THE KNEE Where the measurement below the knee is less than that above the fetlock. A serious **conformational** fault.

TOP LINE The outline of the back from wither to croup.

TRAVOIS A horse sled made of two poles joined to make a platform behind the horse.

TURNOUT Standard of dress of horse and rider. Also of a driven vehicle.

TWIST The waist or narrowest part of the saddle and its tree.

TYPE A horse of no particular **breed** but fulfilling a particular purpose, i.e., cob, hunter, polo pony.

U

UNDERSHOT Condition in which the lower jaw projects beyond the upper. The opposite of **parrot-mouth**.

V, W

VAQUERO Mexican cowboy.

WARMBLOOD In general terms a **part-bred** horse carrying a percentage of Thoroughbred and/or Arab blood.

WEED A poor, lightly-built specimen, often Thoroughbred, hence the term "Thoroughbred weed."

WEIGHT CARRIER A horse capable of carrying 210lbs (95.2kg). Also called a **heavyweight horse**.

WELL-RIBBED UP A short, deep, rounded body with **well-sprung ribs**.

WELL-SPRUNG RIBS Long, rounded ribs well suited to carrying a saddle and allowing for plenty of lung expansion.

WHEELERS The horses in a team harnessed nearest to the vehicle and behind the **leaders**.

WHIP The driver of a carriage. Also an artificial aid.

WHIPPER-IN Assistant to the huntsman of a pack of hounds.

WHITE LINE Band of soft horn round the foot separating the insensitive horn from the inner sensitive laminae.

WHOLE as in "whole-colored", *see* **solid**.

WHORL A circle of hair on the coat or an irregular formation of hair.

WORK In the context of **exercise** and work, the latter is concentrated exercise, usually in the school area, and of short duration.

Y, Z

YURT Mongolian tent made of felt or hides.

ZEBRA BARS Striped bands of dark hair on the forelegs and sometimes on the hind legs, too.

Index

Acknowledgments

Author's acknowledgments

I have to express my gratitude to those without whose help and encouragement this book would not have been possible. I am very appreciative of the wholly professional efforts of my dear friend Sian Thomas BHSI, of the Snowdonia Riding Stables, Waunfawr, Wales, UK, who organized the lessons for us, and for the help and cooperation of our invariably cheerful "model," Harriet Lowe and her supportive parents.

Of course, I have to thank the staff of Studio Cactus for a production that is original and is presented with so much flair, and, also, for resisting the temptation to fall out with their sometimes irascible author.

Nothing would be possible without the quiet efficiency of Mrs. Julie Thomas who manages with easy aplomb the intricacies of a communication technology of which I have no more than a rudimentary knowledge.

Finally, my thanks are due to my wife Mary, who for more years than she would like to admit, has supported me with all understanding in every sort of circumstance.

Studio Cactus would like to thank Peter Cross for his excellent lessons photography; Sian Thomas, Harriet Lowe, Sharon Rudd, and Katherine Rudd for modelling; Claire Moore and Maggie Raynor for illustrations; Jo Walton for picture research; Lesley Riley for proofreading; and Hilary Bird for indexing. Thanks also to Jacky Spigel, Madeleine Day and Sean Moore for providing invaluable support and encouragement throughout the project. Finally, special thanks to Elwyn Hartley Edwards for his patience and unwavering professionalism.

Picture credits

Unless listed below, all photographs in this book are the copyright of Bob Langrish or Studio Cactus:

6: Janez Skok/Corbis
13 top: HorseSource
13 below: Bettmann/Corbis
14: Bettmann/Corbis
15 left: Rex Features
15 right: Swim Ink/Corbis
18: Charles & Josette Lenars/Corbis
19 top: Bettmann/Corbis
20: Archivo Iconografico, S.A./Corbis
21: Archivo Iconografico, S.A./Corbis
22: Archivo Iconografico, S.A./Corbis
23 top: Roger Wood/Corbis
23 below: Gustavo Tomsich/Corbis
24: Charles & Josette Lenras/Corbis
25: HorseSource
26-27: Tim Thompson/Corbis
28: Geoffrey Clements/Corbis
29 top: Hulton-Deutsch Collection/Corbis
29 below: Bettmann/Corbis
30: Minnesota Historical Society/Corbis
31 top: Adam Woolfitt/Corbis
31 below: Corbis
34-35: Brooke Hospital for Animals
36: Hulton-Deutsch Collection/Corbis
36-37: Corbis
38: Richard T Nowitz/Corbis

39 top: Minnesota Historical Society/Corbis
39 below: Bettmann/Corbis
40 top: Bettmann/Corbis
40 below: Hulton-Deutsch Collection/Corbis
41: Bettmann/Corbis
42: Bettmann/Corbis
43: Bettmann/Corbis
50: George Selwyn
53 below: George Selwyn
54: Jan Butchofsky-Houser/Corbis
55 top: Mark L Stephenson/Corbis
55 centre: Burstein Collection/Corbis
55 below: Geoffrey Clements/Corbis
56 left: HorseSource
57 below: HorseSource
62: Mary Evans Picture Library
63 top left: Bettmann/Corbis
63 top right: George Selwyn
63 below left: Kit Houghton Photography
63 centre right: Kit Houghton Photography
63 below right: Kit Houghton Photography
72: Bettmann/Corbis
73 top: Bettmann/Corbis
82: Nevada Wier/Corbis
83 top: Hulton-Deutsch Collection/Corbis
83 below: Kit Houghton/Corbis

129 below: Kit Houghton Photography
145 top left: Keren Su/Corbis
157 below: Kit Houghton Photography
159: Kit Houghton Photography
198: David Samuel Robbins/Corbis
199 top: Kit Houghton/Corbis
208: Lindsay Hebberd/Corbis
209 top: Kit Houghton/Corbis
228 centre, below right: Elwyn Hartley Edwards
229 top, below left, below right: Elwyn Hartley Edwards
230 below: Elwyn Hartley Edwards
231 top: Elwyn Harltey Edwards
232: Elwyn Hartley Edwards

Brooke Hospital for Animals
You can find further information on the Brooke Hospital for Animals on their website:

www.brooke-hospital.org.uk